A Bridge of People

Royalties from sales of this book
are being donated to Oxfam.

Ben Whitaker

A Bridge of People

A Personal View of
Oxfam's First Forty Years

With a Foreword by
Conor Cruise O'Brien

Heinemann : London

William Heinemann Ltd
10 Upper Grosvenor Street, London W1X 9PA
LONDON MELBOURNE TORONTO
JOHANNESBURG AUCKLAND

First published 1983
Reprinted 1984, 1985

© Ben Whitaker 1983

SBN 434 86275 4

Printed in Great Britain at The Pitman Press, Bath

Dedicated
to
R. A. I. W.
and
with grateful thanks to all who helped

Contents

Illustrations

Foreword
Conor Cruise O'Brien

'We'll give ye every assistance in our power, short of actually helping ye.'

Mr Dooley's formula comes to my mind whenever I listen to, or read, statements by spokesmen for the advanced world, about development aid.

As Ben Whitaker points out (in Chapter 12), 'the gap between North and South is not only widening *but doing so at an accelerating rate'*. Also, the contribution of the advanced world to Third World aid has been steadily declining. Mr Whitaker gives some details in the same chapter:

'The 17 members of the OECD's development committee (DAC) gave only 0.35 per cent of their combined GNP in 1981, compared with 0.38 per cent the previous year, and 0.52 per cent twenty years ago. (Holland – where aid is not felt to be a party political commitment that loses more votes than it gains, but a popular issue in which political parties vie with each other for imaginative vote-catching policies – gave the highest proportion, 1.08 per cent of its GNP. Britain's fell to 0.43 per cent, while the U.S.A.'s was cut to 0.2 per cent).'

Mr Whitaker adds, correctly, that 'the heirs of those political leaders and civil servants who said that the Great Irish Famine must be left to be solved by "market forces" and "natural wastage" seem once again to be in control of governments . . .'.

To that, I would add two comments. The fact is that hunger in the Third World today kills as many people *every three weeks* as it killed in the year or so of the Great Irish Famine. The second is that the Great Irish Famine, of more than 130 years ago, has left baneful political and psychological consequences which are still felt today. Specifically, the strong moral, political and often financial aid which reaches the Provisional IRA from men and women of Irish origin in America is heavily influenced by famine and post-famine memories handed down, over generations, to the descendants of the famine emigrants.

We cannot guess what long-term consequences may flow from present policies of the advanced world towards Third World poverty, but it is not likely that these consequences will be agreeable – to us who have acquiesced in the politics of neglect, or to our descendants.

For we *have* acquiesced. The goverments which have been steadily cutting back on aid are not authoritarian governments (not that the authoritarian governments have behaved any better: on the contrary). The countries in question – roughly speaking, the North Atlantic countries – are working democracies, responsive to democratic pressures, and absences of pressure. And Third World development aid is increasingly perceived to be an area of absence of pressure. There are no votes in it, so it doesn't happen. We can't blame our rulers for failing to do things there are no votes in; after all, if they insisted on doing things like that they might cease to be our rulers.

The rulers have not behaved any worse than they know the public (generally) expects them to. In fact there is some evidence, in Britain at least, that the rulers may be (marginally) more enlightened than the public. Polls cited by Mr Whitaker show that the proportion of British people who believe that Britain should give overseas aid fell from 62 per cent in 1969 to 46 per cent in 1977.

Nor should it be assumed that the majority of the public which doesn't believe in *any* overseas aid is drawn entirely from the less educated classes. Intellectuals against aid for anyone are also a formidable little lobby. No topic is intellectually more dowdy than the original Brandt Report, unless it be the United Nations. Among those in the know, the word is that development aid is a nonsense, because it all gets stolen by the receiving governments.

Now the opinions of those who regard themselves as in the know are seldom altogether unfounded, and unfortunately this particular opinion contains quite an amount of truth. Many, possibly most, though certainly not all, Third World governments are corrupt, incompetent, and – in every sense of the word – irresponsible. Aid entrusted to such governments is liable to be stolen, wasted or actaully used – in a variety of ways – against the poor, whom it is supposed to help.

As governmental aid mostly goes through governments, and as so many receiving governments are of this type, it is quite reasonable to be sceptical about governmental aid. But the scepticism should be extended to cover, not only the recipient governments, but also the donor governments. Aid could not have been diverted, stolen and wasted to the extent that has undoubtedly taken place unless the donors, as well as the recipients had consented to that. Unfortunately, in many cases, the donors closed their eyes to what was going on, because in reality it was the corrupt governments they wanted to help, and not their unfortunate subjects. The corrupt are often friendly, and useful; what their subjects want, need or get is neither here nor there. So Foreign Offices often reason, though not aloud and in public.

Quite a lot of governmental aid does get through to its intended destination but even that flow is endangered by the widespread, and quite well-founded, belief that aid is likely to be stolen. The whole thing would benefit from vigorous and well-informed public debate, but the actual level which the debate has attained, in the main democracies, has been rather disappointing. This has been mainly due to the low level of public interest, but the character of the public debate has also been adversely affected by two sets of converging political inhibitions, on the right and on the left.

Those on the right are pretty obvious. The right's vision of the Third World, since the Second World War, has been dominated by rather crude and summary notions of fighting Communism. You fight Communism by helping anti-Communist governments. Now – partly for this reason – the following has become a highly reliable Third World maxim; 'Show me a dedicated anti-Communist, and I will show you a crook.' There are plenty of other crooks around too, of course, some of them spouting left-wing rhetoric – as I had occasion to observe at close quarters during three years in the Ghana of Kwame Nkrumah.

But right-wing governments have larger opportunities for corruption – mainly because the right in the advanced world is always influential institutionally, in relation to foreign policy, even when the left has a parliamentary majority. So the right in the advanced world has a vested interest in soft-pedalling the extent of Third World corruption. In public, that is. In private, and in confidential briefings, the right uses the existence of such corruption as a reason for cutting back on development aid;

while at the same time ensuring that as much as possible of the consequently limited aid goes to friendly, anti-Communist governments, however corrupt these may be, and however probable that moneys supplied in the name of development will not be used for development.

On the left, the subject of Third World governmental corruption tends to be avoided for different reasons, principally because it is felt to have racist overtones. To admit the existence of the phenomenon is felt to be playing into the hands of the right. In actual fact, the avoidance of the topic – because many of the corrupt governments in question are black or brown – is itself a manifestation of racism. Black and brown crooks are no more deserving of respect and consideration than the white crooks who are so often in cahoots with them. And as for 'playing into the hands of the right', again it is the embarrassed silence on the subject that suits the right, since right-wing officials, politicians and businessmen do so much to sustain the system – and also to use its existence to discredit, not the corrupt governments they favour, but the whole concept of development aid.

There are, however, people in all four parties in Britain who are genuinely concerned with development aid. To these, I should like to suggest that they give priority now, not immediately to raising the scale of governmental contribution to development, but to a critical, public analysis of present forms of governmental aid, showing roughly how much of it goes to the people for whom it is intended, and how much to other purposes. Until that is done, and until corrective action is taken, to whatever extent it may seem to be required, the idea of governmental development aid will continue to sink into a sort of vague and unsavoury disrepute – the good along with the bad – and it will not be possible to generate public support for the greatly increased aid which genuine development needs require.

The above – except where I quote Mr Whitaker directly – represents my own personal thinking, and not necessarily Mr Whitaker's, and a fortiori not necessarily Oxfam's. My train of thought was started by the stimulus which Mr Whitaker's data and expertise gave to my memories of African experience: mainly in the Congo and in Ghana, but also in Nigeria and – in Oxfam's wake – in the Horn of Africa. What Mr Whitaker says often gives me a shock, but it is often a shock of recognition. It is an extension of my knowledge, but it is an extension that fits into what I already know.

Oxfam, as Mr Whitaker points out, is relevant mainly because its ideas are relevant to Third World conditions. Its ideas are relevant because Oxfam people – as I have seen in the Horn and elsewhere – are good at listening: listening always primarily to people who need help, but who are also prepared to help themselves. Oxfam projects – often in conjunction with other development workers, religious or lay – are based on the principle of the irreducible, effective minimum of outside aid, whether in irrigation, sanitation, health, or technical training among other projects. Ideally the people who are to benefit do most of the work, while Oxfam, or other like-minded people, supply only those bits of equipment and knowledge which are not easily available locally.

As a proportion of gross international development aid expenditure, the Oxfam effort is quite small; its main relevance is in terms of ideas, as Mr Whitaker points out. Oxfam, and those associated with it, have always been as he says, 'bubbling with debate', and the debate bubbles in these pages. Mr Whitaker himself clearly favours the approach which has been Oxfam's since the sixties, an approach partly summed up in the maxim of the Freedom from Hunger Campaign: 'Give a man a fish and you feed him for a day; teach him to fish and you feed him for a lifetime'. If you take along with that Oxfam's belief that 'for any development to be successful, it must come from the bottom upwards, not to be imposed from the top', and 'never to tell people what they want but instead respond to requests they articulate', and if you add to these the concept of social development and of 'appropriate' or 'intermediate' technology, you have (I think) the main elements in Oxfam's philosophy.

Mr Whitaker has seen many of the fruits of that philosophy and he approves. Yet he cities contrary views, generally without seeking to refute, or even discount, the opposing point of view. Being myself much given to argument, I am impressed by this quietism, and wish I could emulate it. Certainly it fits well into the Quaker-shaped ethos of Oxfam.

Mr Whitaker (Chapter 6) quotes a Zimbabwean woman, now a consultant to Oxfam: 'asked what she thinks are the white voluntary agencies' motives for their work she suggests, 'Besides guilt and the missionary instinct, it's this permanent overriding feeling that they know best.'

That's rather a chilling verdict, in the circumstances, but Mr Whitaker doesn't try to argue. He just leaves it there. What a lesson to some of the rest of us!

In the same spirit, the author quotes in his last chapter a saying of Mahatma Gandhi which seems to call in question the basis of all such enterprises as Oxfam:

'Man is not omnipotent. He therefore serves the world best by serving his neighbour. This is Sivadeshi (local self-sufficiency), a principle which is broken when one professes to serve those who are more remote in preference to those who are near.'

That of course is exactly the point that Dickens had to make about Mrs Jellyby. Dickens and Gandhi might have got on well enough, if they could have managed to keep off the subject of celebrating Christmas!

Mr Whitaker steers well clear of institutional hagiography. He steers equally clear of the danger of numbing the reader's mind by excess of either statistics or pleading. His comparisons and illustrations are quietly telling. This for example (from Chapter 3):

'If during the next two days, we learned that an unexpected tragic disaster struck which claimed the lives of 70,000 children, the British public would respond with generosity, and moralising leading articles in the press would . . . underline the lessons which must be learnt. In fact during the next two days . . . that is the number of children who will perish unnecessarily as a result of malnutrition, thirst, poverty and disease. *We have been given advice notice this will happen. And we could prevent it – if enough people told their political representatives* . . . But we do nothing – or not enough. And the press remains largely indifferent.'

This book appears as Brian Walker's ten-year tenure as Director-General of Oxfam draws to an end. His successor is not altogether to be envied; Mr Walker's will be a hard act to follow. It was indeed a tightrope act, which he brought off brilliantly: to build up Oxfam steadily, while holding on to the advantages of smallness. And he kept administrative expenditure down to 3 per cent – an achievement which must boggle the minds and chill the blood of people in the intergovernmental aid agencies.

Mr Walker has a good sense of limits, and the advantages to be derived from them. He has also a good eye for limits which are absolute in theory, but not in practice; like the distinction between development aid and political intervention. On that matter Mr Walker (quoted in Chapter 11) has this to say:

'Of course, all aid is political. The simplest grant. . . . a new well in, say, a remote African village: clean water to drink, ample water to irrigate crops and water the cattle. A manifestly humanitarian gesture. But political, too – for a well belonging to the people disturbs the balance of power in that village. Whoever owned the watering place hitherto is now disadvantaged. Normally that means the landlord, the moneylender or the local political power boss. Sometimes all three in one. If the people have their own water they do not need to work for the landlord, or pay him a tithe, or vote for him in the election, or turn a blind eye when he looks lustfully on their daughters. The political power structure has been disturbed – with a measure of justice flowing towards the poor and away from the powerful. Even when multiplied many times over (and the combined annual income of half a dozen continental charities is greater than the GNP of some Third World countries) this remains a modest enough gesture, and is neither radical or revolutionary. Nonetheless, it is a beginning – a threat to the power base of the rich and the powerful and hence profoundly political . . .'

It was entirely in accordance with this general approach that Mr Walker took the bold decision to bring Oxfam into Cambodia in 1979. That was at a time when Western governments still, incredibly, recognised the abominable – and by then also nonexistent – Pol Pot regime. The actual government in Phnom Penh, having been installed with the aid of Vietnam forces, was boycotted by the West. So the official advice to Oxfam was to keep out. Mr Walker, however, saw that people in Cambodia were in the direst need, and that the political circumspection which was commended to Oxfam would mean death for them. Oxfam aid could not be distributed without the co-operation of the government actually in control. Oxfam sought and got that co-operation and – with massive public and financial support, partly generated by television – carried out one of the largest emergency rescue operations in history.

The Cambodian operation was a major triumph of humanity,

and the boldness of humanity, over cold-hearted and dogmatic bureaucracy. The bureaucrats were, in the end, powerless, both because Oxfam's extremely high public reputation made it a dangerous animal for elected politicians to tangle with, and because of public sympathy with the plight of the Cambodians. This last was mainly due to John Pilger's television programmes.

There are certain high moments when democracy, and freedom of publication, are not content with just being good things, in a general and teleological sense, but actively prove themselves to be good things, in the here and now. Watergate was such a moment when democracy and the press vindicated the supremacy of the rule of law. Oxfam's operation in Cambodia was such a moment also. Both in its substance and its style, it set a high standard for Oxfam's operations in the future.

PART I

Putting People First

We hold these truths to be self-evident: that all men are created equal; that the inequalities and injustices which afflict so much of the human race are the product of history and society, not of God or nature; that people everywhere are entitled to the blessings of life and liberty, peace and security and the realisation of their full potential; that they have an inescapable moral obligation to preserve those rights for posterity . . . To establish a new world of compassion, peace, justice and security it is essential that mankind free itself from the limitations of national prejudice, and acknowledge that the forces that unite it are incomparably deeper than those that divide it – that all people are part of one global community, dependent on one body of resources, bound together by the ties of a common humanity and associated in a common adventure on the planet Earth. We can no longer afford to make little plans, allow ourselves to be the captives of events and forces over which we have no control, consult our fears rather than our hopes.

Henry Steele Commager

But in the final reckoning, it will not be simply economics and technology that end it. It will be people – people who care. We are those people. We have to ask ourselves – each one of us – where we really stand.

Robert McNamara, Address to
the Governors of the World Bank

One hears young people asking for a cause. The cause is here. It is the biggest single cause in history . . . Many in rich countries are so selfish that they would – and maybe will – be willing to get richer and use the technological superiority which their riches give them to fight off the hungry millions outside. I for one shouldn't like to live in such a world.

C. P. Snow

1

'A Good Friend':
The Cambodia Operation

The vision of Christ that thou does see
Is my vision's greatest enemy . . .
Thine loves the same world that mine hates,
Thy Heaven doors are my Hell gates.
Both read the Bible day and night,
But thou read'st black where I read white.

William Blake

A good friend is to be found when one is poor.

Cambodian proverb

'It is not everybody', observes Oxfam's Deputy Director, Guy Stringer, laconically deadpan, 'who has the opportunity to spend four and a half days crossing 640 miles of the South China seas in a tug pulling a barge the size of a football field, to a port about which extremely little was known and where there certainly was some doubt as to the sort of reception that we should receive.'

The challenge of the Cambodia (or Kampuchea) operation, with its risks and improvisation, showed Oxfam at its best as well as the dilemmas and dangers its work frequently involves.

On 18 September 1979, at forty-eight hours' notice, Stringer flew to Thailand carrying £50,000 and some urgent instructions. These – drawn up at a meeting of European Non-Governmental Organisations [NGOs] chaired by Brian Walker, the Director-General of Oxfam – were to acquire a ship and as large a quantity of food as possible. The action was in response to a priority appeal from Cambodia, where Jim Howard (Oxfam's technical director) reported a horrific catastrophe had taken place, corroborated by two French doctors who had entered the country and Mme de Plaud who had been working in hospitals there.

On his arrival in Bangkok, Stringer rapidly discovered that no official permission would be forthcoming from the Thai

3

government for supplies to be moved either by ship or by air from Bangkok to Cambodia, and he therefore had to fly on to Singapore without delay. There he was told that a majority of governments at the United Nations had just taken the decision to continue recognition of the genocidal Pol Pot as the ruler of Cambodia, despite his having been driven out of the country by the Vietnamese army. This bedevilled and complicated the relationship between the new Vietnam-supported government in Phnom Penh and any outside body, whether a UN agency or overseas NGO. At the same time, several British diplomats took the view – as they still do – that Oxfam were irresponsible and amateur do-gooders and might, through their naive concern to save lives, upset the political applecart.

Undeterred, Stringer delicately but speedily completed negotiations to charter a 250-ton tug plus a 1500-ton barge, which he fitted with iron stanchions along both its sides into which planks were inserted to increase its freeboard. No underwriter would offer all-risks insurance to the venture. A further obstacle appeared: before the Singapore stevedores would load on board the rice he purchased, they required an undertaking that the food would not reach the hands of Vietnamese soldiers. Stringer was able to satisfy them and by 8 October, on the eve of his sixtieth birthday, he sailed with a crew of eight Filipinos, one Indonesian cook, one Oxfam colleague, and an Irish captain (since at the last moment the harbour authorities refused to allow the Singaporian master permission to go). Piracy is prevalent in the area of the route which had to be taken, and would be invitingly easy at the tug's speed of six knots.

'The few facts that we had about the port of Kompong Som suggested that an unorthodox solution would have to be found – we'd no idea of the depth of the harbour, but we knew there was no power, no cranes, no water, no oil, and that the labour force was unskilled, enfeebled by a poor diet over a long time', Stringer recollects. He therefore had loaded on board additional seeds, sack trucks, carpentry tools and wood to make gangways, cooking pots and special food for the dockworkers, besides provisions and water in case they encountered any refugee boat people on the high seas. Sailing against an adverse current – a precursor of the northeast monsoon – they reached Kompong Som on the evening of Saturday 13 October, carrying the first Western food in any sizeable quantity to arrive in Cambodia. A mishap then nearly caused immediate disaster. Stringer and Chris Jackson of Oxfam recall:

> We wondered what sort of reception we might receive. We attempted to raise the radio station with a call sign we had been given. Silence reigned. From courtesy we ran up the Kampuchean flag we had bought in Singapore, forgetting as it turned out in the rush of our departure, that Singapore still continued to recognise the Pol Pot government. The difference between the two flags is small – one having three spires of Ankor Wat and the new one five. In the event it was extremely fortunate we were not shelled and later in the visit we carried out a symbolic burning of this flag on the wharf at the request of, and in front of, the dockers. When the sun rose the next morning, the port continued to shimmer in the light. Nothing moved. But eventually the one tug which the port possessed moved out to us and twelve officials stepped aboard. They were all extremely young and carried only a penny notebook and a biro. On pieces of cardboard they had written their various duties – *douane* and *santé* – and these were pinned on their breast pockets . . . Eventually, all was accepted. When we berthed at Kompong Som wharf – the first vessel from the West to bring supplies to this desperate country – it was for me one of the most agreeable moments that I can remember in my life. On the quay was a high level reception committee: the Minister for Economy and Reconstruction, the Minister of Health, the Minister of Agriculture, the Provincial Governor accompanied by Oxfam's Marcus Thompson and Dr Tim Lusty (Oxfam's medical director who is also a farmer) who has been doing a lot of professional groundwork – together with practically every truck remaining in Cambodia. I felt very proud of Oxfam . . . But apart from the sack trucks we had brought, there was no equipment available whatsoever – no forklifts, cranes, conveyors, not a thing. So everything had to be carried off by a collection of emaciated young men and women, some of whom were really boys and girls. We had more typewriters in Oxfam's head office than they did in the entire country – in fact a typewriter and carbon paper were the first things I gave the Minister of Economic Development. It took nearly five days for 1,500 tonnes to be unloaded, even though the organisation was being personally directed by the third most important minister in the government – who gave a personal undertaking that the food would be used for the most needy civilian population.

Two days later, the convoy of eighty elderly and battered American trucks reached the shattered capital, Phnom Penh. What had once been a city of two million people was a ghost-ridden ruin, its rubbish dumps being picked over by starving shadows who were using worthless banknotes as fuel and attempting to eat roots. The Oxfam team looked at one orphanage, where 500 small children who had lost their parents were sheltering inside a school which had been ransacked and systematically vandalised by the retreating Pol Pot forces: 'The children were very thin. They had literally nothing – no blankets, mats, pencils, things to play with – nothing. They were in rags or naked.'

Oxfam and Dr Lusty, at the local government's request, decided to launch an immunisation programme: for this it would be necessary to bring in not only refrigeration units for the vaccine, but also generators to power the refrigerators, and diesel fuel to run the generators. Obviously, not only was more assistance urgently needed, but transport too if supplies were not to become bottlenecked at the dockside. A second and larger (1,900-ton) barge was ordered forthwith, together with fifty Leyland trucks, plus spare parts. Since these had to have lefthand drive, this meant purchasing in Turkey, and flying them – via Hong Kong – to Phnom Penh. Further trucks were hurriedly freighted in on a ship carrying fertiliser from Greece. Cambodia's needs at that stage were unquantifiable. Over two million people – mainly the best educated – had been killed, out of a total population of eight million. The Ministry of Health's total transport consisted of one Renault car with a flat battery and no tyres.

Oxfam urgently had to choose priorities where its aid could bring most immediate good. Jim Howard discovered that the capital's waterworks was out of action through lack of spare parts and aluminium sulphate: these were included in the next shipment, together with quantities of seed and irrigation pumps for the quick sowing of short-term rice in the countryside. In an abandoned fishing-net factory at Chak Anre, Marcus Thompson and Stringer found unused Japanese machinery, and one small old man who said he was the chief engineer 'since the time of Prince Sihanouk', although he had been put out in the fields during Pol Pot. He turned out to be one of those natural engineers who can mend practically anything with a hair clip. He said he could get five machines into working order, but he had no nylon with which to make the nets. In halting French we determined the specification he needed, and we ordered a quarter of a ton of nylon twine to come on the third shipment. By getting this factory going again, what an improvement to the slogan we have so often used of teaching a man to fish – actually getting him to make the net himself.'

They also encountered less pleasant sights. Of the High School which had been used by the Pol Pot regime as a centre for torture and killing, Stringer said:

In a fairly vigorous life, I have seen a number of bestialities and brutalities, but shown round in the sun by a very pleasant graduate and his young wife, I was positively sickened by the rooms which still bore the signs of murder and cruelty of the most violent type, by the manacles, whips, canes, and shackles, by the tiny cells and the rows of pictures of decent reasonable men and women – doctors, mechanics, lawyers, nurses, the odd film star, who had been brutally murdered in this way. The piles of clothes, the matted blood and the whole air of horror was almost too much to bear. To hear on the BBC later in the week a defence by Mr Blaker in the High Court of Parliament of Her Majesty's Government's decision to continue to recognise Pol Pot seemed to me to be an act of incredible incomprehensibility.

Later when, on 22 October, he and his colleagues went to Phnom Penh railway station, they stepped among burnt pieces of cloth on the main platform: it was explained to them that on the last day before Pol Pot left, his soldiers had deliberately set fire to a train in the station in which two hundred wounded people had been lying. Stringer remembers they found other scenes mingled in the beauty of the countryside:

Twenty kilometres west of Battambang in the wide flat plain there are two small hills with a pagoda on the top of one and a saddle of land connecting the two. It is a pleasant afternoon's walk up a rocky path through young bamboo, acacia trees and honeysuckle from which you look down on the silent land where the cattle stand in the shade and the only movement is smoke drifting from the cottages. I was unprepared for what was to come, as the ancient monastery has been largely destroyed, except one part which had been used for the retention of prisoners – in it were clothes and wire manacles. There was also a sort of execution block in which the blood from the executed man poured down a little pipe through the wall. Fifty yards from the monastery a series of steps led down into a sacred grotto in which lay a huge carved painted Buddha with flowers placed in front of him. As one descended the steps, a sweet smell greeted one, and it took me some time to actually comprehend what I was looking at: the deformed forms of men and women who had been executed at the top and flung down into this holy place. The bodies had then been burnt, but they had adopted in their death the most dreadful positions, like an incredible dance in all sorts of terribly distorted, and at times almost comical, positions. I just did not know what to do or say. Later I was told that they were in fact the last of the intellectuals from Phnom Penh.

Back in Britain, Oxfam was engaged in a fundraising operation that it has never equalled before or since. After a hesitant start, money began to flow in and targets were repeatedly revised upwards. Following John Pilger's powerful articles in the *Daily Mirror* and documentary for ATV – made with the help of Jim Howard and ending with the bleak message that most of the people shown in the film had died – teams of volunteers had to be drafted into the Banbury Road headquarters to cope with the arrival of more than a thousand contributions a day. The largest amount of all was raised as a result of the bring-and-buy appeal made by the BBC's children's programme *Blue Peter*. This made television history by linking for the first time such a charitable appeal to the name of a single charity. Operating through Oxfam's shops, it raised £3.5 million by Christmas, more than three times the original target. In all, Oxfam was given over £6m, and another £14m was raised by a consortium of thirty-two other NGO agencies – a model instance of close international co-operation in instant response to a need – established in Brussels in September 1979. Among the leaders were the Dutch NOVIB, the German CARITAS, the World Lutheran Federation, Oxfam America, and Oxfam Belgique.

'Pinned in a nutcracker between the ambitions and ancient aims of Russia, China, and Vietnam, the best that we can hope for is that we may be able to make a contribution to keeping the Kampuchean people alive, to give them some hope for the future and at least an understanding that there are some men and women who came, albeit late, to help them as good neighbours with no ulterior motives', wrote Stringer the next month, January 1980. Yet while few questioned either the scale of the tragedy or Brian Walker's intrepid initial decision for Oxfam to intervene directly while governments and the UN were still hamstrung by non-recognition of the *de facto* Cambodian government, several controversies rumbled on the sidelines. Some people in Oxfam itself worried that the drama and scale of the operation were diverting Oxfam from its true purpose of the less spectacular pursuit of long-term development, and saw it as a reversal of its recently evolved policy away from disaster relief. Other agencies would have been superhuman if they had not at times resented Oxfam's domination of the media, or given voice to their thoughts that Oxfam was taking a risk in not having ultimate control of distribution. The overwhelming response to the *Blue Peter* appeal evoked grumblings from some quarters that its success was hurting domestic charities. Oxfam itself kept a discreet silence on the issue, but one BBC producer was less reticent and described such complaints as 'obscene and outrageous lies'.

Further argument, fuelled by allegations that the aid would go to feed the Vietnamese army, centred on whether Oxfam and the NGO consortium were politically innocent and being manipulated. These charges were indignantly refuted by Walker and Malcolm Harper who headed Oxfam's team in Phnom Penh for seven months from November 1979 (and is now the Director of the UK Nations Association), who stated, 'We have a fetish about controlling where our aid goes: we pride ourselves on it.' Walker had made a key agreement with the Vietnamese-backed Heng Samrin government of Cambodia in Phnom Penh in September 1979 not to channel aid across the Thai border, and had won in return the right for a team of seven Oxfam representatives to travel, monitor and evaluate what happened to the aid being given. There was no other option if help was to get through in time to the civilian population who most needed it. The Phnom Penh government – understandably – set its face intransigently against permitting any relief that could revive Pol Pot's Khmer Rouge forces in their camps over the Thai border. Aside from its humanitarian motivation, other observers believed the NGOs' aid was in fact politically positive to the West, as being likely to reduce the Phnom Penh government's dependence on Vietnam or Russia. There was a minor drama in January 1980 when Richard Lindley of the BBC reported seeing two of the Oxfam-supplied trucks in use at Ho Chi Minh City airport in Vietnam: fortunately an investigation proved that they were merely being used to collect 24 metric tonnes of condensed milk donated by the Communist party of Japan.

Cambodia gave Oxfam unique experience of working with a Communist government. The one at Phnom Penh they found suspicious of Westerners, like most governments, obstinately reluctant to admit errors, but in general unusually honest. Roger Newton, the co-ordinator of the NGO consortium remembers its greatest success as being the supply of 10,000 metric tons of rice seed – against all the odds, including apparently insurmountable political obstacles in Thailand: 'The FAO eventually got us export permission; the International Committee of the Red Cross arranged a magnificently efficient and dramatic airlift from Bangkok. Meanwhile thousands of tons of seed were coming by sea . . . Then when disaster threatened and cracks suddenly appeared in Phnom Penh's wharf in March and April 1980, UNICEF and Oxfam joined forces to supply flat-top barges which saved the whole rice seed and fertiliser programme. Though there were also some pretty big hiccups, from which we learnt some painful lessons.'

Cambodia was untypical of the challenges of development. Although exceptional, the episode shows – like *War and Peace* – how rarely history is formed by static plans. Brian Walker summed up the operation in reflection as follows:

> 1979 was one of those climacteric years which hit an organisation occasionally and alter its shape and complexion in fundamental ways. None of us realised the consequences which would flow from the Cambodian decision . . . As the weeks and months slipped by, and we become more and more involved in this most hideous of human tragedies – ranking with the worst excesses of Hitler's Germany, of Amin's Uganda or of Stalin's Russia – we realised that we were caught up in a momentum which, across a range of variables, was bound to change the Oxfam we knew. Those variables included the response of governments and people all around the world to our initiative; the magnitude in physical terms, and the complexity in political terms, of the aid operation itself; and the impact all of this had upon our work in other parts of the world, as well as our fund raising and public opinion forming responsibilities here at home. Being bombarded from all these quarters naturally led to a great deal of heart searching at all levels. Pleas were made early on that we were not strong enough to absorb all these kinds of pressures – that neither staff nor volunteers would be able to measure up to the challenge on a sustained basis. Some argued that we didn't have the right to accept the gifts which were pouring in when the political future of South East Asia was so uncertain and that we should abort the appeal. A third group argued that if the Cambodian operation grew to the dimensions predicted, it would throw out of kilter our work in other parts of the world, and, therefore, we should hold ourselves back. Others saw the operation in simplistic terms – people were in trouble, Oxfam ought to help, regardless of the consequences . . . Well, not only did Oxfam survive this complex period, full of high-risk decisions, but I believe it showed the organisation, through all the ups and downs it encountered, as being true to the basic ideas which Oxfam, at its best, represents.

Oxfam's part must be set in context against the large roles played by UNICEF, the International Committee of the Red Cross, the FAO and several other organisations. In April 1981, the Cambodia/Kampuchea consortium of aid agencies was discontinued and the country reverted to being just one part of Oxfam's Asia programme. But the effects of the emergency operation remain significant and lasting.

For the first time a non-governmental agency had shown that, by incisiveness and conviction, it could operate where huge government and international bodies were stymied and politically hamstrung. Pilger recounts how in 1979 the Foreign Office 'applied unsubtle pressure to voluntary relief agencies, warning them of "grave difficulties" if they went ahead and sent relief to the Phnom Penh government; Oxfam, to its great credit, ignored this.' Oxfam believes that for some time afterwards it was the victim of 'black propaganda' from Foreign Office sources as a result.

The gamble could have blown up in disaster: if suspicious communist soldiers had opened fire . . . if the Vietnamese had misused the *Blue Peter* alms . . . if Pol Pot had returned to power. Instead, as Walker says,

> The solidarity and compassion which surged across our nation directly influenced our government, and recognition of the odious Pol Pot was withdrawn. At the United Nations in New York, Britain's ambassador sent a message through his senior member of staff, to say that at a time when Britain's image in the United Nations had been pretty low, the one consistently bright spot for him and his team was the constant reports received from United Nations agencies and foreign delegations of Oxfam's work in Cambodia. Even those who politically opposed what we were doing respected the effectiveness of our work. In Britain, the campaign brought excitement and a sense of purpose into the lives of millions of families up and down the country.

Stringer – more than a little nostalgically – says, 'We shall never be the same again.'

Lastly, but most importantly, what were the results for Cambodia? The psychology and social damage inflicted on the Khmer people can not be repaired, at least for a generation. They had been physically and mentally scarred to the core of their existence. The consortium cannot claim to have 'saved' Cambodia: only its inhabitants are able to do that. But Kom So Mol, the Cambodian Minister of Agriculture, told Oxfam in June 1980 that because of the agricultural seed programme which had been Oxfam's and FAO's priority from the beginning, his country would be self-sufficient in seeds by the next year. Contrary to what Oxfam at the first believed, it was not food aid that Cambodia needed; it was the help and wherewithal to get the whole country's life system functioning again, so that it could produce and distribute its own essentials. Bill Yates reported from Phnom Penh that there was no doubt that the earliest deliveries were the crucial pump-priming which enabled the country to get on its feet again. The hard work of Harper, Lusty, Newton and others helped the survivors feel they had not been abandoned by the world. In August 1979, Howard had found 50 sick and starving children in what had been a pig-pen; ten months later, this site had been transformed into the largest primary school in the country, with desks and footballs paid for in Britain. With the help of a massive UNICEF-Red Cross operation, 300,000 Cambodian refugees returned home in 1980, and 1.3 million children entered schools after a five-year interruption of education – all achieved, as Donald Allen of UNICEF points out, for a cost of less than half what the world spends on arms in a single day.

In Cambodia, Oxfam had an international political role, unwished, thrust upon it. The episode was lucky to command a combination of dramatic press concern and compassionate public sympathy; the real test will be another episode which involves anti-British, politically unpopular victims liable to be ignored or disliked by the media and the public. The journalist Iain Guest believes that the first lesson Cambodia teaches is that relief and aid cannot be expected to exist in a political vacuum; and the second one is how much response depends on opportune journalism.

Jim Howard, whom Pilger describes as seeing all such issues from the point of view of people rather than from any Messianic complex or his career, sums it up:

> I think it will be a pity if ordinary people in Britain, who supported a faraway nation with their hearts and their savings, do not realise how much they have contributed to the rescue of Cambodia. You see, for some of us in the relief business, the old colonialist fervour dies hard. How can the natives possibly have a government which might, just might, know its own people best? Their attitude is that the West knows best. The truth is that real corruption in Cambodia has been negligible. None of the supplies are on sale in the market. The problem, which Westerners have difficulty with, is sensitivity. This is a government whose murderous enemy is still recognised by the United Nations and which feels itself cut off and isolated fighting for its life. In the circumstances, I believe they have done an historic job of recovery.

2

'Into the Dangerous World I Leapt': Oxfam's Birth and Growth

> For a rich industrialised society to be less than assiduous in narrowing the world's present disparities, is to acquiesce in, indeed even to promote, the denial of the most basic of human rights – the right to life itself at a tolerable level of existence . . . All the dictators and all the aggressors throughout history, however ruthless, have not succeeded in creating as much misery and suffering as poverty sustains today.
>
> *Shridath Ramphal* (Minority Rights Group Lecture, 1981)

> It is easier to go to the moon than build homes for people . . . But events or situations are never themselves trapping, it is only our limited and conditioned interpretation of them. There is an alternative to fear and dissolution, the art of bringing new light to bear.
>
> *Dom Thomas Cullinan*

In 1977 Oxfam's income was about half that of Dr Barnardo's. After the Cambodia appeal, donations to Oxfam drew ahead of those to the National Trust, both the major cancer research funds, Dr Barnardo's, the Royal National Lifeboat Institution and the Salvation Army, so that in 1980 it became the British charity with the largest voluntary income of all. Has size altered the humanitarian ideals of its original smaller scale?

Ronald Blythe, in his beautiful anthology *Places* (published the following year by O.U.P. 'for Oxfam – since Oxfam has indeed become part of the British landscape too') wrote:

> It could be an example of something being so familiar it can no longer be seen . . . Although it now operates on a heroic scale it has been able to retain an intimate and even a parochial quality. It is both highly professional in its operations . . . and also approachably amateur so that practically anyone of good will still finds it quite an ordinary and natural business to give it a helping hand.

James Cameron said in his arresting advertisement *I dearly wish Oxfam did not exist*: 'Not everyone feels about Oxfam as I do,

13

and understandably, since not everyone has seen it at work all over the world, as I have, nor seen the places where it has not yet been able to work, which is worse. Before "Oxfam" became part of the language the word itself, I must agree, had a bit of an instant-coffee ring about it. An Oxford association with famine, one of the least hungry English towns identifying itself with those who starve thousands of miles away? Yet Oxfam got itself embodied in the vocabulary – and mercifully so, if one may play with words. Everyone now knows what Oxfam is, some people take the trouble to learn what it does, and how it does it.'

But nobody at the first meeting of the Oxford Committee for Famine Relief would have anticipated its future. It was far from a large gathering, and went scarcely noticed during the Second World War. Half a dozen people, having planned it in the Friends' Meeting House at Oxford, met in the Old Library of the University Church there on 5 October 1942. The minutes, written in a battered threepenny exercise book, describe its objectives as being the relief, to the extent that the law for the time being permitted, of famine and sickness arising as a result of the war. The founders included Professor Gilbert Murray, O.M., the classical scholar and humanist; Rev T. R. Milford, the Vicar of the University Church, who became Chairman; Cecil Jackson-Cole, an idiosyncratic businessman who became Honorary Secretary; Dr Henry Gillett (the first of many Quakers to shape Oxfam), then Mayor of Oxford; and – completing a recognisable Oxfam mix – Sir Alan Pim, retired from the Indian Civil Service, who became Honorary Treasurer.

Their hope was to arouse public concern about the plight of starving civilian families, and especially the children, in then-occupied Greece and Belgium. 'Very little was known', Milford said, 'about what was going on in Nazi-occupied Europe, but what we did know concerned us deeply. Through the Quakers we heard that many people were dying in Greece from starvation, partly through the effects of the Allied blockade of Europe.' It was thought intolerable – a prelude to the cry 'people before politics' heard at the time of the recent Cambodian operation – that even at the height of the war the Allies should say to innocent children in Greece, 'Sorry, you've got to die.'

A similar committee already existed in London. There was a dissident mood growing amongst a number of people in Britain

– led by Dr George Bell, the then Bishop of Chichester – for reconciliation between nations. They were opposed to the pursuit of a total war, which in Mervyn Jones's words (*Two Ears of Corn*, Hodder and Stoughton, 1965), 'had taken dangerous and unworthy forms. They protested against the condemnation of the whole German people, in which they saw a racialist mirror-image of Nazi hatred of the Jews. They thought that the demand for unconditional surrender would merely unite Germany behind Hitler . . . They criticised the bombing of German cities as both wrong and futile. They were opposed to the Allied blockade of continental Europe . . . The blockade was imposing no hardship on the Germans, who ate and lived well until near the end of the war, but meant hunger and misery for millions who were on our side: the people of the occupied countries. Greece, above all, was fast descending into famine.' The outcome was a letter, dispatched to the national press over the signatures of Margery Perham, G. D. H. Cole, and Sir Farquhar Buzzard, together with the heads of four Oxford colleges. But the Minister of Economic Warfare (Dingle Foot) replied that although he sympathised, permission must be refused for food to be sent to Belgium, lest it indirectly help the German war effort.

In Greece, however, the Greek Red Cross was still functioning and it was decided to channel the first donation of £3,200 through this body. In March 1943, the Committee was first registered as a charity with its address at Milford's house, 12 Holywell, Oxford. In October of that year, a Greek Famine Relief Week in Oxford, organised by Jackson-Cole, with Greek dancing, films and concerts, raised £10,700. A shop which had been opened for the week's duration to sell gifts yielded another £2,300. Milford approached the MP for Oxford for support, but without success at that stage: Quintin Hogg objected, first, that he believed the Government had secret information that aid would benefit Germany; and secondly, that other Allied countries which were not included in the relief plan would be dissatisfied. The Committee did not accept these arguments, and £20 was authorised to be spent on advertising an appeal for postcards in favour of controlled relief to women and children in Greece and Belgium.

This is the first recorded expenditure on advertising: by May 1944, 7,044 signatures had been received, including 70 per cent of the members of the City Council. The Greek project was successful. After D-Day the next month, the first appeal was made for clothing (although this was still rationed in Britain) to be sent to liberated countries. An appeal for 'books for Europe' brought in 12,000 volumes. By the next year, people were also sending dried milk as well as sweets and other rationed foods.

When many German people were found after capitulation to be near starvation, the Committee anxiously debated whether Germany should be included in the relief programme: would

AN APPEAL TO OXFORD.

European Relief Fund.

Dear Sir/Madam,

Leaders of our nation have spoken of the unparalleled catastrophe which may fall on millions in Europe this winter. Great numbers have lost their breadwinners or their houses, but above all there is a serious shortage of food. In particular the women and children, the old and the sick will suffer greatly. Many are likely to die of hunger and cold.

Our government have therefore enabled voluntary societies to purchase special food and medicines without affecting our rations. Donations are urgently needed to buy these relief supplies and we appeal for a generous response throughout Oxford City and University to this plea. Your donation will save the lives of women and children.

The Committee have decided to entrust the distribution to the Friends Relief Service (Quakers) whose trained workers are already operating in many parts of Europe. We are assured the supplies will be under their effective control from purchase to distribution among those in distress. Relief

Please turn over

EUROPEAN RELIEF WEEK IN OXFORD. JANUARY 19th to 26th. 1946.

this put people off helping? And if voluntary groups such as themselves contributed, would this only result in the Government doing less? It was decided to take both risks. An urgent appeal for food and medicines for Europe 'where the need is greatest' was signed by the Vice-Chancellor, the Mayor and Bishop of Oxford, both the University MPs (Sir Alan Herbert and Sir Arthur Salter), now joined by the MP for the City (Quintin Hogg), as well as Lord Pakenham (now Lord Longford), and A. D. Lindsay (then Master of Balliol). The decision was proved right: money and clothes continued to flow in. They were channelled through agencies working on the spot, such as the Quakers (£16,000 in cash and £32,000 worth of clothes in 1948): this way of working through local groups rather than starting its own programmes has been Oxfam's strategy ever since.

A similar impetus for post-war reconstruction had led to the start of Christian Aid. The Save the Children Fund, the oldest of the large foreign aid charities, had been founded from much the same sentiment as Oxfam – but one world war earlier in 1919, from the Fight the Famine Council which opposed the Allied blockade of Germany. Oxfam's two initial godparents were the contrasting talents of the widely-respected Milford (later to be Master of the Temple and a Canon of Lincoln, his younger brother being a Canon of Calcutta and later of Bristol), and until his death in 1979, the dynamic Jackson-Cole. The latter was a hectoring individualist in the Beaverbrook mould: an energetically successful self-made shopowner from the East End of London, who converted to Christianity. In Milford's words he was:

restlessly anxious to help the world's needy and he determined to dedicate the rest of his life to giving practical expression to the Christian injunctions to heal the sick, clothe the naked, and feed the hungry. He was to endow several other charities, but not Oxfam: instead he seconded his staff, paid for the first national advertisements, and provided the people to launch the initial appeal through a small business he owned in Oxford. Without his vision, business ability and use of his own firm's resources, Oxfam would never have gone outside Oxford. Later he continued to oversee its fundraising work. With the end of the war and with the tremendous needs he saw arising, he realised that the traditional approach to charitable work would be inadequate. Charities would have to be run on businesslike lines. He decided to extend his business interests to provide the necessary finance. Because he needed people with a certain amount of altruism, he advertised for Christian and public-spirited people to work with him. Those who joined his staff were made to realise that a major part of the company profits would be devoted to building up new charitable enterprises, or to putting new life into worthwhile, but flagging movements. As his business ventures expanded so did his charitable work. Business staff were released to give part of their time to charitable enterprises.

In 1948 the Committee decided against Oxfam closing down just because Europe was on the road to recovery. On 30 September it resolved unanimously that, in Milford's words, 'there could be no reason for stopping while human need remained. Suffering caused by the war had opened the way for a flood of goodwill which must try to meet need anywhere however caused'. It was decided in fact to widen and extend, rather than stop, the work. Oxfam's first permanent gift shop was opened; it still flourishes in the centre of Oxford, at 17 Broad Street, which also became the Committee's headquarters until 1954. The publicity was made more professional by Robert Castle and Harold Sumption, a Quaker who continues to give it expert advice today. The word 'Oxfam', orginally the abbreviation used in telegrams, gradually became a household word though it was not officially adopted as the Committee's name until eleven years later. Those who worked with Jackson-Cole ('JC' as he was irreverently known by some in those days) remember him as a far from easy colleague; often intolerant and so angry on occasions that he had been known to hurl typewriters in the office. But it was he who insisted on advertising nationally for the first Administrative Secretary in 1951: Leslie Kirkley was the result. JC was gradually eased sideways to be Honorary Secretary Emeritus. Jackson-Cole went off to start Help the Aged and, when the pattern repeated itself, founded Action in Distress (now Action Aid). He was one of those who believe ends justify means; but he left behind three impressive ends as a result.

The Leslie Kirkley era

In 1949 the Charity Commissioners approved the widening of Oxfam's registered objects to being *the relief of suffering arising as a result of war or any other cause in any part of the world.'* The first major appeal the same year was for Palestinian refugees; this was followed by victims of the Korean war (1950); starvation in Bihar (1951), when the Indian Government objected to the use of the word 'famine', and Oxfam had to change its advertisements to 'malnutrition in Bihar' with the result that donations fell to 5 per cent of their former volume; the east coast floods in Britain, and the Ionian islands earthquake (1953); the Hungarian uprising (1956); Algeria's war of independence (1957); World Refugee year (1959); the fighting in the Congo (1960) and in Nigeria-Biafra (1967–70); earthquake in Peru and cyclone in East Pakistan (1970–71); Bangladesh-India (1971); Guatemala's earthquake (1976); India's cyclone (1977). . . .

Alongside this roll-call, which echoes the campaign honours of a venerated regiment, the fundraising methods were transformed. Unlike some other charities, Oxfam has never courted royal or titled connections. From the haphazard amateurism of relying on a handful of enthusiastic volunteers who used to call on Oxford householders asking for articles no longer needed from cupboards and drawers, more professional methods developed. In 1950 Oxfam's income in cash and kind was £100,000, with the latter source exceeding the former by six to one; by the end of the decade it was over ten times that figure, and for the first time cash income exceeded the value of donated goods. In 1958 it was registered as a non-profit-making company limited by guarantee.

Richard Exley (a young north-country conscientious objector who is now a writer and publisher) the next year suggested the Pledged Gift scheme, which produced in its first four successive years £3,000, £20,000, £70,000 and £240,000. Originally based on the tallyman of the north, today there are several thousand collectors who visit each month or week people in their streets, offices or factories who have pledged themselves to make a regular contribution for Oxfam's work. (Oxfam's other, crucial, role of broadening consciences is illustrated by Exley's view that 'Oxfam would still be doing a worthwhile job if all the money collected were to be pushed in a wheelbarrow over the cliffs of Dover.')

But the major reasons for the transformation of Oxfam into a worldwide organisation flowed from the vision and skills of (now Sir) H. Leslie Kirkley. He came from a small family paint business in Leeds, and was another instance of what Oxfam has benefited from frequently: an able man who decided to change the direction and value of his career in mid-life. (Since doing so, all without exception seem to have been happier as a result. Perhaps their example will be followed by many more men and women of talent who feel the satisfaction derived from their present work is limited in its satisfaction or meaning?) Kirkley, an internationalist as well as Labour Party man, had been strongly influenced by what he had seen in defeated Germany. Trained in local government and as a chartered company secretary, he had gained from his experience (as the honorary secretary of a European Relief Committee in Leeds) of having welded two hundred separate charitable groups – mainly of friends and their friends – in the north of England during the post-war years. To develop Oxfam, he appointed Regional Organisers who supervised the collection of money and clothing in their particular areas and were later to act as educators too. Mental patients at the Warnford Hospital helped address envelopes, 'thus doing two goods at once.' In the 1960s the gift shops expanded under Joe Mitty. Mitty was the first – and for a long time the only – paid member of the staff, and has just retired after 33 years' work with Oxfam. An ex-Army captain who had served in India, he proved to be a natural trader and ingenious fundraiser.

Previously, no one from the organisation had been to the Middle East, India or the Far East to see the needs at first hand – 'We used to sit in Broad Street waiting for appeals and then send out cheques.' Kirkley made time to travel to identify problems and encourage local initiatives and applicants. The *Week's Good Cause* appeals on the BBC generated strikingly expanding amounts, as knowledge of Oxfam's work spread: in 1950 (Gilbert Murray) £9,689; 1953 (Sir Maurice Bowra) £13,885; 1956 (Lord Hailsham) £30,976; 1958 (Lord Birkett) £46,860; and by 1960 (Richard Dimbleby) £105,941. Kirkley tried to encourage the interest of trades unionists – 'It's essential in order to widen the development lobby, and because of their opposition to cheap imports.' He also regrets not having achieved more to link Oxfam firmly with the 'town' part of Oxford as well as the 'gown' – 'We never really succeeded in involving most of either the workers or the management at the motor works.'

In 1956, in time for the Hungarian crisis, the clothing depot at Bourne Street, Chelsea, was opened. The name 'Oxfam' still continues to puzzle people of every nationality overseas – including Americans who wonder about what possible connection there could be with Oxford, Mississippi. Regular suggestions have been made – by Nicolas Stacey amongst others – that Oxfam should move its headquarters: to London (where the supply of volunteers and managerial talent would, in theory, be greatest), or to Bristol or Leeds (which have easily accessible airports). Being situated in Oxford helps to maintain unity, and human scale; but there are international critics of its 'dreaming spires' location – especially after Christian Aid moved from Sloane Square to Brixton. But it has always been decided that the balance of advantages lay with remaining at Oxford – from where Heathrow airport is more quickly accessible than from London – and where Oxfam 'has first call on talent, whereas in London we'd be competing with many other causes. It is also a popular place to live for most of the employees, as well as being central for committee members from all over England; and we can draw on experts at the University – such as Hourani, Perham, Attiyah, Hodgkin – knowledgeable about every part of the world.'

For Kirkley's first ten years he had to work with parts of Oxfam scattered in six buildings all over Oxford. He, as Director, was to be found up two flights of stairs over a tailor's shop. On the other side of the street, the other staff worked above narrow stairs cluttered with packages of stationery. Committee meetings were held in the back room of a Baptist Church; the card index was kept in a condemned shed lent by the City Council. In 1962, the present headquarters were built at 274 Banbury Road, in Summertown, about a mile north of the centre of Oxford for £75,000 – from a special fund, without the expenditure of any money given for relief work.

Hitherto, most of Oxfam's work had been concentrated on providing immediate relief to hungry, sick or homeless people. During the 1960s, however, Oxfam evolved into a development agency. It was decided to try to tackle the roots of famine and poverty, to implement the Freedom from Hunger Campaign's maxim of 'Give a man a fish, and you feed him for a day; teach him to fish, and you feed him for a lifetime.' 'The man you feed this year will starve next,' as Benedict Nightingale wrote in Charities (Allen Lane, 1973), 'unless he has been taught to irrigate, till, sow or somehow produce food for himself. Symptomatic relief may only postpone a cure; and yet on the other hand emergencies are emergencies, famine famine, and we can hardly allow people to starve because of dogmatic anxieties about their future. It is a desperate dilemma, and most of the major foreign aid charities have come to accept a double responsibility as inevitable.' In his 1960 *Week's Good Cause* appeal, Richard Dimbleby had described Oxfam as 'a sort of financial fire brigade, always ready, day and night, to send immediate help to any danger point, to any disaster in the world.'

But by the end of that decade, it was spending less than 10 per cent of its grants budget on disasters; more than half was being used to improve medical and welfare projects in areas which had suffered no emergency, and 40 per cent on agricultural development and technical training. In the early 1960s, Oxfam's advertisements were still confidently stating 'With your help Oxfam can banish hunger.' In 1958 it was helping in 25 different countries; by 1963 this figure had grown to 72. World Refugee Year (launched in 1959 by Christopher Chataway, Tim Raison, Trevor Philpott and Colin Jones, with the help of Chris Brasher, David Ennals, Robert Kee and others), as well as the Suez debacle and the UN's Freedom from Hunger Campaign, were all catalysts, combining to bring home to a significant part of the British public both the situation of those who were not 'having it so good' and the fact that the British could do something about this. Britain, with Kirkley chairing the publicity committee, raised more for World Refugee Year than did any other comparable nation, Oxfam itself contributing £755,000; for the Freedom from Hunger Campaign it pledged £1.8m, and raised £2.1m.

In 1961 Oxfam appointed its first permanent representative abroad. Kirkley sent Jimmy Betts (a brother of Barbara Castle) as Field Director for Africa, initially to work in Basutoland, Bechuanaland and Swaziland from a base in Maseru, and later moving to Nairobi. 'Back in the 1960s,' Kirkley recalls, 'the world seemed so much more confident that it could achieve something . . . So we sent Jimmy, an ex-forestry man from Nigeria, to find out the best way we could help. He came back with a quarter of a million pound package for development. That was big money for us in those days so we promptly asked him to return, set himself up in the area, and see that the money was spent in the way that donors intended.' Later the co-operatives in Botswana (as Bechuanaland became) were expanded with the help of Bernard Murphy, a trade union organiser who persuaded co-operatives

in Britain to contribute their help. Three years later, Bernard
Llewellyn became Field Director for Asia, and similar posts were
also created for Latin America and for West Africa. Kenneth
Bennett was the first Overseas Director, until 1974 when he was
succeeded by Michael Harris. But some money was always kept
in hand so that in case of emergency a grant could be made in a
matter of hours on the authority of the Secretary and the Chairman
of the Grants Committee. Probably for most people this work still
remains the image of Oxfam. Then, as today, there were doubts
amongst the staff about whether to divert energy to successive
disasters, and worry lest the emotional response to them acts to
distance the reality of basic needs and problems; but funds – as
well as plans – for development in fact are often boosted as a
spin-off from disaster appeals.

The growth of support, as measured by money, seemed – even
allowing for inflation – deceptively inexorable: Oxfam's record
£1 million in 1960 became £2m by 1963 and £2.9m only a year
later. Other agencies expanded similarly on the rising tide of
internationalism in Britain at the time: competition seemed to
stimulate rather than duplicate. In earlier times missionary
societies had been the only overseas charities. Christian Aid
(previously called Inter-Church Aid), started by the British part
of the Protestant World Council of Churches, spent £1.25m in
1964 through the Council of Churches of recipient countries.
Catholics and Jews have their own very active agencies. But War
on Want – a radical campaigning group founded in 1951 and, like
Oxfam, secular – raised £1,125,000 in the same year of 1964.

Factors that have been suggested as prompting this climate of
growth for the voluntary agencies include the cumulative effects
on those enjoying increasing affluence in the rich world of a
liberal education coupled with improved communications such
as television documentaries; easier and cheaper intercontinental
tourism, especially for younger people; the influence of people
who had served as overseas volunteers; a national search for a
new overseas role after the end of the British empire; and, for
others, the attraction of a peaceful way to counter Communism.
Oxfam's trading company, Oxfam Activities, founded in 1965 to
handle goods like Christmas cards and tea towels, soon began to
import handicrafts from poor countries as well. In that year there
were 20 regional organisers and 400 Oxfam groups; by the end

of the sixties the total income rose to £3.4m, with 241 gift shops, and Milford confessed, 'We are sometimes alarmed at the ever increasing scale of Oxfam and watch ourselves for signs of *hubris* lest we should magnify the organisation and forget its purpose.'

In the same year of 1965 Oxfam, after anxious consideration and intense discussions, embarked on another programme in furtherance of its conviction that prevention was easier than cure: it began to make grants for small family planning projects. At that time it was one of the pioneers in this field; no UN agency was working in family planning, and Sweden alone among governments was allocating aid funds for such a purpose. A number of people in Oxfam – not just Roman Catholics – expressed violent opposition, and a few resigned in protest. More soul-searching and agonised debates followed as Oxfam embarked on the complexities of development policies. 'To respond to charity for those in blatant distress requires merely Yes or No', Arthur Gaitskell pointed out at an Oxfam conference in September 1964. 'It is a sign-posted open road. You follow it or you don't. To respond to an interest in world development is a very different matter. This is a jungle of uncertainties and confusing tracks.'

All charities seem to attract more than their share of passionate opinion and tensions, though Oxfam has weathered most of its heated arguments with the aid of its tradition of preferring to take decisions by consensus. As Geoffrey Wilson suggests, the Quaker background of many key figures in Oxfam helps them to resolve most differences more tolerantly than other charities. But like many people with a mission, people working in agencies such as Oxfam believe their organisation is the centre of the universe, and resentment at outside criticism can be one facet of their tenacious loyalty. Tension rose both within the organisation and inside some of its individual personalities, in one employee's view of their work, as 'socialist evidence confronted old liberal attitudes'. Radical staff members have always wished to see Oxfam as 'a cause to identify with, and worth fighting for' rather than being 'a well-meaning charity seeking to pick up the broken bits'. Doubts were raised, for example, as to whether or not to publicise the most controversial grants. There were debates on questions such as the propriety of seeking money from industry (Yes: 'The people of Calcutta need it'; No: 'Much of British commercial money is made out of the very practices and conditions we are working to change'). Malcolm Harper (an able disarmament crusader who spent eighteen years with Oxfam, after theological college and South Africa) says luckily Oxfam has one very important quality: the ability – unlike some political parties and other charities – while sharply criticising itself, to get on with the job at the same time.

The Stacey crisis 1969–70

Division over the future direction Oxfam should take crystallised – and then polarised – around proposals made in 1969 by the Rev. Nicolas Stacey, who had become its dynamic youthful Deputy Director the previous year. In the key confidential memorandum he wrote on 16 October, Stacey – 'intelligent', 'not a natural Number Two', 'ten years ahead of his time' according to colleagues – stated with perhaps more candour than tact:

> The present turning point in Oxfam's history has much in common with the one that faces all charities when they are a quarter of a century old. Charities are usually started by a handful of people with great vision, dedication and drive; as the charity grows in size and significance, the founder members get older and invariably more cautious (although this is sometimes rationalised as increased wisdom). The committee structures become more rigid, bureaucracy increases and the initial enthusiasm and vision become eroded . . .
>
> Oxfam has been a product and expression of the national mood in the late 1950s and first half of the 1960s . . . I believe there is evidence which shows that the tide which was flowing for Oxfam, and which has been the fundamental reason for its success, is now on the turn – and may have been for two or three years . . . Some of my reasons: . . . Increasing comments by regional organisers that Oxfam has a middle-aged image. Our inability so far to catch the imagination of the young professional and technocrat classes. The vulnerability of Oxfam is shown by the way a shortfall in our budgeted income plays havoc with our expense ratio, and the virtual impossibility of achieving an immediate, effective reduction in expenditure to bring it down to 20 per cent . . . Because the problem of world development is now acknowledged as being so vast, and the donor never sees the result of the donation, once disenchantment about overseas aid sets in, charities in this field may suffer more quickly than a home charity operating on a narrower front and able to show results. War on Want has already suffered a severe drop in income.

The solution Stacey proposed was a drastic one: to change Oxfam primarily into an education and lobbying body; that it should reverse its priorities, and concentrate on building up a pressure group to make the Government change its policy. 'Any organisation involved in the relief of suffering in the Third World must inevitably be involved in education, and bringing pressures to bear on the points of power in the developed world . . . My first recommendation is that Oxfam Activities and Oxfam shops should be merged to form a separate company whose profits would go into an Oxfam "educational" trust . . . It could be argued that few pressure groups outside the USA have ever had funds on this scale at their disposal, and to transfer the Shop and Trading Company profits of nearly £0.75m per annum is overdoing it. I would argue that there could have been few causes of greater significance to the peace of the world and the future of mankind than the challenge the developing world presents to the developed world.'

Fired by the example of Des Wilson's success at Shelter, Stacey advocated that Oxfam should employ a full-time political adviser who would organise local groups to lobby an all-party parliamentary group of MPs; and that Oxfam's staff should become proselytising crusaders arousing the country. He proposed a new 'Oxfam Sponsorship' department, which would 'run city and town campaigns, spearheaded by mobile flying squads using Kennedy-type election techniques. In these short, sharp campaigns the whole community would be mobilised to raise funds for a particular project from which there would be an important educational spin-off.' Overseas, he also thought it 'desirable, though not essential, for Oxfam to be operational in a limited number of imaginative projects.'

Opposition to Stacey's plan coalesced around two arguments. First that, while education was permitted, the Charity Commissioners' report for 1969 clearly stated: 'It is a well-established principle of charity law that a trust for the attainment of a political object is not a valid charitable trust and that any purpose with the object of influencing the legislature is a political purpose.' The second objection stemmed from doubts whether the bulk of Oxfam's own volunteers and traditional supporters would welcome or accept any such change: the more staid members of Council raised the spectre of 'elderly widows on the South Coast who would cease supporting Oxfam if it didn't continue with its work of putting pants on foreign babies'. On the Council and Executive there is an element of chance in policy-making, dependent on who attends; as with most such bodies, it is the older and retired members who are most likely to come to meetings frequently. Against the background of the Nigerian civil war then raging, Oxfam's Council of Management decided to maintain its traditional role, while giving support to Young Oxfam, Third World First, and the World Development Movement. *The Guardian* commented: 'Stacey's plan was a major gamble. If it had failed, Oxfam could have ended up with nothing: no change in political attitudes achieved, and its charitable status and efficiency compromised. And that is a very relevant consideration when what you are spending on a political campaign at home is not just cash but lives – the lives of those suffering human beings which that money might have saved if you had not diverted it to other ends. There will be many who will regret, nevertheless, that the gamble was not taken.'

Stacey, who had been thought of as heir apparent to Kirkley as Director, resigned in May 1970 and later became Director of Social Services for Kent. He wrote in *The Sunday Times* the weekend following his resignation:

Oxfam's decision was almost inevitable, and it will continue to do excellent work as I saw for myself in a recent tour of Oxfam projects in seven African countries. It is an organisation worthy of everybody's wholehearted support. I have resigned because I think it has missed an opportunity of attempting to influence events which will dominate our history in the remaining years of this century, and I do not fancy myself primarily as a fund raiser. But I accept that the whole tradition of charities in Britain makes it extraordinarily difficult to combine fund raising on a large scale with education, propaganda and political pressure. The sincere and well-meaning but elderly and cautious people with a high threshold of boredom who dominate the web of committees that control most charities shrink from the cut and thrust of the political arena. While the typical donor, thought to be elderly, female and middle class, probably considers politics dirty, pressure groups irrelevant and controversy ungentlemanly. (The good people who subscribed so generously to the soup kitchen for unemployed miners in the 1930s run by the vicar from the vestry of the parish church would have been hurt, shocked, surprised and confused if they had heard the recipients of their bounty shout 'Damn your charity, we want justice'.)

Leslie Kirkley fully recognised the difficult crux of Oxfam's dilemma. He had written in the previous year's Annual Report: 'Our allocations for overseas aid and development topped £3 million for the first time in our history. What now? We can go busily on. We might treble our income; we can then treble our aid to the developing world. But what does this mean if governmental and inter-governmental aid from the rich nations continues to diminish while public apathy about the Third World spreads – and the world poverty gap goes on widening. These trends are swallowing up many times over, all that voluntary agencies can do. To go on increasing the size of our income is just not enough in itself – unless we are satisfied to end up as a mere sop to the national conscience – a gesture in the face of crisis.'

An endless succession of policy discussions, memoranda and meetings ensued. Kirkley circulated this minute on 4 March 1972 after an internal conference at Charney Manor, a discussion centre owned by the Quakers:

> Over the week-end I met with Divisional Heads and discussed Oxfam's current situation and the future of the organisation. We agreed that our primary objective is the meeting of desperate needs and to achieve this end we must significantly widen our constituency. Our great strength lies in our very substantial resources of funds and people, which should enable us to recruit and mobilise a popular movement. While not contracting out of the legitimate exercise of political influence we did not see Oxfam as an intensive political pressure group – this is a function to be performed by others, probably with our blessing and support from time to time . . . Top priority should be given to winning *new* friends and for this purpose we must make a simpler basic appeal than employed recently. Parallel with this activity we must look afresh for new ways of *involving* people once their interest has been aroused and educating them in the main issues confronting the Third World.

Sackur, Wood Associates were asked to devise a new communications strategy. The next January they presented their recommendations:

> Oxfam's image with the public is not the same as the perceptions of Oxfam by its own staff. . . The public think of Oxfam as an agency principally involved in relieving hunger in the world. The staff mostly think that Oxfam should be either largely involved in economic development or largely concerned with opinion forming or influence in the UK. The lack of consensus among staff, and between staff and supporters, has dangers for Oxfam . . . No meaningful communications strategy can be put into effect unless it reflects a commitment to a clear line of policy by the whole organisation. Management in Oxfam has traditionally encouraged autonomy and freedom of expression among the staff. This style is appropriate to a young, rapidly expanding organisation, but Oxfam is now mature and relatively large . . . We recommend a radical review of the range of activities throughout Oxfam, to establish medium and long term priorities. This should lead to a greater concentration of effort in overseas aid on certain types of project at the expense of others. It will require setting clear objectives, and justifying all activities in terms of their contribution to

the objectives, e.g. in the fields of fund raising and education . . . The publicity of most charities involved in overseas aid has presented Third World people as children calling for a parental response. Today, perceptions of the Third World by the majority of people in the UK and other rich countries conflict strongly with this idea. The Third World is seen increasingly as particularly prone to violence and the people as selfassertive. Oxfam publicity should recognise this reality and present Oxfam's role as alleviating the grounds for resentment and creating bonds of friendship. It should at the same time create an image of the organisation as effective and socially approved. The purpose would be to widen the constituency of supporters, and increase the consciousness of the need for Oxfam.

In 1974 Oxfam's Council, in an attempt to reconcile the conflict which Stacey had left behind, agreed that up to 5 per cent of income could be spent on educating people at home about the causes of world poverty. The Public Affairs Unit was set up to research and publicise particular topics in depth. But in June of the same year Robin Sharp, writing on behalf of a group of radicals amongst the middle-level staff, put forward further proposals for a realignment of Oxfam's policy:

We, Oxfam, are a partnership of people rich and poor reaching across the barriers of power and oppression, privilege and deprivation, and working to eliminate these inequalities that divide us. Bringing people together in an understanding of their common humanity, it is our purpose to strive for the justice, freedom and equitable sharing of resources without which more than half the world's people are presently deprived of their dignity and self-respect: *justice and freedom*, so that through surrender of the obstructive powers and privileges concentrated in the hands of the few, all may become the subjects of their destiny instead of its objects. *A sharing of resources*, so that the products of the earth and collective labour of its people be distributed to ensure for all the basic human rights of food, shelter, education and reasonable conditions of life . . . recognising that our role in working for these objectives is one small part of a universal struggle, the direction and scale of our activities must be calculated to take a maximum advantage of (i) Oxfam's influence and authority in Britain and other industrialised countries, and (ii) our direct knowledge and experience of development in the Third World. We reaffirm our belief in Oxfam's direct role in the development process, firstly through the financing of community projects which meet the criteria set out above and secondly through the activities of the trading company in providing employment and markets. This direct role should be sustained on account of its intrinsic merits, its value as an example of what can or should be achieved, the scope for innovation and experiment which is not afforded by larger official aid schemes, and the continuing, close contact with practical community problems which enables Oxfam to keep its other activities in a proper perspective. At the same time, recent history has shown that aid programmes alone will never resolve the conflicts and inequalities which concern us. Any significant improvement must depend on a fundamental change of attitudes between rich and poor. In parallel with the direct action programme, therefore, equal emphasis must be placed by Oxfam on activities conducive to this kind of change, both through the medium of public opinion and through those who directly influence the course of public affairs.

To further the thrust of this realignment (which was largely to be adopted over the next few years), Sharp proposed a new educational and political division at headquarters. This would include a department assigned to the question of 'How the rich should live', that would research and publicise (possibly through the example of Oxfam staff) ways in which people in the advanced countries can reduce their consumption to levels required for a more equitable distribution of the world's finite resources.

Finally, the next year Oxfam's Council agreed and published the following interpretation of the charity's objectives, which remain the same today:

In view of the great changes which have occurred in the last year few years in our understanding and approach to poverty and aid, Oxfam's Council of Management has approved this interpretation of our primary legal object: 'To relieve poverty, distress and suffering in any part of the world . . .' It is not a definitive statement of policy, nor is it the only interpretation possible, but the Council feels that it expresses well the ethos and purpose of Oxfam.

Oxfam believes in the essential dignity of people and their capacity to overcome the problems and pressures which can crush or exploit them. These may be rooted in climate and geography, or in the complex areas of economics, politics and social conditions. Oxfam is a partnership of people who share this belief – people who, regardless of race, sex, religion or politics work together for the basic human rights of food, shelter and reasonable conditions of life. We believe that, if shared equitably, there are sufficient material resources in the world to enable all people to find fulfilment and to meet basic human needs. We are committed, therefore, to a process of development by peaceful means which aims to help people, especially the poor and underprivileged overseas.

This development will sometimes generate conflicts of choice both for us at home and our partners overseas, but it must be a commitment to a process whose elements are dignity, criticism and change in which people decide their own priorities within their own cultural styles and their own scale of values. Oxfam's contribution is modest within the constraints of our limited resources. But we have learned that we can serve as a small scale social catalyst; helping and encouraging people to realise their full potential; helping small groups to become self-reliant and to combat the oppressive factors in their environment.

If we are to be effective and authentic, Oxfam staff, volunteers and supporters must function as an integrated movement. Fundraising, trading activities, the stewardship of our resources, and our patterns of consumption both personal and corporate should reflect the same values we work towards in our overseas development programme. The lessons we learn there should help to shape also our public opinion forming work, and our educational work. We recognise our responsibility, as citizens, to influence, where appropriate, the organisations and institutions in this country, including Parliament, that are involved in the wider aspects of our relationships with the poor countries.

In all of this we are aware that we too live in the same changing world. Our own organisation and the policies we pursue must keep pace, therefore, with new insights as they develop. We must be sensitive to the need to change ourselves. All people, whether they be rich or poor, strong or weak, privileged or deprived, are interdependent, and share in the common task of seeking to achieve mankind's full potential. Oxfam provides people at home as well as overseas with the opportunity of playing a small part in a much larger struggle to eliminate poverty and to help mankind develop in a spirit of love, brotherhood and solidarity. ·

The arrival of Brian Walker in 1974

This text had been drafted by Brian Walker, the new Director who took over in 1974, to heal the fissures left by the Stacey crisis. In the first letter he circulated to employees Walker wrote:

Director's Office, 11 February 1975

Dear Colleague,

During almost 20 years of industrial management the most important lesson I learned was that the only 'real' problems encountered were what I call 'people' problems. Money can always buy the skills needed to solve every other kind of problem – marketing, technical, financial, or whatever. 'People' problems derive from that tangled and complex web of human relationships which undergirds every organisation. They cannot be resolved by the application of skills or expertise. But in organisational terms, problems of human relationships usually do have much to do with a failure in the communications network. People misunderstand, don't know or somehow get the wrong impression. And that spells trouble. Your colleagues are scattered to the four corners of the globe. It is very difficult to keep in touch with one another – to communicate and to exchange ideas – especially when we are going through not only a period of radical change, but have a new Director at the helm as well. And so, as one small part of a much wider strategy of improving our communications, I intend writing to all our staff three or four times a year – but only when there is something worth saying, or explaining.

In this first letter there are two points I want to make: In the later summer, financially, we were in bad shape. Hugh Belshaw [the Finance Director] reported that we were running £108,000 behind budget; my own first overseas tour had already confirmed that inflation in the Third World was hitting 40–50 per cent per annum and if we took those commodities in which we are especially interested – cereals, fertilizers, cement, petrol and the like – one could justifiably strike an average rate of 200–300 per cent. At home it was little better . . . our liquidity dried up in the autumn and we had to start borrowing to cover current expenditure.

However, by the turn of the year some of our decisions were beginning to take effect. People, especially in the Regions, were redoubling their efforts and by the end of January Hugh Belshaw was able to report that we had turned a £108,000 shortfall into an £80,000 increase over budget requirements. A turn round of £188,000 at the beginning of a countrywide recession is a rather remarkable success story. A great encouragement for us all as we move into what the experts predict will be the toughest year this century.

But it isn't just the straight improvement in our liquidity which I want to stress – it is a whole host of 'straws in the wind' which are important. First, there was the response of our own staff. Some gave up their threshold payments, some their holidays, some put in extra effort, some found ways of improving their performance. Then, at Christmas, an unexpected number of old age pensioners sent us their entire 'Christmas bonus' – putting our own sacrifices into perspective. Tins rattled in Oxford chalked up almost £700. A farmer walked into Oxfam House one day and gave us £9,000. He said '. . . Good husbandry has looked after me and my family and now I want to share my wealth with farmers in India and Africa.' Then there was the bank manager in Chicago who asked his customers to give $1 to charity, which we would split between a home charity and 'the most efficient overseas charity I can find' – and came up with Oxfam as the answer. Or the British Cabinet Minister who, following a speaking tour of American universities during the Christmas recess, gave instructions that all her fees should be made payable to Oxfam. Or the Bristol man who signed over to Oxfam all his property worth £250,000 and which, when eventually realised, should bring in double that amount, and who told me he had done this because Oxfam was 'sincere' and 'efficient'. Or the school teacher who signed over the whole of her recent teacher's pay rise to Oxfam and began a campaign to urge her colleagues to do likewise. Or the City Editor about to retire from the board of one of our leading quality papers who offered his services to Oxfam . . .

Change never is easy. But each one of us, when faced by the need to consider changes of attitude or method of working (let alone changes in lifestyle which the whole of industrialised society is having to contemplate) would do well to ponder: what right have we to urge the poor to change, or the rich to alter their style, if we ourselves are disinclined to experiment and adapt? . . . So my second point is – try to make the changes work successfully . . . Discount rumour, trust and respect your colleagues and have faith in our work. Oxfam is a resilient movement. We are rather like the amoeba – our shape may be ill defined, we may be highly sensitive and even vulnerable in certain areas – but like the amoeba, we have a very high survival rate and are virtually indestructible. It's going to be a tough year – but it will be easier to fight it together. Good luck, and thank you.

Dr Don Sutherland, a Canadian outsider who has helped in Somalia, suggests that Oxfam's strength has always been its ability to attract able as well as good people to work for it. Brian

Walker faced a difficult task. Leslie Kirkley was an extremely hard act to follow, because for more than two decades he had been 'Mr Oxfam', combining diplomatic skill at bridging gaps between the radicals and the elderly ladies with a likeable human personality which remembered the names of all the staffs' children. But Bill Yates, who has been working there for twelve years, commented that Oxfam's size has just about outgrown the informal stage of being run as a friendly extended family, and that Walker's new ideas were the necessary next phase.

Walker and his wife came originally from Kendal in the Lake District. A former Methodist turned Quaker, he had developed considerable managerial ability working for an American company in Northern Ireland, and had acquired conciliatory and political experience (which was soon to be needed at Banbury Road) as the founder Chairman of the New Ulster Movement which in 1970 launched the Alliance Party there. During an Easter holiday in the Lakes he discussed with his wife whether they should move back to England, since his life was being threatened and he had been burnt in effigy by Paisleyites, and his wife and children were also bearing the brunt of these pressures. The next day he saw in *The Guardian* an advertisement of the Directorship of Oxfam – though the process of ordeal by selection committees was to take many months. (Guy Stringer, who became the Commercial Director in 1969, was similarly screened eight times at different interviews before he was admitted.)

The job Walker was eventually appointed to is an almost impossible one, so many are the contrasting demands and constituencies requiring to be reconciled. He saw his role as to know when to use the accelerator and when to brake. The technique of survival is not unlike how Harold Wilson described leading the Labour Party: when the rattletrap is moving in a forward direction, the passengers remain occupied and mostly refrain from mutiny, but as soon as there is a holdup the atmosphere changes.

Walker and Stringer set about professionalising Oxfam with the help of outside consultants, declaring, 'We have even less right to misuse money than a normal business.' The Lancaster School of Business Studies drew up a management accounting system. Oxfam's organisational divisions were modelled on those of ICI on the advice of Conrad Jamieson. Today management analysts use Oxfam as a case study so that Oxfam benefits free from the results. Out went the days when Oxfam leaned unduly on amateurs with private incomes; in came a salary structure for the paid workers that was reasonable though still well below the market rates. The post of Walker – energetic and able, occasionally thought to be abrasive or impulsive – was changed from being that of Director to that of Director-General.

Stringer, a man of compassionate warm charm and dry humour (who had moved from being Marketing Director of a Pilkington subsidiary because 'I reckoned I had answered most of the questions I would meet, and I felt that the same questions would be coming around again and again'), has an extraordinary flair for fundraising. He started several new remunerative ventures for Oxfam, including the Wastesaver scheme (described later) and a foreign stamp business. To the regret of many, however, it was decided to close a secondhand book business, on the advice of the Manchester Business School. Stringer and Geoffrey Wilson (the Chairman) were both skilful and busy at pouring oil on the personality conflicts which the changes engendered. Decisions at Oxfam are wherever possible arrived at, democratically, by consensus rather than vote, with employees at different levels being painstakingly consulted. (The Stacey episode has shown how resistant Oxfam's character is to charismatic leadership.) Wilson describes progress at its best as 'inspired ad-hocery', while Stringer admitted that 'the unstructuredness is disconcerting for the first few months'. One of Oxfam's divisional heads commented, 'I'm always amazed how the mix manages to stick together; the meetings help, and I think it's easier than it would be if we were in London.' Sometimes moral dilemmas were not easy to resolve: a property in Bristol of more than two hundred houses, which had been left to Oxfam, was sold, at a profit less than possible, because the charity did not wish to become land-lords. In 1976, it was decided to use only recycled paper for letters, and to write all internal notes on the backs of used paper; at the next staff conference it was also determined to try to reduce all paperwork in the organisation by 20 per cent. The idea of using lotteries to raise money was turned down, after a 50-50 split of opinion (in Quaker terms, the suggestion was 'left on the table'). But another move, to persuade Oxfam's shops not to accept war toys, narrowly failed.

A member of Oxfam's Council reflected, 'People with a mission and a feeling of involvement always want to persuade more than to listen.' Musing on the problems of running Oxfam, Walker says:

> Managing people, so that they (we) can grow and maximize their innate potential in pursuit of the objects of the charity – this is the starting point. Everything else flows from it. The first requirement of staff selection is 'commitment'. Dedication to the cause, commitment to the purposes of the charity, is pre-eminent. This overrides all other requirements. Recruits are required to take a 10–15 per cent reduction from average market rates in their salaries. At the senior management levels this reduction increases to 50 per cent or even 60 per cent, for we seek upper quartile people in terms of professional, technical or general management skills. But the contradiction is there – for highly motivated people who step aside from the normal pattern of career development, almost by definition, are very difficult to 'manage'. Powerful creativity is highly volatile material. Commitment is only one step removed from fanaticism. Dedication can degenerate into dogmatism. Zeal can become zealotry.
>
> This is the challenge – how to retain balance at the human level. It is further compounded when the financial success of the operation is based largely upon an unpaid voluntary 'labour force'. With over 600 shops run by some 20,000 unpaid volunteers, servicing over three million customers, and providing 40 per cent of our income, the problems of management are self-evident. Ultimately what is management's authority? Legally, the laws of charity provide the framework in which we try to work, but, except in a strictly legal sense, they are difficult to interpret, and at times are confused and confusing. The elimination of waste, the care of resources, the dedicated input and ideas and energies by people, represent a kind of Holy Grail, sought after by industry and commerce alike. They come naturally in a charity like Oxfam – but it is like controlling quicksilver; a bush fire with the wind at its most erratic. The basic techniques can be taken almost for granted. Public funds entrusted to an established charity – in our case £15–20 millions per annum – demand great probity and accountability. We set ourselves the target of being at least as good as the best companies in terms of the stewardship of our resources. Market research, cost control, sophisticated selection procedures, computer usage and data analysis, budgeting, O & M, training and development, R & D, are all an intrinsic part of the operation. Public opinion forming, the 'educated pound', are well researched techniques. Yet, throughout it all, there runs this streak of volatility. The maverick card is the one to watch. The inner dynamism which ensures we pursue widespread consultation and shared decision making in staff and volunteer relationships, can also push us towards anarchy, and away from accountability. The activists, running, as ever, well ahead of the 'common people', are persuasive in their articulation. And, it is not necessarily wrong – just difficult and at times self-contradictory. The purity of logic can lead a charity up blind alleyways. Soul-destroying, theological debates can become ends in themselves. Energy can be dissipated and the ground rules assaulted for no apparent reason.

Meanwhile, Oxfam's main work overseas continued apace under Michael Harris, the Director of the Overseas Division, a dedicated administrator with wide experience, who is very good at choosing field staff as well as showing intense loyalty to them. He had been an ambulance-driver in China and Secretary to the Cabinet in Malawi. (Two of Oxfam's other senior men – Charles Skinner and David de Pury – had been in the Diplomatic Service.) Oxfam's own Field Directors now number twenty-seven. The programmes benefit from Oxfam's great strength: its capacity to renew itself as it develops, allied to the advantage it enjoys over many other agencies from having fieldworkers permanently abroad. This makes it easier for policies to be continuously adapted to increase their relevance and sensitivity to local needs. Walker explains:

> As we have gained a deeper understanding of development and a greater trust in the people we're working with, so we have tended to give more grants to local groups, getting down deeper into the grass roots where the people themselves can decide on their own priorities rather than outsiders like us imposing our ideas on them. Giving an ox plough so that people can till the land sounds like second best to us in the west: we are used to tractors. Yet when land holdings are very small – to say nothing of the oil crisis and inflation – a very strong case can be made out for the traditional ways. Adopting a local approach to local needs means that local people have a quicker understanding of those needs, so we now recruit local people to work with us in the field. We are always deepening our understanding. Political and economic processes are making it harder and harder to work with the people who most need our help. We must always grasp new insights and learn from new experiences. This is even more vital in the 1980s.

The weakness of traditional charities' appeal is that it is often not until disaster strikes that much money starts to flow – and then that can be too late. But the necessity of Oxfam's disaster relief work often provides offspin benefits that help the longer-term development projects. In 1971 Oxfam had learnt from the enormous scale of the East Pakistan tragedy, when in the space of a few months 10 million people had fled to India. Housing was nonexistent, so experiments were started to produce the best forms of emergency shelter using all that twentieth century technology could devise. Two related problems tackled by Jim Howard (the technical officer) were sanitation and the threat of cholera – a disease transmitted through polluted water and endemic in the East Bengal floods. In 1974 a solution was worked out that was capable of being shipped in a single packing-case. It was a self-contained sewage system able to cope with 1,000 people a day. Large butyl tanks, originally designed for military use, were connected to a series of lavatories placed at a higher level and enclosed; the tanks sealed off the contents from the air, killing the cholera germs. After a settling period the harmless liquid could be drained away, and the solids remaining used as good and safe fertiliser.

Walker himself was responsible for the establishment in 1977 of the world's first comprehensive Vegetable Gene Bank, one of Oxfam's most striking innovations. Sited at Wellesbourne in England, the purpose is to conserve for future plant breeders all the key tropical and temperate vegetables under carefully controlled conditions, by a Gene Bank in which seeds can be reproduced true to type as required.

But not all the projects are successful. Oxfam has no miracle formula. The basic development policy strategy, of 'teaching a man to fish', has come under repeatedly insistent questioning throughout the last decade, because in several areas it was realised by Oxfam's workers that their clients had no access to – or any prospect of – any such 'water' in which they could 'fish'. Increasingly, debate and concern turned to such questions as how poor people might gain access to water or land so that they might have a chance of being able to support their families – whether in Latin America, Africa or Asia. Oxfam's wish to help 'the poorest of the poor' made it impossible or irresponsible to ignore the political constraints in which it worked. One catalytic turning-point was provided by the experience of the energetic Reggie Norton in the wake of the 1976 Guatemalan earthquake, when the work of reconstruction was felt to be blocked by the local social and political structure. (Norton later left Oxfam to work in Washington because he believes that the realistic way to help Central America is in fact to try to influence US Congressional Committees.)

'Poverty,' Michael Harris said recently, 'is so often allied with peoples' search for justice and basic human rights. Faced with the terrors and murders within the countries of Central America it is becoming increasingly difficult to remain uninvolved. It is the refugee who is becoming the political weapon of the countries concerned. Can we refuse aid? *Can we pass by on the other side?* In my view this would be impossible; we must always respond to human need whatever the cause. What we must avoid at all costs is involvement in violence of any sort; and ensure that any help we can offer is made available to all who require it, as well as ensure its proper and correct use. . . . Allied to this is the crucial task of how we communicate on the home front. We must put across in our own country our views of the problems of the poor world and our belief that the rich world must identify itself with these problems. Time is running out and the failure of the North to make any real sacrifices to assist the South is something that must be fought as hard as we know how.'

The process of thinking through the implications and root causes of development problems experienced overseas has led Oxfam to an increasing succession of recent campaigns. In the 1981 'Brandt lobby' 10,000 people went to Westminster to press their MPs about overseas aid policies. Internationally, Oxfam has joined the campaign to press for the adoption of a Code of Practice for the marketing of baby milk. In 1982 it published hard-hitting books on food aid, pesticide abuse and medicines in developing countries. The year 1983 began with the launch of the new campaigning network, Oxfam 2000.

The challenges faced by Oxfam aged 40 are even harder and more complex than the task faced by the original handful of founders who first met in an Oxford room in 1942. Despite its striking expansion, Oxfam's development has succeeded to a surprising degree in remaining true to the founding spirit of its original values. Today, it supports some 1,350 projects in 80 countries overseas. Palestinian refugees and hunger in Bihar still feature in the current programme in 1983, just as they did in the early days. Just under £½ million was raised by Oxfam for its Lebanon appeal – meanwhile news was arriving of new refugee disasters in the Sudan and Ghana. The work is supported by 620 shops (compared with only 5 in 1963) and 55,000 long-term donors (compared with 8,000 in 1963). The full-time staff now numbers 563. How political, how professional, and how big Oxfam should try to become, are now among the main issues being debated within the organisation. David Manasian wrote in *Management Today* in February 1980: 'Some people, both inside and outside the organization, feel that there are definite limits to how institutional Oxfam should become. The public wants its contributions to be used efficiently, but quite illogically, prefers charities to appear amateurish.' Yet when Norton was struggling to cope with the Guatemalan earthquake, he said the first and prime requirement he needed in that situation was not food, blankets, clothing, housing, or money. It was an accountant. Harris fears that 'our bigger size carries the danger that we lose the common touch. I don't think we should get any larger. If we do, we'll have to go the whole hog – computers, job descriptions, a much more formalised structure – and personalities will cease to count.' But Walker and most of the rest of the staff have few such doubts: 'Commitment and drive are still very close to the heart of Oxfam: it's the yeast in the lump. What we've tried to do is build on that. There is no fundamental conflict between growth and efficiency on the one hand and commitment on the other.'

3

People to People: Why Private Development Agencies?

We were given a Gospel that was a wild tiger; we tame it and
domesticate it into a pussycat.

Dom Thomas Cullinan

We have the means and we have the manpower to eliminate hunger
from the face of the earth. We need only the will.

John F. Kennedy

The effects of voluntary development organisations like Oxfam
are felt by several million people. Besides those who benefit
directly from their programmes and the others who support
them with labour or money, the work does something to alter the
nature of society – both in the relations between nations and in
Britain's domestic concerns.

The effects are at the same time two way. A body such as
Oxfam, lacking reserves and investment income, cannot survive
without the public's support: if its policies become markedly
unpopular or if there is any breath of irregularity, its oxygen –
together with that of those it supports abroad – would be cut off.

In the forty years since it was founded by a handful of people
in October 1942, Oxfam has allocated over £100 million in aid
overseas. Since 1980 it has become Britain's largest overseas aid
charity, with an income in 1981–2 of £16.2 million (compared
with the Save the Children Fund's £13.2, Christian Aid's £7.8,
Action Aid's £5.1, the Methodist Church Overseas Division's
£3.3, the Catholic Fund for Overseas Development's £2.1 and
War on Want's £1 million). But while its growth is evidence of
public confidence, can such a size budget be of much relevance
to the scale of the needs of the world's poverty? The impact of its
ideas, however, may be. This is what this book tries to weigh
with an objective eye, encouraged by the fact that Oxfam gave
the writer complete freedom to be independent and critical.

Oxfam's shops have now become part of the landscape of many High Streets, and a stock feature in cartoonists' repertory. In 1982 the word 'Oxfam' entered the new *Oxford Dictionary*. Those who only see its jumble-sale image might be surprised how professional and big it has become. But all institutions, including charities, should regularly re-examine why they still exist. What justifies their continuation? What are their real ends; which are their best means? And what are they in fact achieving? Are they a moral panacea for our collective conscience – or might they, in effect, be an alibi for society avoiding or postponing wider necessary action? Could a little bit of charity on Sunday be a cover-up for business as usual the rest of the week? And isn't it colonialist or paternalistic for white Europeans to continue interfering and suggesting to the rest of the world how they should live?

Voluntary agencies' employees – unlike government or UN ones – often work and live among 'the poorest of the poor', and feel some satisfaction, as well as frustrations, from seeing at first hand the results of their work. But most Oxfam people sometimes have doubts about the effect of what they are doing. Could private aid agencies in fact be relieving pressure on governments and the UN to provide the necessary development policies and programmes whose size only they are in the position to fund? Is the role of charities the equivalent of a token Victorian soup-kitchen when what is needed now is a proper welfare system – based on a just and equitable sharing of the limited resources of this earth? And what are the motives of mainly rich white people sparing a few crumbs from our tables? Might we in fact be making the poor even more dependent on us as a result?

'People give money to people, not to concepts', Oxfam was warned by one of its consultants. 'They will assent to concepts, even work for them, but they will not donate to them. In its anxiety to sell the concept of overseas aid, Oxfam is robbing its human face.' 'The further Oxfam moves away from the soup-kitchen role to the task of comprehensive community development – the permanent abolition of hunger in a region – the nearer it moves towards an involvement in the politics of the country which it is endeavouring to help,' argues Anthony Smith, now Director of the British Film Institute. 'It also involves an extraordinarily difficult leap in the kinds of knowledge and expertise that Oxfam must provide. This kind of grass-roots social engineering involves long-term and constant cash flow and a different kind of dedication from the old-style relief work. It is precisely the kind of work which governments cannot do well and voluntary organisations can. The voluntary agency can free itself from local red tape and from the politics of the receiving country more easily than a donor government can. An Oxfam Field Director can give help to local labour to build a brace of wells while the visiting dignitaries from the World Bank and the local politicians are still being photographed at the airport – but in fact Oxfam's problems at home merely begin as its overseas role becomes clearer; the kind of message which the public responds to most readily is precisely the kind which Oxfam has to abandon.'

There is the connected problem, Smith suggested in *New Society*, of the British paradox that many members of the public are liable to feel they need no longer support a charity which becomes over-successful. The matured policy of Oxfam necessarily involves explaining to the public that medium-term development is as important a focus of charity as is the relief of immediate starvation. But 'if a donor hears that the charity he has been giving to is a success in achieving its objects, he tends to move to another charity' is the warning of one of Oxfam's professional advisers. Another liability is that the fact of being so well known has caused Oxfam to become synonymous for many people with all overseas aid and its limitations – including, ironically, the government aid of whose form Oxfam is often highly critical.

But alongside the dangers Oxfam risks as a result of its success, and through changing from appeals about starving babies to urging more thorough development, it cannot evade the fact that the need for its work – far from withering away – has not only increased, but is becoming more urgent. The absolute and relative gaps between the rich and poor nations have widened because – as similarly between rich and poor individuals – to be rich means that credit is forthcoming; setbacks can be cushioned, losses absorbed; specialist expertise, information or know-how are accessible. Rich people offer contacts and mutual advantages to each other, providing institutional networks besides financial and technical support. If disease threatens an individual's family or a country's crop, which income group is most likely to be able to get an antidote in time, and which to lose all? Whereas zero growth for a rich country is hardly a traumatic disaster, in Africa, Asia, or Latin America it can mean condemnation to a life sentence of hopeless destitution.

At the start of this century the average person in a rich country was estimated to have 4 times as much income as a person in a poor one; *by 1970 the disparity had become 40 to 1*. (See 'Is the gap getting worse?' below.) Within the most recent lifespan the less developed countries (LDCs, *alias* developing, underdeveloped, or non-industrialised countries, the Third World or the South) have progressed, socially and economically, to achieve what it took Western Europe a century to accomplish. But today the pay rise which an American person can expect annually is still greater

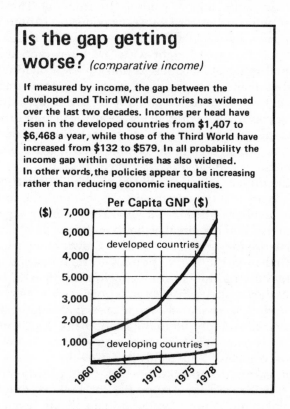

Source: U.S. and World Development Agenda, 1980.

than an Indian can hope for in 100 years. In 1981, for the first time in a generation, the per capita gross domestic product of the world's developing countries *actually declined*. Yet it is now clear that the rich countries' response to such inequity is growing protectionism and neo-isolationism. The anti-aid winds blow increasingly strongly, generated by xenophobic self-interest often thinly disguised as patriotic nationalism.

The Reaction against Aid

Recent surveys in Britain show a marked change in public opinion away from all foreign policy issues or altruism in favour of domestic and self-interested preoccupations. A chorus on the left demands import controls to shut out Third World products, thus further weakening the poorest: a curious reversal of socialism's basic tenet of 'to each according to his needs'. Similar policies on the right wing are often propounded by intellectual refugees, anxious to pull up the drawbridge over which they themselves escaped – perhaps to prove themselves *plus royalistes que le roi* or possibly to live down a liberal or left-wing youth. But at present we are all the victims of a vicious circle whereby, because rich nations feel insecure against the poor, they waste ever more of their privileged economy on armaments.

The £55 million which the World Health Organisation spent over ten years to eliminate smallpox is less than the cost of one strategic bomber. While the superpowers' military expenditure has risen this year to more than half a million pounds *per minute*, the assistance they give development is dwindling. (As foreign aid shifted from big capital projects to rural development, its advocates have less influence on governments than the business lobbyists they replace.) Even more serious, *a smaller proportion of the aid itself is being allocated to the poorest countries which need it most*: according to the World Bank, less than a third of official development assistance is now going to low-income countries, compared with nearly half in 1970.

As the current recession deepened, it hurt the poorest – the countries with least fat – most. But the bulk of United States development aid is now sent to military clients such as Israel, Egypt and Turkey. The American administration has recently signified its intention to halve US multilateral aid and tilt even further its concentration to 'strategic' countries. Official aid from the industrialised to the developing world fell in real terms by 4 per cent in 1981 – with some of the world's richest countries registering the most severe cutbacks – resulting in only half of the target level set by the UN. The right-wing government which took power in West Germany in 1982 decided to cut overseas development aid by 27 per cent. The multilateral aid outlook is equally bleak: a reduction in donors' contributions – the first ever – has forced the UN Development Programme to cut its 1982 funding by 40 per cent; over the next four years it will have to terminate more than 1,200 projects. Meanwhile the total external debt of the developing countries increased from $180 billion at the end of 1975 to $626 billion at the end of 1982. Even developing countries hitherto regarded as among the strongest, such as Mexico and Brazil, are threatened by economic collapse. Not only liberals, but Robert McNamara, Edward Heath and Geoffrey Rippon have warned of the disaster facing the rich countries if they persist in lending money at extortionate rates of interest while continuing to refuse to buy poorer countries' products.

In Britain – despite the fact that it remains one of the twelve richest nations in the world, and one of the few to run a current account surplus – the government at the start of the 1980s sliced its aid budget by 11 per cent in real terms: the biggest reduction ever recorded. In 1982–3 it cut a further £26m – at the same time as it was willing to spend over £1,600m on the Falklands affair. But it is not only the quantity of British aid which has suffered. The change in its character has been severely criticised for switching away from helping the lowest-income countries, and for its new preference for commercial contracts such as exported steel mills in place of Judith Hart's and Frank Judd's emphasis on programmes to help the poor. *British overseas aid has recently been reduced by approximately four times as much as the average cut in public expenditure; the cut made in 1981 was some seven times the whole amount of funds collected by all the voluntary agencies such as Oxfam.*

All these factors place heavier burdens and responsibility on the voluntary aid agencies. But meanwhile the recession in Europe has squeezed their budgets between the hammer of inflation and the anvil of falling incomes: in 1981 total voluntary

U.K. Net Aid Spending as a % of Total Public Expenditure

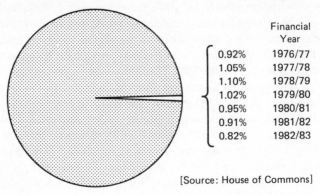

	Financial Year
0.92%	1976/77
1.05%	1977/78
1.10%	1978/79
1.02%	1979/80
0.95%	1980/81
0.91%	1981/82
0.82%	1982/83

[Source: House of Commons]

contributions to charities in Britain fell by 3 per cent, with grants from trusts dropping by 8 per cent and donations from companies falling by 11 per cent.

People are never at a loss to find reasons why they should not give to charity. As we waste fertiliser on our lawns, golf courses and cemeteries, despite being told that many families lack any fertiliser essential to grow necessities on their desert soil, we say, 'Shouldn't charity begin at home?' In fact, Oxfam helps not only Mother Teresa, but also projects in the United Kingdom. It gives employment to handicapped people; assists for example the Child Poverty Action Group, and Helen House at Oxford where Mother Frances runs the first hospice in Europe for dying children; it helps the victims of flood emergencies in Yorkshire and Norfolk in the same way as it does in Bengal.

Brian Walker, the Director-General of Oxfam, asks sceptics who advocate that Third World countries should 'stand on their own feet' what this means for those in totalitarian states, or where all the power is concentrated in the hands of a small elite. 'In fact,' he points out, 'Third World countries provide 80 per cent of the money they spend on development, receiving only 20 per cent from the richer nations. Oxfam's contribution is through small-scale projects, linking people at home to poor people in the Third World, and while the poor clearly benefit from the money we allocate, we receive as much as we give – perhaps more. We are reminded that elementary honesty among the poor is often of the highest order. Loans to landless farmers in India, who have no collateral to offer, consistently maintain a return of "honoured debts" at a rate of more than 90 per cent, although no Western banker would take those risks. After the earthquake in Guatemala, many people who had lost everything, including the land on which their homes had been built, refused handouts and insisted on working for what they were given.'

Kevin Rafferty recounted in the *Financial Times* his own experience of the contrast between Western and Eastern ideas of charity:

> The biggest tragedy is the meanness of the rich nation 'friends' of the refugees. If one creams off the layer of self-interested businessmen and politicians, who have dealt too much with men from the power blocks of the West whose concern is money, the people of India and Pakistan are simple and poor – but hospitable and loving. When I first went to India a complete stranger in Delhi offered me his room in his three-roomed house, fed me and looked after me when I was ill and would not take anything in return . . . Yet we – Christians! – cannot cough up even half a per cent of our annual defence budget to rescue these poor people, whose plight is not their own fault.

Third World leaders have suggested that the most important work that organisations like Oxfam can do is to educate and better inform the general public about developing countries' problems. President Nyerere of Tanzania asks them to 'change public opinion in your own country. For the rich countries use democracy against equity. By that I mean that when I go to Europe, your Prime Ministers and Trade Ministers and so on, say, "Yes, yes, Mr President, we understand your problems – but our voters don't and they won't let us do anything about them". In Scandinavia and the Netherlands they take a lot of trouble to develop public opinion – and as a result their governments have much bolder policies towards the Third World.'

The British like to think of themselves as generous supporters of overseas charity. *The figures in Tables 1 and 2, however, show otherwise* (see pp. 55, 56)

Only about 100 of the 150,000 charities registered in Britain in fact work primarily overseas. Depending on which definition of a 'Non-Governmental Organisation' (NGO) is used, the total number of such voluntary donor groups in the richer countries is between 1,100 and 3,200. The combined development grants they make from the funds they raise are at present growing faster than the rate of inflation (from £0.9 billion in 1979 to £1.01 billion in 1980, including just over £0.43 billion derived annually from governments' contributions – the equivalent of just under a tenth of governmental development assistance from the donor countries). *From Britain, however, the total voluntary contribution is less than 85p annually per head – less than one-fifth of what the average Swiss person gives, and making British people, contrary to how they like to imagine themselves, among the least generous in this respect.* Nevertheless, a survey carried out for the British government by the Central Office of Information in 1978 showed that one-third of the people questioned thought that the NGOs give more money to help the poorer countries than the government does.

What Good can Private Development Agencies do?

But isn't the scale of the problems of world poverty so huge that only government aid can make any real impact, and NGO agencies merely scratch the surface?

One answer to sceptics is that NGOs have a valuable role by pioneering innovative methods and pilot projects (especially unpopular or politically controversial ones), which are often copied later by the larger bodies. Pathfinding Oxfam work which has recently been replicated includes refugee health planning in Somalia, and community health programmes in Bangladesh. Besides many communities having received quick and flexible help through NGOs which they would not otherwise have had (some examples of which are described in Part Two of this book), independent judges speak highly of the quality of most NGO's projects. One such health report concludes: 'The main problems arise in translating successful voluntary agencies' projects into national programmes . . . Their success hinges on factors which cannot be replicated. These include charismatic and dedicated individuals in project leadership and, often, highly motivated persons within the programme generally [as well as] freedom from government bureaucracy . . .' Michael Jay, who until recently was the senior UK diplomat in charge of economic development in India, said of Oxfam's work there:

> Visits to projects left me with a high regard for Oxfam's work. Without exception they were aimed at very poor people, and in every case except perhaps for one, they seemed to me well conceived and executed. The agencies

through which Oxfam worked seemed to have been chosen carefully and well, and I was impressed by the extent to which Oxfam were building them up through help and advice, which is essential if they are to continue to do good work after Oxfam's financial help is withdrawn. I was also impressed by the calibre of Oxfam's own staff, both expatriate and Indian. I may have seen some of Oxfam's better projects, and the general picture is perhaps less rosy than I have painted it. But the impressions of others tend to confirm my own. Officials of the Ministry of Social Welfare in New Delhi, which is responsible for relations with voluntary agencies, spoke well of Oxfam, and particularly of its secularism. (Christian agencies tend to be viewed with more suspicion.) After my visit to one large Oxfam project, the Collector of the District concerned wrote a highly commendatory letter about Oxfam's work, including a request that the High Commission use its influence to prevent Oxfam withdrawing from the project in the following year as was planned. On another occasion, an official from the state of Madhya Pradesh spoke highly of the tact and sensitivity with which Oxfam were supporting very worthwhile projects in tribal districts – a sensitive area for any foreign agencies. Oxfam is also highly regarded by other voluntary agencies. I have no doubt therefore that Oxfam are doing good work and that funds channelled to them by members of the public, or through ODA's joint funding scheme, will be well spent.

One of the ablest British ambassadors, before taking up a major post abroad, asked Oxfam to give him a course to brief him about the reality of his new country. Some observers think that all diplomats would benefit from similar training, which would include truths not found in official telegrams or urbane briefs.

Another senior diplomat-economist in the Overseas Development Administration said he considered 'Oxfam are excellent at doing the things they're good at' – though he added that he thought 'they shouldn't tackle big projects, because they can't employ the "higher blackmail" against corruption that governments can by threatening to pull out'.

Oxfam alone obviously cannot solve world poverty. But a further very considerable argument (and one not likely to be advanced by countries' Foreign Offices) in favour of people-to-people nongovernmental development work is that it is freer from political bias and distortion than official governmental programmes. Despite the average Gibraltarian already having 20 times the level of income an Indian does, he receives 1,300 times as much British aid assistance as the latter. The Soviet Union does not believe in charity at all. Both Eastern European and United States aid programmes too often seem adjuncts of the Cold War. At present, Britain and West Germany are following the United States's refusal to sign the International Sea Bed Treaty, which had been painstakingly agreed and would give some of the poorer countries a share of the world's resources. Such political postures have recently increasingly spilt over into multilateral aid, with vetoes by the US at the World Bank and by Britain (against Argentina) at the UNDP, and Britain's efforts to prevent EEC aid from going to Vietnam and Nicaragua. Food aid, insensitively used from international or domestic political motives, can worsen the situation in a recipient country by increasing dependency and depressing peasant farmers' prices.

By contrast, NGOs can operate in countries their governments do not favour – as we have seen several did in Cambodia when neither Western governments nor the UN would recognise the *de facto* government there – and have recently done so in Vietnam, Ethiopia and Nicaragua. *Unlike some governments with their aid, NGOs do not seek to turn recipient countries into political colonies.* And unlike the IMF and World Bank, NGOs do not dictate internal economic and social policies.

Whereas the UK government's aid projects and those of the United Nations and World Bank have to be channelled only through governments (which themselves may be contributing to the causes of underdevelopment), projects from organisations such as Oxfam can reach the poorest direct. For example, in the co-operative which Oxfam is helping in Mali through the EuroAction consortium, the co-operative's members themselves are making the decisions – thus keeping employment and money in rural areas, where both are badly needed. Nigel Twose, working in Ouagadougou in Upper Volta, assesses the result:

> Clearly, many aid programmes are not working. The complacency of the sixties development experts is slowly disappearing, and we are at last coming to terms with the fact that none of us have the absolute answers. But a few things have become clearer. One is that unless the local population is involved in the selection of the programme's contents from the beginning, there is little chance of success. The smaller a programme is the more likelihood that the people themselves have actively participated in the project design. And the best results of all seem to come when the programme is based on requests coming directly from the village groups or local associations of the area.

Sir Geoffrey Wilson, the Chairman of Oxfam (and previously the head civil servant at the Overseas Development Ministry), said: 'When asked what difference these often tiny projects make, the answer is first: they give hope and help to individuals of initiative; second, they are often the kind of projects which governments cannot or will not help. Her Majesty's Government will only do certain types of projects, and often insists on United Kingdom procurement in return.' In fact it seems to be an unnecessarily unbending British view that government aid has to be channelled only through other governments: Norway, Sweden and several other governments have for many years funded work through other bodies, including voluntary agencies.

It is true that private aid agencies do not have the formal accountability that the public sector's aid programme has in a democracy, through parliamentary debate, special committees' scrutiny, and ultimately the ballot box. But private sector agencies are accountable to the donors and voluntary helpers without which they cannot work. Informing and educating public opinion about development is therefore essential to their work.

The experience of working for Oxfam radicalises many of its staff. A number of them expressed pleasure at the cut in the government's aid budget because they are critical anyway of its programme. To these radical critics, the motive for official government aid is suspect: 'Doesn't it make the recipient countries less likely to make political adjustments? And instead spend money on economic infrastructure items which are necessary for the profitable operation of foreign businesses, and also make them increasingly dependent on loans to repay past loans – and therefore more compliant?' They cite President Kennedy's words in 1961: 'Foreign aid is a method by which the US maintains a position of influence and control around the world and sustains a good many countries which would definitely collapse or pass into the communist bloc', and President Nixon's unfortunate (but, sadly, accurate) reminder in 1968: 'Let us remember that the main purpose of American aid is not to help other nations but to help ourselves.'

British government ministers have recently echoed this, stating in Parliament that, apart from a small amount of disaster aid, all British aid must first carry political, trade or military advantages to the UK – with the result that it is the voluntary agencies alone who have been left supplying disinterested development assistance. Teresa Hayter calculated, 'If repatriated profits on foreign investments, interest payments, royalty payments, debt repayments, private capital sent abroad and so on, are added up, they exceed capital inflows in the form of official aid and private loans and investments,' and she went on to argue that government aid is a form of bribe to make recipient countries continue to co-operate in the drain of capital from their countries (*The Creation of World Poverty*, Pluto Press and Third World First, 1981).

Lord Beveridge once proposed the creation of a voluntary service grants committee, funded by the state as well as trusts and individuals, to help charities doing work of an unpopular nature. As a compromise substitute in the field of overseas development, the British government's Overseas Development Administration (ODA) under the Joint Funding Scheme provides matching funds for certain approved projects of NGOs (see Table 3, p. 57). The criteria necessary include:

(i)   The project must be a new one (projects funded for more than 3 months before submission are disqualified).

(ii)   The total grant must exceed £2,000 (though NGOs are increasingly finding the small grants most effective).

(iii)   Projects must be developmental, not humanitarian (a difficult dividing line in, for example, refugee work).

(iv)   There is a proscribed list of countries, such as Cuba, Argentina, Vietnam.

(v)   Projects will not be funded for more than 5 years (though it can often take at least this time for a new project to become properly established).

(vi)   Imported equipment for the project must come from Britain (sometimes a complicating constraint).

Geoffrey Wilson considers that, in order for Oxfam to maintain its independence, 10 per cent of its gross income or 20 per cent of project money is the maximum it ought to accept from the government or the EEC. At present it is, unfortunately, not permitted to use any British government aid funds to support work by overseas agencies or research institutes – unlike the policy of many other donor countries (such as Canada), who find this a cost-effective way to target aid to the poor and to bypass bureaucratic or corrupt official systems.

The People behind the Figures

It is not easy to keep sight of the fact that welters of statistics are composed of human men, women and children. And so much of the language of the whole subject is inappropriately impersonal and sanitised – or else biased in its meaning through the Western use of words such as 'developed'. *What the numbing statistics show is that the majority of people in our world today – unnecessarily – never have a chance to enjoy the bodily, intellectual or spiritual life of which they are capable.*

What we are looking at briefly in this book are life and (unfortunately often) death matters for the ordinary families in the world (see Life Expectancy Chart below). These number over 800 million, and have an annual income of about £50. Out of this they have to feed their children, bury their dead, buy their seeds, maintain their home and their land, and try to save something by to cope with visitations of nature such as crop failures, flood, fire, disease or drought.

If during the next two days, we learned that an unexpected tragic disaster struck which claimed the lives of 70,000 children, the British public would respond with generosity; and moralising leading articles in the Press would castigate politicians and underline the lessons which must be learnt. In fact during the next two days – perhaps the time you take to read this book – that is the number of children who will perish unnecessarily as a result of malnutrition, thirst, poverty and disease. *We have been given advance notice this will happen. And let us equally be clear: we*

Life expectancy

	Yrs. at birth	Country, territory, or area (1975–80)
✳	35–39.9	Ethiopia; Yemen.
✳	40–44.9	Afghanistan; Angola; Bhutan; Burundi; Chad; Democratic Yemen; East Timor; Gabon; Gambia; Guinea; Guinea-Bissau; Lao Peo. Dem. Rep.; Mali; Mauritania; Nepal; Niger; Senegal; Somalia; Upper Volta.
✳	45–49.9	Bangladesh; Benin; Botswana; Central Af. Rep.; Comoros; Dem. Kampuchea; Equatorial Guinea; Ghana; Ivory Coast; Liberia; Madagascar; Malawi; Mozambique; Nigeria; Oman; Papua New Guinea; Ruanda ; Saudi Arabia; Sierra Leone; Sudan; Swaziland; Togo; Utd. Rep. of Cameroon; Vietnam ; Zaire; Zambia.
✳✳	50–54.9	Bolivia; Burma; Egypt; Haiti; India; Indonesia; Iran; Lesotho; Namibia; Pakistan; Southern Rhodesia; Uganda; Utd. Rep. of Tanzania.
✳✳	55–59.9	Algeria; Guatemala; Honduras; Iraq; Jordan; Kenya; Libyan Arab Jam.; Morocco; Nicaragua; Syrian Arab Rep.; Tunisia.
✳✳✳	60–64.9	Brazil; Cape Verde; China; Colombia; Dominican Republic; Ecuador; El Salvador; Korea, Dem. Peo. Rep. of; Korea, Republic of; Malaysia; Mongolia; Paraguay; Philippines; Reunion; South Africa; Thailand; Turkey.
✳✳✳✳	65–69.9	Albania; Argentina; Chile; Costa Rica; Guadeloupe; Guyana; Hungary; Kuwait; Lebanon; Martinique; Mexico; Panama; Portugal; Singapore; Sri Lanka; Surinam ; Trinidad & Tobago; USSR; Uruguay; Venezuela; Windward Islands; Yugoslavia.
✳✳✳✳✳	70–74.9	Australia; Austria; **Barbados**; Belgium; Bulgaria; Canada; **Cuba**; Cyprus; Czechoslovakia; Denmark; **Fiji**; Finland; France; German Dem. Rep.; Germany, Fed. Rep. of; Greece; **Hong Kong**; Ireland; Israel; Italy; **Jamaica**; Luxembourg; Malta; Netherlands; New Zealand; Poland; **Puerto Rico**; Romania; Spain; Switzerland; United Kingdom; United States.
✳✳✳✳✳	75+	Iceland; Japan; Norway; Sweden.

Source: 'Population Facts at Hand' United Nations Fund for Population Activities' 1980.

KEY   Excellent ✳✳✳✳✳   Good ✳✳✳✳   Fair ✳✳✳   Poor ✳✳   Appalling ✳

could prevent it – if enough people told their political representatives clearly and firmly enough. But we do nothing – or not enough. And the Press remains largely indifferent.

Of the 17 million children who will die this year (a year during which it is worth remembering the UK is spending £225 million on cat food), 90 per cent have not been immunised against the six most common and dangerous diseases; this would only cost about £2.50 each. As Dr Elizabeth Bryan and Ronald Higgins wrote to *The Times*: 'The needless death of children is not a party issue. It is an insupportable rebuke to all of us.'

The Cambodia holocaust shocked everybody; yet the equivalent number of *preventable* deaths happen every 10 days. Today alone, several tens of thousands of people are likely to die through malnutrition, and the World Bank estimates a further 30,000 will die because they had not enough clean water to drink – just as others died yesterday and more will tomorrow. *The situation can be stated very simply: these deaths are preventable, because we live in a world where there is amply enough to give everyone sufficient to eat and survive healthily.* Since distribution, not growth, is the key to solving the problem, it is political will which is needed, and hard decisions about priorities cannot be evaded.

Machinery in the rich countries is lying idle because the debt-crippled developing nations can no longer import our products. 750 million people remain underfed at the same time as Northern grain-stocks are so high that American farmers face bankruptcy and in 1983 agreed to take more than 80 million acres out of cultivation. £4 billion of the European Community's CAP's £6.5 billion cost is currently being spent on the problem of surpluses. We in the EEC today have, for instance, a surplus of 350,000 tons of milk powder we cannot think of any use for; we pay the owners £334 for every ton they deliberately spoil by having animal feed added to it. Meanwhile, in the Zebbaleen part of Cairo, the only aid is a water trough provided by a British animal welfare organisation.

Mightn't the human skill and imagination devoted at present to creating inessential consumer demands be used instead to fulfil the really vital human needs? Mightn't the human ingenuity which can achieve space travel, or produce the Concorde's few hours' saving for the few, be capable – given the will – of solving these somewhat more important problems?

TABLE 1

Donor countries' grants by private voluntary agencies for development 1980:

	£ million	£ per capita	NGO grants as a % of ODA
Australia	17.26	1.17	6.0
Austria	10.22	1.36	13.6
Belgium	19.57	1.99	7.7
Canada	44.35	1.85	9.8
Denmark	5.61	1.10	2.8
Finland	6.74	1.41	14.6
France	15.52	0.29	0.9
W. Germany	182.91	2.97	12.0
Italy	1.35	0.02	0.5
Japan	11.48	0.10	0.8
Netherlands	34.22	2.42	5.0
New Zealand	2.96	0.94	9.4
Norway	14.35	3.51	9.6
Sweden	24.35	3.08	6.4
Switzerland	27.48	4.31	25.7
United Kingdom	45.52	0.81	5.9
United States	565.65	2.54	18.2
Total or average:	£1030.83	£1.54	8.9

NGO = Non Governmental Organisation [Source: OECD/DAC]
ODA = Official Government Assistance

TABLE 2

Who's most generous? Donor countries by rank, 1980:

	NGO grants per capita	Gross National Product per capita
Switzerland	1	1
Norway	2	3
Sweden	3	2
Germany	4	4
United States	5	8
Netherlands	6	9
Belgium	7	7
Canada	8	11
Finland	9	10
Austria	10	12
Australia	11	14
Denmark	12	5
New Zealand	13	16
United Kingdom	14	13
France	15	6
Japan	16	15
Italy	17	17

[Source: OECD]

TABLE 3

UK Joint Funding from the Government to Overseas Aid NGOs

Government Grants

1976/77	£
Oxfam:	130,000
Christian Aid:	40,000
Other agencies:	249,000

1977/78	
Oxfam:	425,000
Christian Aid:	90,000
Catholic Fund for Overseas Development (CAFOD):	20,000
Save the Children Fund (grant-in-aid):	9,000
Other agencies:	240,000

1978/79	
Oxfam:	800,000
Christian Aid:	200,000
CAFOD:	35,000
Save the Children Fund (grant-in-aid):	5,000
Other agencies:	308,000

1979/80	
Oxfam:	1,000,000
Christian Aid:	200,000
CAFOD:	50,000
Save the Children Fund (grant-in-aid):	6,000
Other agencies:	400,000

1980/81	£
Oxfam:	1,000,000
Christian Aid:	250,000
CAFOD:	75,000
Save the Children Fund (grant-in-aid):	9,000
Other agencies:	516,000

1981/82	
Oxfam:	1,200,000
Christian Aid:	300,000
CAFOD:	90,000
Other agencies (including £275,000 for Save the Children Fund):	588,000

1982/83 (provisional figures)	
Oxfam:	1,200,000
Christian Aid:	330,000
CAFOD:	100,000
Other agencies:	710,000

In 1981/82 in all 276 projects undertaken by 16 agencies were assisted on this 50-50 basis by ODA funds. The total government grant amounts to less than 5 per cent of British overseas aid NGOs' expenditure of £50 million a year, and represents about one five-hundredth of the ODA budget.

PART II

Quiet Revolutions:
Oxfam Overseas

Any man's death diminishes me
Because I am involved in mankind
John Donne

What improves the circumstances of the greater part can never be
regarded as an inconveniency to the whole. No society can surely
be flourishing and happy, of which the far greater part of the
members are poor and miserable.
Adam Smith, The Wealth of Nations

If you want to do good, do it in minute particulars.
William Blake

Author's note: The following five chapters are not in any way intended to be a complete picture or account of Oxfam's work abroad,
but are personal sketches of some of its settings, problems and
projects.

4

Latin America:
Ecuador and Peru

There'll come a day when men make war on death for lives, not men
for flags.

Wilfred Owen, The Next War

Because his spine is twisted
because he is past shouting
because he stinks
because he is too weak
to go on living
the system
that is to blame
shall not go on living

Because his spine is twisted
your explanations are twisted
Because he is past shouting
you cannot shout him down
Because he stinks
your whole system stinks
too strongly to go on living
to high heaven
where he won't get

Erich Fried, Child in Peru

The medical prognosis for those in upcountry Latin America is
not encouraging. Hepatitis in many areas is endemic, as are
malaria and Chagas's disease (sleeping sickness) – both notoriously difficult to treat. Most new arrivals get dysentery; many as
well suffer from altitude sickness in the Andes. Several types of
snakebite and rabies – also carried by vampire bats – can often be
fatal (every village greets you with its barking dogs, and it is
impossible to tell which are rabid and which are not). If you walk
barefoot, you're likely to get hookworm; when you go in rivers,
you are vulnerable to bilharzia and/or to being attacked by
piranhas, if not worse . . . And if you are thinking of becoming a

61

development field worker, remember that recently two of Oxfam's most experienced overseas workers who had both taken the prescribed anti-malarial pills and had the anti-hepatitis injection were still laid low by malaria and hepatitis.

But the worries and fears of the many million poor who live in Central and South America are of different dimensions altogether. If you are not yet too ill, your own body is your final hope of something you can try to barter. An increasing number of Latin America's unemployed people sell their blood for 100 cruzeiros to one of the subcontinent's 10,000 blood banks, which markets it for 500 cruz. to hospitals which then retail it to select patients at a mark-up of 6,000 cruz.

In this paradigm of the subcontinent's social economy that Jonathan Swift might have relished, most of the raw material of blood – 3 million litres a year – is siphoned off for export in a trade which now exceeds £87 million a year. Containers of it now follow the route of the gold the conquistadors drained, to Europe. In 1979, the United Kingdom imported £3.5 million worth.

Since inevitably it is the poorest and least healthy members of the population who sell their blood, the risks of contamination are high. In 1978 the President of Brazil died from hepatitis, contracted from a blood transfusion. Four out of every five people who sell are estimated to be anaemic; many of them are consequently bartering their lives as well. Haiti has recently made a breakthrough in productivity by cutting restrictive practices in this trade: a new method of blood extraction, plasmateresis, has been perfected, which now enables up to two litres to be drawn from the same person day after day.

Most Haitian blood is flown to the USA. One US senator recently protested that his children might be in danger of receiving black blood; it is therefore now classified and labelled according to the source's skin colour. (See *The Leveller*, May 1981, and Sergio Rezende's documentary film *Ate a Ultima Gota* – 'To The Last Drop'.)

There is no room for Eurocentric smugness about the poverty in Latin America: parts of western Sicily are just as fatalistic and destitute. ('Most of us go abroad to escape from ourselves – perhaps even out of self-hatred,' said one Oxfam man working in Latin America. 'The first thing you must learn in this kind of work is that you can't change the world.')

The Magnet of the Cities' Slums

But whereas at home we think of 8 per cent unemployment as a tragic disgrace, in Ecuador – not one of the very poorest of Latin America's countries – the unemployed number 40 per cent of the urban population, and 60 per cent of the rural.

This is only one symptom of the great urban/rural imbalance of political power. Urban incomes in the developing world, when work is obtainable, are on average 2.5 times higher than rural ones; in Latin America the differential is 4 or 5 times. Roughly two-thirds of people in the developing world live in rural areas; yet investment and development plans alike have largely ignored the rural poor. Cities offer the lure of opportunities for the resourceful, whereas country areas stagnate through neglect. Whatever public services are available – whether clean water, schooling, doctors, transport, drains, roads or electricity – are immeasurably more likely to exist in a city than in the country. These provide, as Paul Harrison says, an 'invisible or social income; migrants are well aware that they improve their life chances and those of their children' there (*Inside The Third World*, Penguin, 1979). Hence the never-ending spread of barrios and favelas round Lima, Rio, Bogota, Mexico City – like the bustees in India and bidonvilles of Africa. Sixty per cent of Bogota's inhabitants live in shanty or squatter slums. Older people remember when Lima's population was 175,000; today it is over 5,000,000, and continues to grow by a thousand arrivals every day. Mexico City has swollen by more than half a million people each year throughout the last decade, and is already more than twice the size of London.

Middle class people in a city buying fashion goods look remarkably different when you're with their poorest neighbours who are asking to be allowed even access to a water-tap for their children. 'Why is it so difficult for the rich to help the poor?' asked Dr E. F. Schumacher. 'The all-pervading disease of the modern world is the total imbalance between city and countryside: an imbalance of wealth, power, culture, attraction and hope. Yet the cities, with all their wealth, are merely secondary producers, while primary production, the precondition of all economic life, takes place in the countryside.'

In Latin America there are additional historical factors. The invading European conquerors replaced communal systems of landholdings by societies of huge estates and landless labourers. The inequity of land tenure remains a major overall problem in most areas today: more than four in five of rural families in Bolivia, El Salvador and Guatemala are landless. The several million subsistence farmers and campesino families throughout the developing world have no protection against inflation, which constantly erodes any savings they try to make in efforts to escape poverty.

When political independence arrived in the nineteenth century and slavery was abolished, many landlords substituted almost equally oppressive forms of indentured labour and debt bondage. Farm labourers were – and still are – given loans to buy necessities of food and clothing, which then have to be spent at inflated prices at the landlord's own store. Because of oppressive rates of interest, the loan, which has to be paid with labour, never diminishes. When a man dies, his debt and obligation is inherited by his children.

What can Oxfam best do with a few hundred thousand pounds among several million people in such a situation? Brian Pratt, the energetic young economist who was recently Oxfam's Field Director covering the Northern Andean regions based in Lima, says: 'Often the scale of the problems is such that Oxfam can do little more than seek to assist people find solutions through official channels – for example, putting together a claim for water services, etc.' (The barriadas of Lima are so short of piped water that tins of it are regularly stolen.) 'We've tried to work with not so much the concerned intelligensia whose popular contacts may not always have many roots, as with local base-groups' initiatives that can help to strengthen communities – and which may also be able to serve as examples for other areas. There is a great deal of money available for certain types of charitable and developmental work in South America. Many agencies are willing to approve large sums of money for relatively untried groups, sight unseen. I strongly believe this sort of funding can be corrupting – more detrimental than beneficial. We've come to assume that other large financial agencies will fund bigger projects and that Oxfam should identify the smaller groups and work in those areas of the country not assisted by other agencies. I'm now travelling in far greater areas – including the most isolated and dangerous parts of the countries. Once small community groups are identified, it's our experience they can only realistically absorb quite small amounts of funds. Also, their forward planning is at best rudimentary . . .'

One Oxfam grant in the Peruvian Andes helps a small Indian group to run a snake farm, from which venom can be traded as antidote serum. The amount of this grant is a mere £432 but it is meticulously costed, accounted for, and later evaluated. In another area I listened for an hour while a Field Director debated with a priest running a project whether the two bicycles requested were really necessary, or whether one would do.

Generally speaking, Oxfam itself is not an operational agency. *Wherever possible, it works by helping local resources – investing in people more often than in physical materials.* Any sizeable grant has to be recommended by the Field Director (the Oxfam man or woman in charge on the spot); no project is supported until it has been visited by Oxfam's own representative. After that, an application can be scrutinised by as many as four further bodies back at Oxford – perhaps being over-vetted by comparison with the procedure of other agencies. Is it really necessary for it to be discussed by the Latin America Field Committee and the Overseas Director as well as the relevant Field Secretary and Area Co-ordinator and possibly a consultant dealing with the region? The paperwork regarding projects has become increasingly thorough. (The details this contains could in fact endanger people in some dictatorships. On the other hand, what are the ethics of foreigners working in a country without the knowledge of its government?) The average grant Oxfam makes overall is around £1,000. On purely cost-effective criteria, how justifiable can it be for a Field Director to travel – often in considerable danger as well as physical strain – several thousands of miles each year searching out tiny projects scattered over Colombia's Mosquito Coast or the Amazon headwaters, when all of Oxfam's allocation for the whole region could usefully be spent in part of Peru alone?

Oxfam however is surely right to give priority to trying to tackle the problems of rural areas – however intractable these may appear and however appalling many urban slums are. For this in fact is the only effective way to help the slums: to try to stop, or at least slow, the flood of yet more refugees from rural poverty crowding into the cities. By contrast, when a government bulldozes newly-erected shanties of squatters, it is merely attacking the messengers who bring bad news.

Problems and Projects in Peru and Ecuador

In the biggest inter-government project ever seen in the Andes, West Germans and Russian aid teams are co-operating on a gigantic irrigation plan to pipe water from the tributaries of the Amazon westwards through the mountains. But not many kilometres away at Sechin – where pre-Inca ruins thirty centuries older than Cuzco and Machu Picchu stand in the desolate Peruvian desert between the Andes and the Pacific – the local smallholders have had no water for five years. Their sole irrigation channel (originally pre-Inca, extended by the Spaniards) was destroyed by an earthquake; having no assets, they were unable to obtain a loan to rebuild it. Oxfam has given them £5,000 to do so. At present the surroundings look like a Biblical wilderness, littered with unexplored sites and a ruined colonial corral where slaves were once penned. But the area's name (the 'Place of the Llamas') and the quantities of the animal bones found there testify to its former fertility. Soon it will be growing crops again. As he walked along the aqueduct, Brian Pratt said, 'It's good to have some tangible projects like this, whenever one feels uncertain about the results of community development grants.'

Isabel Q. was two months old when she was found in the Ecuadoran cave where she had been tied by her mentally defective mother. (In many areas mental illness is considered a source of shame and people of all ages who are thought to be suffering from it are kept hidden away.) The Tribunal de Menores took her away from her mother and she was sent to live at the SOS Aldea de Ninos (children's village) that Oxfam and other agencies support at Quito, Ecuador's 9,000-feet-high capital. When she arrived she was critically undernourished; now she is lively and trusting, seeming happier than many British or American children.

In the village, six or seven orphans live in each of the dozen family-sized homes (one named 'Casa Kirkley') with a friendly mother-figure in each house, looking after their own gardens and pet animals in between lessons and helping to run the community's market-garden and chicken-farm. This is one of the few sponsorship projects that Oxfam supports: each child is adopted by a financial supporter in Europe or North America whom they have never met, but with whom they exchange letters. The personal link of sponsorship is increasingly popular with donors (see Part III). But having to translate these letters into or from several different languages adds to the overhead costs; and in a number of cases the sponsor's relationship can degenerate into possessiveness or paternalism. (Frequent and firmly worded suggestions about birth control made by the sponsor to one family in a Peruvian fishing-port were resented as an unacceptable interference with their personal life and privacy.)

I asked the local 'Partners' – as Oxfam now prefers to call the people it gives grants to – what they thought Oxfam was and what are its reasons for doing the work it does. One group of small farmers replied that they believed Oxfam wanted to show solidarity with their problems, just as they themselves felt solidarity with the problems of the people of Bolivia and Nicaragua. A teacher in a neighbouring village wondered if Oxfam might be connected to the university he'd heard of, and went on to enquire what was the reason why there always seemed to be a famine in this place Oxford. Other local people asked me if Oxfam workers were missionaries in disguise (though Adrian Moyes said, 'Many of us joined Oxfam because it is *not* religious').

At a Peruvian co-operative trying to market products for an impoverished community of 70,000 people, one rural leader's perceptive answer to this question was: 'Some groups in Europe are conscious of having exploited the Third World, and such programmes are a repayment for the underdevelopment of Third World countries.' (It is interesting to wonder what would be the average British reaction if middle-class Peruvian or Argentinian ladies held sales to raise funds for H-block support groups or even trade unionists.) Some such European guilt might indeed be felt. From an estimated population of 2–6 million when Europeans first arrived in Brazil during the sixteenth century, its Indians have been winnowed by war, massacre and epidemics to fewer than 200,000 today. Some were intentionally infected by means of smallpox-riddled clothing given them by land speculators. (Any British people tempted to feel superior about Portuguese and Spanish pogroms should not forget that our British ancestors were exterminating the original population of Tasmania as late as the nineteenth century.)

In the Pastaza region of central Ecuador, Oxfam is supporting the Indian foundation Fecip to organise literacy campaigns in jungle villages whose only communication is by river. The Andean road southwards near the Equator falls in a distance of 300 km. from the snow-line to tropical haciendas of bananas, rice, cotton, and sugar (including one giant sugar mill where three years ago 180 strikers were shot dead, their bodies thrown into the cane as a deterrent). South of the Ecuador–Peru border begins an amazing stretch of eerily blighted coast. Every tree or shrub is dead; the wretched fishermen's shacks have no paint; there is no shop, no church, not even a cemetery. Southwards the landscape stretches even more aridly: not even a stick of dead vegetation is visible, only oil donkey-pumps nodding silently in the desert.

A community development centre in this part of northwestern Peru produces its own popular health manual, vivid with anecdotal illustrations. The workers there spoke warmly of the self-respect their relationship with Oxfam allowed them; they compared this with their experience with another larger Dutch development agency which had once appointed a Director (a highly qualified man but an outsider) to recast their organisation along model lines. Even if such an approach does not lead to personality conflicts – which in this case it did – there is a danger that it can create a new dependency. By contrast, Oxfam had been felt to have respected the autonomy of the community; the centre's committee members stated their view that a donor agency had the right to advise and criticise, but not to take over.

Family planning – and the emotions it arouses – most easily brings out the benevolent dictators among development agencies. (A project in India – not sponsored by Oxfam – surreptitiously inserted IUD coils into women patients in hospital.) It was at one time suggested (but rejected) at Oxfam that no health project should be approved that did not include family planning.

Oxfam, for reasons both of philosophy and of policy, has no wish to dictate. Yet any selection and value judgement about

Por que nos enfermamos de Bronconeumonia

Se dice que es causada por el frio,
pero, en verdad es causada
por microbios
llamados neumococos, estreptococo
y estafilococo

Se produce por tomar gaseosas frias
y heiadas
cerveza y agua fria.

Cuando sudamos y nos da el aire,
cuando nos mojamos con la lluvia
y no nos secamos a tiempo

'Why do we get ill with broncho-pneumonia? People say that it's caused
by cold but really it's caused by microbes: pneumococcus, streptococcus,
and staphylococcus . . .' An extract from the locally produced health
manual.

projects cannot escape being interventionist to some degree. Conversely it can be argued that every development advance which benefits people is in fact common human property, and therefore should be shared. (The wheel was unknown to the Incas when the Spaniards arrived.) There is a further major dilemma. Oxfam historically has always preferred to work by responding to applications rather than by initiating its own project: *yet this approach carries the endemic problem that the people who apply* ipso facto *already possess some initiative, while those in even greater destitution do not, and are therefore not being helped or even contacted.*

Pratt believes there is a 'special need to work with indigenous groups in the jungle – even though it's time-consuming: they are not only the most marginal (equivocal term) people, but also the ones often liable to lose the most from the developmental policies of national metropolitan governments' political and economic priorities – e.g. the incursions of colonists and multinational extractive companies.' Whereas some church agencies vie for 'the hearts and minds of the natives', Oxfam's policy towards the Amerindians is equally based on the belief that 'you cannot put people in a museum, as some anthropologists want'. (The Director of one reserve in southern Peru will not allow 'his' Indians to buy modern artefacts. But as they are a hunting people, they want a gun.) What Oxfam can do is to try to help prepare them to cope successfully for inevitable modern influences – for instance, by helping a local clinic to inoculate them against measles, or by assisting a co-operative to organise their marketing.

The women in Latin America have the worst lives of all, because they have to suffer machismo on top of the common poverty. Wherever possible, Oxfam might consider funding projects through women organisers and leaders, to try to redress the effects of the past four centuries (see Chapter 12).

One 45-year-old Peruvian woman asked: 'Since several of the priests here have children, how dare they go round forbidding birth control to women?' It is quite common all over Latin America to see costly and pristinely-kept churches and cemeteries situated alongside desperate families overflowing appalling shacks which English people might be prosecuted for keeping a dog in. A peasant near Piura told a bittersweet joke about a person watching the Pope at the airport in a fleet of Cadillacs: 'Not bad, considering his business started with one donkey.' Oxfam, like other agencies, often has to work through existing Christian institutions in order to help poor people in Latin America. This can cause problems. It has the effect of excluding those members of the local population who, for whatever reason, did not want to be associated with church bodies. Many of even the most liberal priests are, subconsciously or otherwise, unable to accept women's participation as equals or leaders. Several other religious missions – particularly in emergent Amazonia – behave like new frontiersmen, empire-building. One powerful mission-station in that area of eastern Ecuador where the Amazon rises is particularly unloved by its flock – and unfunded by Oxfam – because it recently publicly flogged some Indians for not attending mass. In parts of Central America, where development workers struggle in highly political settings, fraught with violence, death squads, corruption and civil fratricide, there is at present increasing intervention by extreme rightwing American evangelical groups of a fundamentalist cast.

Yet on the other hand some of the most courageous individuals acting as catalysts for change are priests or nuns. One man, who has worked for thirty years in a mission, declared: 'Among such violence, not to take sides is to take sides.' As a Catholic father confided, 'We can get away with much more reform through our church links, though it depends a lot on which bishop you have.' Modesto Arrieta, a courageous priest supported by Oxfam in southern Ecuador, ran into actual physical opposition from his whiter parishoners when be began to work with the Indian community in his parish. He was one of the lucky ones: he was backed not only by his bishop (who locked the main church to prevent the parishioners using it without the priest), but also by the country's reformist President Roldos, who personally came (shortly before he himself was killed in a plane crash) to open Father Arrieta's new church for the Indians.

The balance sheet of the net effect of the Catholic church on Latin American society is difficult to draw up. Much of the fatalism which inhibits any change or reform in local culture has been blamed by anthropologists on many years' indoctrination that poverty and inequality are God's will – part of a preordained

pattern of life, to be accepted, not questioned. Now that individual priests and bishops are the radical vanguard – in some
areas, the only hope of reform outside the guerrillas, many of
the faithful are (not surprisingly) disturbed and confused. This
dilemma of the church's pivotal position is one of the several
paradoxes not least where I next went to look at Oxfam's work,
in Haiti.

5

Caribbean: Haiti

Nobody made a greater mistake than he who did nothing because he could only do a little.

Edmund Burke

In 1968 we did not know what a community was. We of Choatalum were like coyotes in their burrows – we were isolated from one another and alone. Then the agents of motivation sent by World Neighbours and Oxfam began coming to us. Anacleto Sajbochol, an Indian like us, came to wake us out of our sleep, to motivate us to what we could do for ourselves and our families.

Jose Cupertino Sunac in Guatemala

A notice greets travellers arriving at Duvalier airport, Port-au-Prince:

HAITI IS LIKE NOWHERE ELSE.

The average annual per capita income in Haiti, £128, is the lowest anywhere in the Western hemisphere. In the table of protein consumption for 129 developing countries, Haiti occupies 129th place. Some 20,000 Haitians die of starvation each year; among all but the corrupt elite, almost half the children die before they are five. 92 per cent of the rural population live below the accepted minimum income of £220 a year; in 1978 more than 60 per cent lived on less than £33 annually.

Recent statistics, like the government's financial accounts, are conspicuous by their absence. One is impressed by the very extensive coverage of overseas events in Haitian newspapers . . . until one realises that the reason for this is because any controversial home news has been censored.

It was not ever thus. Colombus said of the place: 'In all the world I do not believe there is a better people or a better land.' The same remains true today, despite the change of inhabitants since 1492: the people are courageous as well as likeable, the land is potentially fertile as well as exceedingly beautiful.

Haiti was the first black country to win its freedom from colonialism: in 1791–1804 it fought and won the first Latin American war of independence, mainly due to Toussaint L'Ouverture's brilliant military and diplomatic rout of the European superpowers, including for a while Napoleon. Once France's richest possession, it was developed purely to supply European needs: in the eighteenth century it provided all of Europe's sugar. Its import and export trade then exceeded those of the thirteen American colonies and all of Spain's possessions. Haiti must be one of the few countries in the world where today production is lower than it was a century ago. The European powers left behind them a major crippling legacy which continues to handicap the whole Caribbean: the chance outcomes of naval battles in the seventeenth and eighteenth centuries have resulted in neighbouring islands speaking different patois-languages from each other, which form barriers to trade, unity and understanding.

Haiti is a textbook example of the interdependence of economic and political human rights. The economies of all the Caribbean and Central America are currently depressed as a result of the fall in prices of sugar, coffee and bananas. But in Haiti there are other, special, factors. Farm work, associated with poverty or plantation life, is increasingly despised throughout the Caribbean; but because small farmers in Haiti have no security, traditionally they have tended to exploit and erode the land rather than invest in or reforest it. Lacking confidence, deeply mistrustful – particularly of the government – people have little goal to work for beyond their own short-term survival. Most of the qualified and ablest Haitians are amongst the almost one million who have emigrated or are in exile. There are more Haitian doctors practising in Montreal than in the whole of Haiti itself – where there is only one doctor for every 11,500 people (1 for 33,000 in the countryside outside Port-au-Prince, the capital), compared with 1 for 1,900 in the neighbouring Dominican Republic.

Meanwhile, one per cent of the country's population enjoys 44 per cent of the national income and owns 60 per cent of the land. According to the World Bank, the 4,000 families in Haiti who earn over £50,000 a year are almost totally exempt from tax.

The national system of government has been described as 'kleptocracy' – government by thieves. The presidential family's own fortune – mainly stored in Swiss accounts – is now estimated to exceed £222 million. For years monopolies such as of tobacco and matches have enabled the Duvalier family (who have ruled since 1957) to drain some two-fifths of the state revenues into private bank accounts; recently this has been supplemented by an annual sale to the Dominican Republic of 15,000 Haitian cane-cutting workers at £450 a head (itemised discreetly to the World Bank as 'revenues of undetermined origin'). While over 98 per cent of people living outside the capital still have no electricity supply, in 1981 the IMF found that several more million dollars had been diverted from the bankrupt national bank to the personal use of 'Baby Doc' (the 32-year-old president for life Jean-Claude Duvalier). The previous year the palace was reported to have commandeered from the airport a consignment of supplies sent as hurricane relief from the US. To be fair, his father François (Papa Doc) Duvalier's reign of killing and terror has given way under the son to mere institutionalised violence and corruption – though following Reagan's election in the US, Baby Doc in November 1980 re-arrested Haiti's leading opposition and trade union figures, together with most of the few independent journalists and broadcasters. For the majority of officials, government position is not a responsibility, but a prize to capture and enjoy; public posts – as in Restoration England – are sinecured investments. All except the highest ranks of the Tonton Macoutes (VNS – the Volunteers for National Security – who outnumber the army by 15,000 to 6,000) are unpaid, so they have to live from the proceeds of corruption or extortion – for example, by arresting people on false pretexts and then making them pay for their release. News circulates by samidzat rumour: a priest told me one night that when some human rights investigators from the US recently arrived to inspect Gonaires jail, the prisoners there were first moved elsewhere, and beds from the hospital were temporarily moved in, together with soldiers dressed as prisoners.

Can Oxfam operate in such a situation? Should it try to do so, and if so, how?

Of the 5.5 million people of Haiti, 95 per cent certainly meet Oxfam's criterion of being 'the poorest of the poor'. They live in a peculiar isolation internationally: cut off from Latin America and the rest of the Caribbean, their government is felt to be an embarrassment by other black states, and is shunned by whites perhaps for more complex reasons.

To cut off outside development aid to countries such as Haiti, as some voices demand, might give an easy and inexpensive moral glow to people in Hampstead, Greenwich Village or Georgetown – but at whose real cost? It is scarcely the fault of the victims – least of all, their children – that they are born under the rule of a Duvalier or an Amin. That is bad enough for them, without their knowing that we – who are lucky not to be in their place – are refusing them any hope of a basic health clinic or of a clean tap in their village. It is better to try to determine how best to help such situations: Oxfam is I believe right to support in Haiti their largest number of projects in the whole Caribbean area. The problem is the difficulty of achieving any spark, let alone momentum: only political change can bring the latter. One essential aim of the community development programmes which Oxfam supports in many countries is to try to give people, besides hope, some faith in the potential of their own unity.

Haiti is none the less likely to remain under a government dedicated to inequality for the immediate future. Does Oxfam want to channel its scarce resources to such places, or should it rather concentrate aid to countries whose governments are trying to promote development? Adrian Moyes, now running the Public Affairs Unit at Oxfam, answered, 'That depends on whether Oxfam can do anything to help the people, and on whether anything that Oxfam does can help or hinder the government. Helping the people does seem possible even under governments uninterested in development – though one should beware of being used as a showcase which the government could use to demonstrate that its policies were not as bad as critics made out. So Oxfam-supported development work in Haiti ought to make bad government more difficult. This would be mainly at a local level: we must not exaggerate the ability of Oxfam-financed development projects to influence whole countries. 'In fact,' he went on, 'the task of such work is one that *only* voluntary agencies can carry out – for both government-to-government and multilateral aid can in some cases only serve to strengthen the recipient government's control over the governed. So perhaps the conclusion should be that if Oxfam *can* sponsor development which strengthens people's ability to assert their rights and protect themselves from oppression and injustice, it should concentrate on doing so in these countries where other forms of aid tend to strengthen the forces of oppression.'

Oxfam accepts that this decision cannot avoid entailing major difficulties. First, development work in places like Haiti often costs much more than in other countries, because the government is not likely to provide any infrastructure or support – rather the reverse. This fact can be used as an argument for Oxfam spending its limited funds elsewhere, where it can help more development for the same outlay. Equally it can support the view that the desperate political situation makes the need in countries like Haiti all the greater – in that without an outside stimulus little or nothing can be done, compared with those countries with a more benevolent government.

A second problem is that a government such as Duvalier's is extremely unlikely ever to take up or replicate any successful Oxfam-financed programmes – which is one of the reasons why Oxfam launches small-scale projects elsewhere. Nevertheless, argues Moyes, it still must be right to try to 'enable people to take advantage of any change in the government's approach. (In most cases in history so far the people have been unprepared to take advantage of the opportunities that reforms and revolutions offer.) It is also surely right to try to enable people to control a bit more of their lives. These may sound modest aims. In Haiti they are quite ambitious.'

Lesley Roberts, the second of Oxfam's too few women Field Directors, opened Oxfam's regional office in Port-au-Prince in 1979. An efficient and dedicated economist who has previously worked in a bank, she taught herself Creole as well as Spanish. It was her decision to site the Oxfam area base in Haiti – the most dangerous as well as the poorest country she had to administer – despite the isolation of life there: 'You cannot avoid the real problems if you live here, whereas there would be a self-reinforcing tendency to ignore them if one lived more comfortably in Barbados – one would not want to visit Haiti much because one would not understand it, and one would not get to understand it properly because one did not visit it . . .'

In parts of Haiti, like Guatemala, many of the fields are so steep

that, when a farmer dies, Haitians say, 'He fell out of his field.'
(Guatemalans speak of 'sowing with a shotgun and reaping with
a fishing-rod'.)

Cap Haitien on Haiti's northern coast – Colombus's first
landfall in the Americas – used to be the richest cultural centre
in the New World, a second Paris with several theatres. Now it
is a sleepy and decaying port the size of Lyme Regis. In the
surrounding mountains lie two of the most fantastic sights un-
discovered by mass tourism: the beautiful crumbling Sans-Souci
Palace, with on the summit above it, the Citadelle, a gigantic fort
constructed by 200,000 Haitians to guard their independence at
the beginning of the nineteenth century. But the Citadelle turned
out to be only the first of several prestige projects in Haiti to end
in disaster: it was on the wrong site militarily, and after the
Emperor Christophe had ordered a platoon of his crack guard to
march off its parapet over the cliff-edge in order to demonstrate
to an English diplomat their loyalty to him, he shot himself with
a silver bullet.

Down below, at an open-air community meeting of the inhabitants of a slum area of Cap Haitien, Lesley Roberts asks:
'What are your worst problems?' – it being a cardinal Oxfam
principle to get people to articulate their needs, rather than to
suggest to them what they want.

A middle-aged man replies (his wife taking the minutes of
the meeting, as in Europe): 'Overcrowding – the church and the
Oblate fathers own the only empty land here. When our 15-year-
old daughters have babies, they still have to share our huts. Then
when the grandchildren arrive – sometimes there will be 10 or 15
children to a shack like that one there.'

'Why have so many children?' (Haiti's density of population is
greater than that of India.)

'The more there are, the more chance you have. Perhaps one of
them may get some education or a job, maybe abroad when he
could send us $50 a month and support us.'

'What about family planning?'

'People aren't interested – it also causes illness.'

Lesley Roberts: 'Why aren't the men more responsible then?'

'Because there is no work, they just sleep all the time.'

'They have enough energy to make children?'

'That is all they have the capacity to do.'

All around, as everywhere else in Latin America – and not only in Africa and Asia as well – women worked while the men talked.

Haiti has had long experience of Europeans arriving bearing poisoned gifts. A nun said she assumed Oxfam worked there because 'like other agencies, it was trying to find out things about the country.' (In a sense this is true – though not in the CIA way she was suggesting – because any development involves two-way learning.) Another priest, a shrewd sensitive man working for Caritas in the northern countryside, phrased his explanation more tactfully: 'There are many egoistic people who are like deformations in our society – including even many of those who have been educated. But *really* educated people are like Oxfam and feel a responsibility for doing something about human misery.'

In recent years Haiti has seen 145 different overseas development agencies trying to work there – one for every 33,000 of the population. In 1980 multilateral and bilateral aid totalled £58 million, amounting to nearly 60 per cent of Haiti's entire budget. Much has been food aid, but in Greg Chamberlain's words in the *New Internationalist*, this has been 'a major factor in the further destruction of Haiti's economy. If you can get free food, you do not need to buy any from the local farmers. And if they cannot sell any, they do not grow it. The entire community becomes parasitical.' Food now comprises well over half of all imports. Although the Haitian government eagerly solicits prestige international development projects – because it wants something to show – these have an abnormally high failure rate: due to the fact that they are almost all 'from the top down' in character rather than 'from the bottom upwards' – and are working through a government which in reality has little wish to see its people gain strength or cohesion.

As a result of both its historical experience and present political situation, it is very difficult to develop a community project in Haiti. 'They do not realise their power as a group', a Catholic sister there told Tony Swift, Oxfam's former Press Officer. 'They think as if they are alone and they are afraid. If forty went in a delegation to Port-au-Prince, they would turn back one by one and no-one would arrive.' In the 1970s, Oxfam enthusiastically tried integrated schemes, where health, education and marketing projects were concentrated in one limited area. 'With an integrated approach', recommended a 1972 Oxfam report, 'the local people have to consider which is the most important subject, how it affects other ones, what is needed to take full advantage of it, whether it would be better to do it after doing something else, etc. They are also more likely to consider the whole community and its development needs . . .' Consciousness-raising is the key, stressed a further Oxfam internal analysis of Haiti three years later: 'This means alerting people to their capabilities and responsibilities. It involves helping people to both an awareness and understanding of how the world in their vicinity works, and the means to transform it. It is the vital component in the programme: without it any success can only be short-term.'

Although there were a few encouraging results (some members of the Volunteers for National Security resigned saying they had not realised what sort of organisation it really was), the larger integrated programmes have not yet achieved many of the other aims hoped for. It is possible that their size inhibits people from becoming involved and participating in a project which they feel is really their own. This is an argument for restructuring the means, not abandoning the ends. *For the key to changing unjust societies lies in giving the victims more confidence: altering the conviction of those at the bottom that it is right or inevitable they must belong there. People too often come to see themselves as the rest of society sees them – unworthy or incapable of being anywhere else but down. So a crucial task development faces is to alter that self-image, to give people the confidence to assert their rights and use their skills.*

So Oxfam perseveres with its work to encourage co-operatives in Haiti, to give beggar children some education and if possible teach them a trade, and to train Haitian 'animateurs' in their efforts to try to counter fatalism. A local translation has been made of the invaluable handbook *Where There is No Doctor.* (Oxfam has also given a grant of £476 for a welfare programme for destitute British citizens in Port-au-Prince.) Roberts has successfully worked as well to develop links between Haiti and other Caribbean countries. Fish are abundant in the seas round the coast but are not being caught or marketed, so that Haiti imports fish: this might be a project for Oxfam in the future . . .

At an adult education centre which Oxfam supports, local

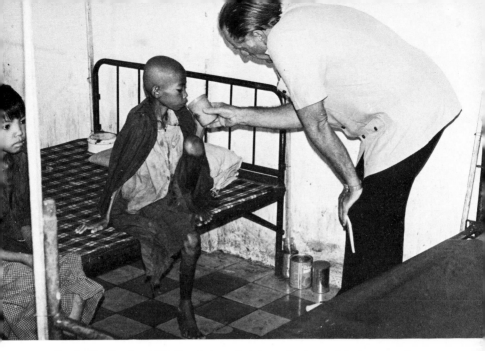

Cambodia, October 1979: Guy Stringer helping to feed one of the large number of severely malnourished children in a hospital at Phnom Penh. Pol Pot's brutal policy had been to destroy the cities to revert to a primitive rural form of communism.

January 1980 – the same two boys released from hospital and now in Orphanage No 1. Their diet was the Oxfam recommended one, for which the equipment and constituents had been brought in on Oxfam barges.

An Oxfam barge being unloaded on the wharf at Phnom Penh on the river Mekong. The sacks contain rice and the boxes, hoes and cooking oil. (See Chapter 1)

One of the fleet of Oxfam lorries being delivered on Phnom Penh Airport. The lorries, bought in Turkey, were flown in large transporters to Hong Kong and then in Hercules aircraft carrying two at a time to Phnom Penh. The unloading time was two and a half minutes. Note the diesel fuel packed in the back.

Oxfam-imported rice – largely the high-yielding hybrid variety – being planted in the Cambodian countryside.

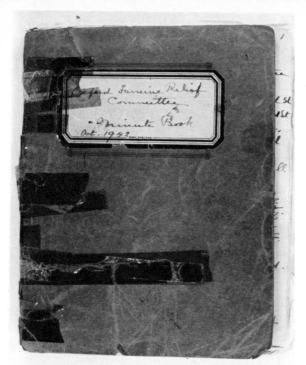

The minutes of the first ever meeting of the Oxford Committee for Famine Relief on 5 October 1942 were recorded in this battered exercise book.
(See Chapter 2)

The first permanent Oxfam shop, opened at 17 Broad Street, Oxford in 1948. Originally it sold donated clothing that was unsuitable for refugees.

people choose their own teachers and raise the money for their pay, selling part of their meagre crops to fund this. (Educational reform is overdue: 190 years after independence, Haitian children are taught a French curriculum in a language that is incomprehensible to the majority of them, who only speak Creole. This is a major reason for the 84 per cent illiteracy rate, and why many children drop out of school before completing even their primary years.) 'There is nothing tangible or glamorous about this sort of aid, but it is investment in people which increasingly Oxfam Field Directors are recommending', said Elizabeth Stamp, Oxfam's Information Officer. Such small-scale projects seem particularly appropriate for Haiti, since larger ones lend spurious prestige to the government.

Neither is emigration any solution: rather the reverse. Such reformers as there are in Haiti wish enterprising people would stay and help to change society. Ironically, the government on the other hand welcomes this safety-valve and wants dissidents to leave – thus making it easier to control those who remain.

Voudou, which is the traditional religion originating from Dahomey in West Africa, still has a wide hold in rural Haiti ('instant voodoo' kits have lately been put on sale to try to attract tourists). It is the religion of independence, while Christianity is the creed associated with colonialists, the European invaders and the not-to-be-trusted whites. Catholic churches still alienate their black congregations by presenting exclusively white images of God and saints. A disturbing thought crosses one's mind: might the European wish to change this society be in danger of being yet one more manifestation of paternalism, however benevolent?

6

Africa: Zimbabwe

Until the lions have their historians, tales of hunting will always
glorify the hunter.

African proverb

For centuries the capitalists have behaved in the underdeveloped
world like war criminals . . . We are not blinded by the moral
reparation of national independence: nor are we fed by it. The
wealth of the imperial countries is our wealth too . . . So when we
hear the head of a European state declare with his hand on his heart
that he must come to the help of the poor underdeveloped peoples,
we do not tremble with gratitude. Quite the contrary; we say to
ourselves: 'It's a just reparation . . .' Nor will we asquiesce in the
help for the underdeveloped countries being a programme of 'sisters
of charity'.

Frantz Fanon

Few people involved in (or writing about) development work
have firsthand experience of the problems or needs of destitute
families. Aid employees are usually selected for their professional
skills or their ability to disburse funds responsibly; their talent
more often lies in the direction of reliable integrity and administrative capability than in originality or intuition. Ironically,
Schumacher pointed out, while there is an increasing trickle of
qualified people in rich countries who are interested in doing
some work to alleviate world poverty – but until the recent
growth of the UN and NGOs could find few outlets to do so, poor
countries' privileged elites more often follow another fashion set
by richer societies and prefer to concern themselves with any
problem except that of the poverty of their fellow-countrymen.
*'If you are not part of the solution, then it must be you are part of the
problem itself', was Eldridge Cleaver's verdict.*

But it is wrong to see development only – or even primarily – in
a material sense. It is perhaps more accurate to think of the truly
un- or underdeveloped human being as a person who knows
that other people are starving or dying from preventable causes

and fails to do what he can to rectify this. *Similarly, are not the really undeveloped nations those which refuse to share surplus resources with others in urgent need?*

Many, though not all, people working for voluntary agencies such as Oxfam have obviously found a personal fulfilment, which impresses like some positive mirror-image of the negative disaffection frequently found among rich people. Michael Behr, Oxfam's Field Director in Zimbabwe, a highly radical man from a background of Russian emigré banking in England, enjoys an immediate sympathy and rapport with Africans, ranging from villagers to government ministers. 'Thank you for listening to our problems', a group of impoverished rural Zimbabweans once said to him. *'They're not your problems. They're all our problems'* was his answer.

Moral indignation – however easy and vicariously enjoyable an emotion it may be – is not enough. It is necessary to progress from outdated *de haut en bas* charity to tackling the complex and often unspectacular real problems involved in development: to move on from helping, and then assisting people to help themselves, to seeking solutions which give greater justice for producers as well as consumers in the Third World. This necessitates examining any 'structural injustice' of which we ourselves are part. 'People are living,' Yilmaz Güney (the Turkish director of *Yol*) says, 'but they are blind and deaf to the way they are living.'

Oxfam has concentrated its help in Zimbabwe on three main areas: a basic health programme; projects relating to the disabled (especially rehabilitating victims of the war); and projects of rural development (including the provision of supplementary feeding for undernourished children). At the time it became independent in 1980, Zimbabwe's problems were legion. 1,400 of its schools had been destroyed by its white rebel army. Some two million of its black nationals had been driven from their homes by military sweeps, so that their land had run to weed and their livestock atrophied. The new nation had an overall inheritance of potentially inflammatory racial injustice, with white wage-rates over ten times those of blacks and primary educational expenditure on white children exceeding that for black ones by a ratio of 15:1.

Because Britain failed to take effective action for so many years against the rebel minority in a colony for which it claimed full legal responsibility – thus shielding it from UN action – the price of restoring law and justice had to be borne by black Zimbabweans and by the neighbouring African states. Brian Walker on behalf of Oxfam has urged that Britain should be much more generous with post-independence aid for reconstruction. In Zimbabwe's first year, Oxfam itself provided £375,698 for projects. Michael Behr is more accepted and popular amongst black Zimbabweans than almost any other British person in the country, but even so, he says, 'Because Oxfam didn't support the liberation movement, some Zimbabweans ask, "Why should we allow you to operate?"'.

As long as apartheid continues in Zimbabwe's southern neighbour, the Western nations' tacit support for South Africa remains a complicating factor. Oxfam's fieldworker in South Africa, Alex Mbatha, has recently had to take refuge in Zimbabwe, after he and his wife Khosi were detained without charge for six months and tortured by the South African security police. Their release in 1982 was obtained with the help of a persistent campaign by Oxfam, though Khosi was so badly treated in prison that she suffered a stroke. Alex Mbatha explains:

Today we are outside South Africa – my whole family – as refugees, because of the type of work I was engaged in. The authorities thought that the job I was doing was subversive – because in that country you do not talk about 'development'. Development in South Africa is synonymous with agitating, being a troublemaker. If you speak in terms of motivating people for self-help, if you intervene to give them hope, reminding them that there are people outside their country who are at one with them in this struggle, then you are branded as a terrorist. But I knew I had done no wrong – I had neither killed nor maimed anyone. At the depth of torture, I knew I had been right to take on that job – to help those people in the homelands who had lost hope, the sick and the old who had nothing, the helpless, the voiceless and the voteless people. I was paying the price of having identified myself with the sufferings of my people.

The longer any Field Director remains in a post, the more he tends to identify with the local people rather than with the headquarters in Oxford – 'going bush' as diplomats say about some of their colleagues who have been abroad for any length of time. But being abroad also gives most people a very different insight into their own country. (I myself found it amusing to read, while bumping up a farmtrack near Zaka in Zimbabwe's eastern highlands, a report from the *Financial Times* that spray-on aerosols of mud were being sold in London to make rich city-dwellers' Range Rovers look more authentic.) Behr believes strongly that Oxfam should be helping projects in Britain similar to the ones it supports abroad, employing at home the expertise it has learned overseas. '"What right have you to be giving us advice about development, when you don't act the same way at home?", Africans would ask us. At present we're trying to be all things to all people, and one day we'll have to choose.'

From his own previous experience with Oxfam's work in Upper Volta – where the grim position is that food production is shrinking by 2.8 per cent each year – Behr said:

> There's no way a developed country would allow to happen in its own towns and villages what it is doing in the developing world. Official development is not working because lack of cultural, political and social sensitivity makes it impossible for the worlds of the 'developers' and of 'those to be developed' ever to meet. We should actively produce evidence through our field offices that would show the irrelevance and failure of the majority of the large international and bilateral programmes. We should not be afraid or too humble to go to these organisations or to the press where necessary, with evidence of the counterproductive effect of these agencies. We have done this in the case of natural disasters, so why not with this particular disaster? I suggest this, not so that we can try and prove that Non-Governmental Organisations are better, but in an attempt to remove some of the barriers that prevent the kind of development taking place which Oxfam's own Guidelines suggest.

He points to a fundamental dilemma, at least for the radicals in Oxfam:

> Although we are constantly pointing out injustices of economic inequality, we hesitate to actively support any real change in the rich world's own system which might be a threat to our own heritage and way of life. By not taking sides, Oxfam in fact contributes – even in a small way – to an increase in the frustration and hate that leads to violence. Of course I'm not saying that everything in the socialist world is rosy and everything in the capitalist world is decadent. But it would be just as naive and misleading for an organisation such as Oxfam not to understand and have links and a working relationship with individuals, groups and countries in the socialist world. It would be sad if Oxfam were to fail to understand, and therefore unable to explain to its public , various expressions of change taking place in the Third World simply because these changes are called socialist or marxist.

Throughout its existence, Oxfam has steered a pragmatic course. How much and when it should use political protest requires a delicate judgement. There are strong arguments why any foreign organisation working in an overseas country should avoid interfering in local politics. There is the additional danger that a change in government may lead to the expulsion of a NGO if it had been seen to be too closely associated with one political group which has lost power. As I saw in Haiti, the more the inhabitants of a country have a bad or repressive government, the more they are likely to need Oxfam's work; but once Oxfam embarks on the slippery course of political involvement, it risks being thrown out and jeopardising all the projects it supports. Brian Walker's view is that Oxfam has moved much more into the political arena in the last six years, and now does as much as it can in this direction without losing a significant part of its own constituency of donors and volunteers.

Behr remains troubled, by something more than deep white liberal guilt: 'Are we not, despite our stated objectives, an organisation that is so identified as a "Giver" that it makes it difficult for us to form any genuine partnership that is based on equality and mutual respect with those who seek a change in their social, economic or political status?' As Sithembiso Nyoni, a Zimbabwean consultant to Oxfam puts it: *'We in the Third World don't want to feel we're the objects of development. We want to be treated as human beings and partners.'* Asked what she thinks are the white voluntary agencies' motives for their work she suggests: 'Besides guilt and the missionary instinct, it's this permanent overriding feeling that they know best.'

The solution Behr proposes to this dilemma is that Oxfam should channel much of its budget for Zimbabwe into setting up an independent Rural Development Foundation where it would be Zimbabweans, not expatriates, who allocate the funds. This would absolve the giver from any feeling of neocolonial interference. But would Oxfam – as trustee for those who had contributed to it – have any say if the Foundation used its funds in (for example) corrupt, racist or anti-female policies? And if a crucial ingredient of the Foundation's effective role is to act in a markedly different way from – and even to criticise – the government's own rural policies, for how long would it retain its independence?

Zimbabwe in 1981–2 still enjoyed the honeymoon of its liberation. Robert Mugabe's government not only contains more able and qualified people than Ian Smith's but, given the circumstances of its arrival, shows a forgiving toleration towards its former enemies that few European countries would be likely to offer to those who had recently fought them in a bitter prolonged civil war. While the capital city's streets have a prosperity and appearance similar to North America's, the worst economic problems are concentrated in the rural areas which are the heartlands of the African population and had been grossly neglected by the white settlers. Black farmers – who outnumber white ones by a hundred to one – are crowded in the 'tribal trust lands' – that half of the country which has the poorest soil. Only 2 per cent of Africans living in the countryside have any access to electricity. *Rural poverty in every country is perpetuated by 'marginalised' people's lack of influence, their dearth of communication with – and understanding of – the world outside the local community, and their (often justified) mistrust of official representatives.* The mutually reinforcing cause and result are economic and political underdevelopment and dependence.

Not only the land of Zimbabwe, but the whole continent of Africa, has the potential fertility to feed all of its population. At present however more than 68 million Africans have an inadequate amount to eat. Most of the former colonist powers were more interested in exportable profits than in local food needs; and unfortunately too many of Africa's new elite concentrate on prestige urban projects rather than rural development or living standards. 'In less than a generation,' comments René Dumont (the great French expert about Africa's development), 'African politicians have forgotten the circumstances of life and death experienced by ordinary villagers.'

In an impoverished rural village near Musiso 150 miles to the southeast of Harare, the Oxfam-funded Sri Lankan Dr Murugasampillay, together with Brian Walker and Michael Behr, sits listening at a meeting where the villagers are stating their problems and needs – in accord with Oxfam's policy not to tell people what they want, but to respond to requests they articulate. About a hundred men sit on benches one side of the spread of a huge tree. An equal number of women and restless babies are standing and squatting facing them. The teacher at the local primary school – which possesses one textbook to be shared between forty children – chairs the meeting.

The first man to speak says they need a hospital.

The doctor replies, 'We can't have hospitals everywhere; how about a clinic?'

'Yes, yes, a clinic!'

There is a general shout of 'Viva ZANU-PF'.

A woman gets up and makes the practical point that a clinic will need an ambulance for distant patients to be able to reach it; a younger woman adds that even that would be no good without a bridge over the river. Others with increasing confidence join in to ask successively for a secondary school, for help for crippled children, training for school-leavers, boreholes, some pre-schools, adult education . . .

Walker thanks them for the growing list of proposals and invites them to choose which is their most urgent priority. Finally he asks them why they are asking foreigners for these things: 'You've had the strength to win the war; why don't you now also have the strength to win the peace?'

Their reply is that the war exhausted them; they're bankrupt; what's the good of independence if one starves; and that they've been exploited – 'emptied like calabashes'.

Before beginning to disperse the gathering sings a song, as the sun sets and babies start to wail in the dusk breeze.

Very few staff from the official international agencies attend this type of democratic gathering (with its echo of a Quaker Friends' meeting), which has now become an integral part of Oxfam's method of work. 'Outsiders are to provide support systems. They are no longer to lead or to impose their own visions and expertise on situations that will be lived by others, not by themselves. Rural people want to be the centre not the recipients of development,' reads an Oxfam report. One carries away from the meeting, however, a nagging worry that many of those people who attend must inevitably expect some consequential manna to arrive from the rich visitors. Nevertheless consciousness-raising is an essential step in getting the channels of political process flowing, particularly in a country which has only recently gained majority rule and independence.

Immediately after the village gathering the *ngangas* (traditional healers, formerly known as witch doctors) huddle together with Oxfam's doctor. It's the first time such a meeting has taken place; the atmosphere is delicate and tense on both sides.

Two-thirds of all the people in the world today still use the age-old medical traditions of their ancestors – frequently from preference, even when it is not the only kind of health care available where they live. In Africa, with only one Western-trained doctor for every 5,400 inhabitants, the 25,000 ngangas remain the choice of many people including those who live in the expanding cities. Research has confirmed that more than half of the ngangas' herbal remedies have ascertainable medicinal value, besides that crucial factor of faith which plays a major part in the recovery of most patients – whether their treatment involves aspirin, placebos or ground rhinoceros horn. Health remedies are used in Africa to treat both physical and psychic injury, as well as to achieve success, execute revenge, or to exorcise evil spirits. Several African states are now trying policies of integrating their traditional doctors into their national medical service, encouraging the ngangas to learn hygiene, to become members of professional associations and to join hospital staffs. Dr Gordon Chavunduka, the chairman of the sociology department at the University of Zimbabwe, is president of the 8,000-member Zimbabwe Traditional Healers Association. On occasions, traditional doctors have been accused of inciting ritual murder, or of blaming an illness onto a personal enemy or scapegoat who is as a consequence attacked. But they also can possess unique advantages. They are a familiar and trusted part of people's culture; they are cheap to employ as well as available almost everywhere; and they use a holistic approach – concerned with a patient's mind as well as his body – treating him in the context of his relationship with his family, community and gods.

To revive the basic modern health system in Zimbabwe's rural areas after the devastation caused by the war as well as the refugees' ebb and flow, Oxfam has financed one of the largest teams it has ever employed outside an emergency (five expatriate doctors and four nurses). It is based on rural clinics and the hospitals of religious missions. The team does excellent work, but complications are latent. Many of Africa's present problems have their roots in expatriate involvements. Employing expatriates – especially white Britons – is also unpopular when so many Zimbabweans are unemployed (there are few African Oxfam field staff in Africa and no black person at all on the Africa area committee of Oxfam). But Zimbabwe itself hasn't enough rural doctors yet. One of the British doctors, when offered medical students from Salisbury, stipulated these would have to be acceptable politically to the people he worked amongst, who happened to be strong supporters of Nkomo. To be identified with European-led Christian missions – even though many of these supported Africans in the war – also invites suspicion and non-cooperation from Africans who are not Christians. Yet no other hospital structure is at present available in many parts of rural Africa. Oxfam's work, as always, rests on the art of making the best of the possible.

7

Africa: Refugees and Disasters in Somalia and Ethiopia

Those who help today, tomorrow may need help. Those who today are helped, tomorrow will be able to help.

Oxfam poster

Little by little, an egg will walk.

Ethiopian proverb

If Oxfam and other agencies were able to work in clinical static situations, relief and development would be easier to plan. But usually the work can only continue by means of inspired 'ad-hocery' in a constantly shifting kaleidoscope – often with the agencies struggling to keep faith with the poor while at the same time trying to avoid involvement in the power struggles that determine their problems.

In 1967 the number of refugees in Africa was estimated to be 750,000. Today the continent accounts for approximately half the world's total of 12.6 millions, and the Horn of Africa – its northeastern corner – alone contains some 2,000,000 displaced people. Up till now the governments, with the help of the United Nations High Commissioner for Refugees and the voluntary agencies, have managed to keep them alive, but on a precarious tightrope. The lifeline for the scattered camps is permanently vulnerable, exposed to threats of a renewal of the simmering fighting; to drought, flood, outbreaks of contagious disease; to the sudden cessation of necessities such as food, fresh water, firewood, or petrol with which to maintain the supply-routes (the Iraq-Iran war cut off Somalia's oil). As a final gift from Nature, many of the camps happen to be sited in fatal contiguity to the earthquake zone of the Great Rift Valley.

Out of every 100 refugees in Somalia, 61 are children and 30 are women – a high proportion of them elderly or sick, since it is the healthiest people who leave. While I was with the Oxfam medical team working in the camps round Hargeisa (the main town of northern Somalia), months of crippling drought suddenly broke. Within twenty-four hours, the opposite extreme of flash floods had turned the camps into quagmires of excrement, where mosquitoes began to spread malaria and humidity sapped undernourished children, generating pulmonary infections and gastro-enteritis.

But Somalia, once again, had not prepared itself to use the rains. Nobody had made the reservoirs or tanks which are an essential part of every Indian village, or even had any water butts to catch the precious water – which instead swirled into the desert, sweeping away with it equally valuable soil and vegetation. All of Somalia, in and out of the camps, would benefit from both water tanks and waste pits, which are neither difficult nor expensive to make: unemployed labour and stones are two of the country's few surpluses.

But voluntary agencies in the neighbouring country of Ethiopia – where Oxfam also supports projects – envy the comparatively widespread amount of sympathy and aid Somalia receives from the Western world. The second most populous country in Africa, Ethiopia is given less development aid per capita than anywhere else in the Third World – despite the fact that its people have the shortest life expectancy (39 years, cf. 51 in India), the lowest percentage of population with access to safe water (6 per cent), and the smallest per capita GNP except for Bangladesh (£60, cf. India's £90 and Haiti's £130 – even though this is a less than reliable criterion because it masks the crucial factor of its distribution). It currently has at least 2.4 million people uprooted by war and drought (of whom the UNHCR estimate 1.5 million are in urgent need of assistance) – men, women and children who have involuntarily fallen victim to Western governments' dislike of Addis Ababa's alliance with Russia and Cuba. On political grounds, the USA blocked a $40 million plan for Ethiopia by the World Bank. Britain's ODA (following the change of government in 1979) cancelled a badly needed water project – which was a model developmentally, being well planned with appropriate technology – though the result is to make President Mengistu even more dependent on Moscow.

As a contrasting example of how nonpolitical NGOs are

able to respond to need, Oxfam's Michael Miller a few weeks afterwards was able to be given £50,000 within forty-eight hours with which to make local purchases of supplementary food for refugee children. This displays a speed of decision and action envied by certain other organisations. Conor Cruise O'Brien, when he visited aid projects in the area, gave as his verdict: 'Oxfam is a relatively lean, unbureaucratic operation, highly effective in proportion to its relatively small size . . . The struggle for development among the world's poor is one of more fundamental importance than the struggle between East and West, and may even determine the outcome.'

In Jijiga, an Ethiopian desert town near the Ogaden border, 12,000 people displaced by drought and the fighting are being helped by Christian Aid, Oxfam, and Mother Teresa's Missionaries of Charity. Oxfam is also supporting self-help projects initiated by local *mehabers* (peasants' associations) in Ethiopia, which is Africa's oldest nation, possessing a Christian culture that goes back 1,700 years, and is proud and suspicious of foreigners – not excluding Russians and Cubans. But, says Michael Miller, 'It's vital donors don't give up on Ethiopia. Relief and development work should be planned to intermesh – the drought is equivalent to a permanent disaster.' Hawkish strategists in Moscow and Washington joust to the local people's cost by 'fighting to the last African'. But if the Great Powers must vie in the Horn – as they have been doing for over a century – let them do so with rival irrigation and development schemes, instead of by hooking client states to dependency on their respective arms supplies. The winners would perhaps be the Chinese, whose disinterested projects of water supply and medical aid are admired as much as they are appropriate to the area's real needs.

One of the very few encouraging sights in the Somali camps are the 26 solar pumps bought by Oxfam and installed by Rob Fraser and Eddie Thomas, two water engineers (the latter seconded by Halcrows). A spin-off from the American space flights – where weight prohibited other forms of fuel – these have small movable photovoltaic units which generate electrical power from sunshine.

Oxfam is now also installing some of these in Bhutan. Together with wind pumps and biogas-plants, solar pumps are technologically right for almost every Third World country, besides having the advantages of being simple, silent, pollution free, and easily movable to where they are next needed. Compared with a petrol or diesel engine, their capital cost pays for itself within three years – earlier, if oil prices rise again. Their present price of £3,500 each could be drastically reduced if they were mass-produced: at present only a small number are sold, but Africa, Asia and Latin America between them could use several tens of thousands – and will indeed have little other alternative when in the foreseeable future they exhaust their wood supplies. Some supply of cheap, renewable energy will be crucial to support the basic necessities of life, especially for the maintenance of rural societies. The future supply of oil is finite, besides demanding prohibitive amounts of foreign exchange. *Here is a challenge for some UN agency to commission an imaginative and massive programme of simple solar technology – preferably by arranging to have it manufactured in co-operative factories in the Third World itself.*

When I put the question to Ogaden refugees what they thought Oxfam was, they suggested it might be an oxen farm. Apart from coping with the priorities of nutrition and immunisation, Oxfam's two volunteer doctors and six nurses working in the northern Somali camps concentrated on training Somali and refugee health workers to be able to take their place. Don Sutherland, an original-minded and talented doctor over from Vancouver for six months, was attracted to the job because it allowed him to practise the ideas of community medicine he would like to see implemented back home. The Oxfam health workers function as a team, meeting at the start and end of each day to discuss planning and casework in the light of the practical and ethical dilemmas caused by overstretched resources. (In one area of Somalia, a single doctor was recently carrying responsibility for the medical welfare of 130,000 refugees.) The greatest good of the greatest number requires inevitably that primary health work for prevention must take priority over any attempts at cure.

Dr Ann Kinmonth, who came from Oxford to take over from Sutherland when he returned to Canada, is in her first week at Saba'ad Camp. She is asked to decide whether they should attempt to treat a baby with very advanced meningitis. 'Yes: its mother brought it to the health clinic, which is what we asked.'

'It looks a pretty hopeless case,' the nurse reported, 'but perhaps we should go through the motions for the sake of the relationship.' Two minutes later, Kinmonth is called to another of the akul huts made of twigs and empty food sacks, to diagnose whether the phantoms a prostrate woman is seeing are because she has pneumonia or because her mother believes she has the evil eye and has administered a traditional remedy to her.

John Woodland, Oxfam's assistant Field Director in the area, is a gentle Dorset farmer sensitive to the complexities of Somalia. 'I don't think many people back in the UK realise the patience required for the problems of everyday existence working here or in Uganda. Getting the Land-Rover's puncture repaired, for example, involves a major operation with arguments as to whether this is your tyre – or if indeed you ever brought one at all.'

For six months after he returned home from his previous post in the Karamoja region in Uganda, where 50,000 people starved to death in 1980, Woodland found himself appalled by the 'den of iniquity' – the overconsumption and overeating in the UK. A woman doctor who returned from Ethiopia to Oxford, agreed: 'Yes, it's like having your head in a huge jam doughnut.'

If you are working on your own, the isolation can be exhausting. Very few expatriates have made any friendships amongst the local people. Some workers from another agency who decided to integrate with the refugees' lives and shared their huts were summarily expelled as a result by the Somali government. It can also be a dangerous job: when a British water engineer working at the most distant camp for the Save the Children Fund in 1981 was seriously injured in an accident, he had to be carried bumpily over a very rough track for several hours since there was no radio or telephone link with which to summon help.

An Australian woman doctor working for another NGO, World Vision, said: 'We come out here for adventure.' This fundamentalist Christian agency, based in Los Angeles, has grown through sponsorship schemes to £68 million a year – four times Oxfam's size. It aroused controversy in Honduras when some of its members there threatened Catholic refugees to withdraw their food if they did not attend Protestant services. But it also has a policy of employing not only multinational but also multiracial teams which might well be adopted by other agencies. One of the most important side effects of the relief programme is for Somalis to see not only women doctors and nurses in charge of teams, but also skilled black Zimbabweans and Nigerians.

Refugee families have nostalgically named sections of their camps after the oases and riverbeds they left behind. 'They become so completely dependent on us expatriates for medicine, food, water', said one English nurse, 'it becomes all too easy to forget many of them are grown men and women equal to ourselves.' Apathy among refugees is natural if they are allowed no control over their lives. All too frequently they are never told anything about their future: but in truth, what is there to tell them? There was a totally different atmosphere of activity at a vegetable farm I visited later in Djibouti, which had been started as a combined co-operative venture by twelve Djibouti and twelve refugee families.

The Horn of Africa so far has escaped the death toll of Cambodia. But it is permeated by a different tragedy. *Everybody agrees it is urgently necessary to treat the cause, not merely the symptoms, of refugee crises: to find some effective political solution – but this is not an area which NGOs like Oxfam can embark upon, despite the drain the present deadlock causes to their budgets.*

Furthermore, success can be taxed in a vicious circle: the more successful organisations are at coping, the more people they find they have to look after. Ethiopians allege that hundreds of people are still moving to the camps because the food available there is preferable to that outside. Many workers, haunted by the example of other refugee camps such as the Palestinian ones which have become permanent, have an uneasy feeling that the outside world's humanitarian effort – unthinkable though it would be to stop it – only postpones any longer-term solution being faced by local politicians. Refugee relief aid has become the biggest source of foreign exchange for the Somali economy. Somali leaders see the refugees' plight as a means of obtaining from the developed world aid, sympathy, and food (a proportion of which finds its way to the scarcely-any-better-off Somali population). At the same time they do not wish the camps replaced by proper permanent settlements or to be comfortable or integrated because they want the refugees both for propaganda and one day to retake their homeland.

With 40 per cent of its modest resources taken up by its defence budget, Somalia (the seventh poorest nation in the world) has enough inherited problems of its own to prevent it unaided from resettling many of those who have fled from the Ethiopians in the Ogaden region that both countries claim. Oxfam's Field Director, Robert Mister, was recently told of one village which lost 32 children suffocated in their sleep by a sandstorm. Every single one of Somalia's medical doctors departed within six months of its independence. Its per capita income has dropped from £1.25 to £0.75 a week, during a year when inflation has accelerated by 40 per cent. The water table is increasingly exhausted and dropping, and the scant supply of brushwood will soon be all burnt by the unprecedented new concentrations of population.

Many of the people in the camps are former nomads, who would not take easily to settled cultivation – still less to fishing, which is one of the few resources which might help the Somali economy to develop. (In 1980 the catch was 10,000 tons, but the F.A.O. has identified a potential yearly harvest of 211,500 tons.) Many refugees are now starting their fifth successive year in the 35 Somali camps; they are forgetting their traditional nomadic skills, and have become a new permanently destitute people. Another problem is that the inevitable 'seepage' of relief food out of the camps (partly through its being bartered for unobtainable items such as sugar) has depressed prices for locally grown food, so that less is likely to be planted in the future. This adds to the resentment amongst some Somalis who have an unfounded suspicion the camp families are being better treated than they are.

Andre Sabbe, a Belgian worker in Somalia, has attempted his own drastic personal solution by legally adopting 30,903 refugee children, for whom he is now trying to obtain £19 million in family allowances from the Belgian government. The United States has admitted a small quota of refugees, choosing the ablest and best qualified, leaving even less hope amongst the less advantaged core who remain. But most of the oil-rich Arab countries have done little for their fellow-Muslim refugee neighbours – nor do they seem likely to while the UNHCR carries the bulk of the current burden at a cost of over £100m a year. However, neither should we forget that – at the time of a refugee explosion in Africa, Central America, Afghanistan and southeast Asia – the present UK government cut back its contribution to the UNHCR from £6m in 1979/80 to £4.75m in 1980/81. Britain now contributes per capita less than 20 per cent of what Sweden does.

The Somali Minister for Refugees wryly said that if Somalia had put the refugees adrift in boats in the Indian Ocean, like some other countries did, the world would quickly have found homes for many of them. Ethiopia and Somalia require another £250m of emergency aid in 1983. Chad and Uganda at present urgently need enormous subsidies. Sudan's refugee problem has now swollen to 600,000.

Refugees throughout the world have become a manmade disaster. The future outlook for them – more than two decades after the end of World Refugee Year, penned in semi-permanent concentrations not only in Africa and in the Middle East but also now in Central America and in western and south-eastern Asia, appears to be 'a cumulative nightmare', as Dr Frances D'Souza said in a report for the Minority Rights Group, *The Refugee Dilemma*, in 1981. The year before, the UN High Commissioner for Refugees had reported that his budget, fixed at an unprecedented figure of £120 million only three months earlier, needed to be doubled forthwith because of new emergencies. Thanks to the UNHCR and voluntary agencies, refugees may not actually be dying of famine or disease, but the world prefers not to consider their future. It is ironic that, as an Oxfam doctor in Somalia pointed out, the success of a relief operation in fact may increase the danger that outside concern and financial contributions may fade away once there are no pictures of actual corpses – just as the world community forgets the continuing disasters in South Africa, East Timor, the Sahel or the Palestinian camps.

But overall, 'Disasters, whether natural or manmade, assume the magnitude they do as far as human suffering is concerned, largely because they occur within a social environment of poverty and deprivation', Brian Walker pointed out in November 1982 to the UN Disaster Relief Organisation (UNDRO, whose creation Leslie Kirkley had suggested).

Even in the rich world this is true, as the Italian earthquake in 1980 demonstrated . . . Coastal flooding in India, Bangladesh or Vietnam, is that much worse because of endemic poverty . . . To struggle out of a cruel stroke of misfortune requires not only significant material assets to rebuild one's life, but demands equally strength of body, agility of mind and determination of spirit, all of which may have been eroded, from the time a person was conceived, by the effects of poverty. The disadvantaged are disadvantaged from conception onwards; the dispossessed sometimes are dispossessed for generations before they were born. The development of the brain of an unborn child in the womb can be adversely affected by its mother's malnutrition . . . malnutrition and poverty through childhood and adolescence will lead to gross deficiencies in the body, leaving that person weak and inadequate to face the effects of disasters . . . *It is important, therefore, to stress that disasters should not be considered separately from their basic social and physical environment. For us, disasters are essentially a reflection of man's traditional enemy – poverty.*

Secondly, there is little long-term value in responding to disasters 'mechanistically', as distinct from 'organically'. The former means the essential distribution of blankets, clothing, basic medicines, shelter and food, while the latter style of response focuses upon the continuing social development of the people within their family, their community, and their cultural structures. In other words, as quickly as possible, following a disaster, those who wish to help must first understand in depth the cultural milieu within which the disaster has taken place . . . and then the attempt to respond must be in terms of a community response which has as its hallmark co-operation and community solidarity. To put this in the reverse way, the imposition of an ideological or cultural style which is inimical to the community being helped, could well be more disastrous, in the long term, than the disaster itself. The world is littered with the unintended effects of kindness, generosity and charity which have gone wrong.

Thirdly, for an agency to move effectively and rapidly from the immediacy of disaster response to longer-term development, it is essential for the planning and work to be done not *for* the community, but *by* the community itself . . . There is considerable evidence that we tend, in our sympathy, to over-emphasise the shock and disorientation, *and to under-emphasise the inherent potential, with its therapeutic effect, which enables people to pick themselves up and tackle their disaster.* We believe that that potential is always there, and that it is a prime duty, at once humanitarian and professional, which requires the donor agency to help stimulate that kind of response from the community itself.

My fourth point is the self-evident one that none of this is really possible unless the donor agency has access to carefully compiled knowledge about the community it is trying to help . . . idiosyncracies which are fundamentally characteristic of a particular community, and which provide pitfalls to the unthinking generosity of donors, can be identified – Hindus are vegetarians and so when the harvest fails, cans of American beef are an insult; the use of Western medicines in isolated, very poor communities throughout most of Africa can be of little real value to the people; the hurried and thoughtless sinking of wells which merely deplete and exhaust a limited water table (as happened in the Sahel in the mid-1970s) can merely inhibit long-term development. The donor agency must also be tolerant of local myths, superstitions, and habits which, while annoying or incomprehensible to us, are nevertheless very real to the people we are trying to help.

Similar warnings are given throughout Tony Jackson's book *Against the Grain* (Oxfam, 1982), which argues that much of food aid can actually be counterproductive to the best interests of the people it is trying to help. Massive food imports that were poured into Guatemala after the earthquake in 1976 – essentially as a way to dispose of surplus American food stocks – destroyed the local market and spelled ruin for many local peasant farmers.

The apathy and despair rife in several refugee camps and communities arises from the fear that the disaster of their predicament is permanent, isolated and ignored. The response of a constructive NGO to such situations should be to plan to integrate developmental goals into its relief work. The structures – both communal and material – that it leaves behind when it withdraws from a disaster should serve as a continuing help for the needs of the people, after the disaster has been forgotten. In the projects which Oxfam and a few other agencies developed in Somalia, this became a prime objective. When they withdrew from Saba'ad and other camps, trained Somalians were able to carry on the community health, water and agricultural projects within their own cultural pattern. Not all donor agencies have this approach; the suspicion is aroused that a few of them – presumably for income-raising purposes – need the refugees more than the refugees need them.

Dr Paul Shears, one of Oxfam's doctors, described the change in refugee health policy which has taken place while maintaining day-to-day care – a task which he describes as 'like trying to overhaul a car with the engine running':

> It is increasingly evident that in most cases there are local and refugee resources and personnel that can be mobilised to provide most of the necessary health services. It is important to move away from the concept of an operational expatriate team approach – which in many cases can replace potential local initiative and create inappropriate aspirations of levels of health care – to the provision of key individuals, to assess new refugee situations and to co-ordinate, rather than replace, local resources and personnel, where possible in conjunction with existing Oxfam-funded projects.

In this way, a disaster can be given the potential to become a springboard for an ongoing pattern of development. This is the challenge Oxfam is tackling with the Ghanaians expelled from

Nigeria in 1983. Michael Harris of Oxfam emphasises another very important guideline for charities' response: 'The challenge of improving relationships and working agreements with other charities working in the disaster field. How easy it is to strive to be first in the field: to steal a march on a "rival", which appears on television the next evening. Often however there's duplication of effort; much more could be done with better liaison and co-ordination, to join together in common endeavour to meet the needs we are facing. At times of disaster we join together in fundraising – let us see if we cannot carry this a step further in the operational field.'

8

India

With God's help I can enter every heart. If I can be the agent of both the rich and the poor I shall be glad. For the poor I am striving to win rights. For the rich I am striving to win moral development. If one grows materially and the other spiritually, who then is the loser? Besides, what is land? How is it possible for anyone to consider himself the 'owner' of it? Like air and water, land belongs to God. To claim it for oneself is to oppose the very will of God. And who can be happy if they oppose his will?

Vinoba Bhave

The problem of getting people out of poverty is not how to get them enough to eat and drink; this is the condition for sustaining them in poverty.

Mary Douglas and Baron Isherwood, The World of Goods

Considerable – and widening – as the gap is between the richest people and the poor in Britain, the disparities in developing countries are often greater:

In Britain, the poorest fifth of the population have 6 per cent of the income, the richest fifth have 9 per cent.

In India, the poorest fifth of the population have 7 per cent of the income, the richest fifth have 49 per cent (59 per cent in Nepal).

In Malaysia, the poorest fifth of the population have 3 per cent of the income, the richest fifth have 57 per cent.

In Brazil, the poorest fifth of the population have 2 per cent of the income, the richest fifth have 67 per cent.

[Source: *World Development Report*, World Bank, 1980]

India, with one in five of the globe's population (approximately as many people as live in Africa and South America combined), is too huge and too complex for generalisations not to be misleading. It is a powerful nation, with vast potential. India has the tenth largest industrial output, and the third greatest pool of technically trained manpower in the world. Less fortunately, it is also the world's largest exporter of doctors: as many as 15,000 – trained in India at great cost – are now overseas, working mainly in Britain and the USA. The result is that there are less than 2.2 doctors per 100,000 people in India itself – and considerably fewer in rural villages or in urban slum areas.

Contrasts abound. For the Asian Games which took place for two weeks in 1982, huge stadia and flyover bridges costing several hundred million pounds were built in Delhi – but built painfully, with techniques scarcely changed from past centuries, by thin, ill-paid women and men living night and day on the sites in tents made of rags and cardboard. The extremes of destitution suffered by the poorest in India – its landless people, tribal Adivasis, and Untouchables (also known as Harijans, 'scheduled castes', or Dalits) – are due not to lack of national resources but to the inequity of their distribution. Amartya Sen argues persuasively that most hunger and famine everywhere is not caused by declines in the total food available per head, but by failures of 'entitlement' in market economies. In British India during the 1943 Bengal famine which caused some 3,000,000 deaths, people died in the streets of Calcutta in front of shops well stocked with food: Sen documents that there was in fact very little, if any, decline in the total amount of food available in Bengal (*Poverty and famines: an essay on entitlement and deprivation*, O.U.P., 1981).

Today, within sight of an Indian aircraft-carrier or one of her atomic reactors, the subcontinent's cities have miles of Brueghel-like alleys, teeming with craftsmen and crippled beggars – providing the visitor with a time-change that enables him to glimpse his mediaeval ancestors, going about their lives in a hierarchical society still fired by faith or superstition.

Calcutta

Calcutta has an appearance more of the age of Dickens and Doré, especially at night, when the smoke of cooking fires and nineteenth-century factories makes the city's few lights sulphurously pale. But the population who live and sleep crowded on the pavements or in shacks display enormous resourcefulness and courage in their struggle for survival. Families – their children helping alongside – ingeniously recycle anything from rags to shards of wrecked cars that are thrown away in most other countries. Some pavement-dwellers, however hungry, remain too proud to let their wives work. Spasmodically, official attempts are made to encourage the creation of more traditional slums, by the current policy of providing 'site and basic services' such as a water pipe and electricity, but leaving it to families to fashion their own homes as and how they can.

Most newly arrived travellers from richer countries, once they have surmounted their shock and incredulity, try to ignore such sights as the price of avoiding despair. But out of cardboard hutches, eyes silently speak to the visitor: 'Are we not human like you?' The most frightening part when faced with such poverty, is how easy (and tempting) it is to forget the victims' common humanity with us.

Calcutta's population has five times the density of New York's, which is the most crowded city in the Western world. Since the arrival of many thousands of refugees from East Bengal, Calcutta supports twice as many inhabitants per square metre as any other Indian city. But its harbour – the original reason for its existence – has now irreversibly silted up. Rampant water-hyacinth is choking the arteries of its canals with its beguiling flowers and tendrils. Since it elected its popular Marxist adminis-tration, West Bengal has been given only minimal Federal government help; industrial investment has been switched to Bombay. But hard as marginal existence is in Calcutta, there is more economic opportunity and less violence there – and hence more hope – than in the totally destitute rural villages of areas like Bihar.

Some years ago the United Kingdom's Overseas Development Ministry considered a plan to devote virtually its entire budget to a concerted attack on Calcutta's problems, in an attempt to achieve one major change as a result of its work. But on second thoughts it concluded that, even if this plan ever succeeded, it would be like trying to empty a bath whilst the taps were still running, because any significant improvement in living con-ditions would attract another million migrants. *Calcutta's problems can only be alleviated by helping the rural areas: just as those wealthy countries which worry about immigration should be helping labour-intensive rural projects in the developing nations.*

The pavement dwellers in Calcutta number more than 85,000. To deter new migrants, the administrations of both Marxist Calcutta and capitalist Bombay regularly demolish their pathetic shelters and bustees – especially since these people do not have any vote in the city, because they are still on the register of the villages they came from. Demolition continues even during the monsoon, so that families, unable to construct waterproof shelters, exist in a state of permanent discomfort and apprehension. When the police evict them, they lose any tenuous chance of local work that might provide them with a precarious living. Bombay civil rights lawyers are taking cases on their behalf to the Supreme Court, arguing that the government has no right to expel them without providing any alternative accommodation.

Meanwhile, Oxfam's Field Director for East India, Alok Mukhopadhyay, is supporting schools on the pavements to teach basic literacy to both the adults and children living there. At the same time Oxfam is giving priority to helping projects that are designed to provide work and improve basic conditions in the catchment area of the countryside around Calcutta. Mukhopadhyay and two assistants have to see 120 different projects twice each year, including ones 6 days' mule-ride away in Bhutan. His Assistant Director, Lincoln Young, told me: 'I like this work so much, I feel it's extraordinary to be paid to do it.'

Several small-scale Oxfam-assisted Bridge employment projects are focusing help in particular on the hard-working and courageous women of India (who – unlike those in the West – have a mortality rate that is worse than men's and is deteriorating further). Despite the Mahatma's teaching, most leftwing reformers neglect women's plight more than Indira Gandhi does, under the pretext that to focus on women's problems *per se* divides the ranks of the poor. Reports of wives being burnt to death for the sake of their dowries continue to recur. Many wives who have been deserted by their husbands, and other destitute women who are trapped in debt bondage, are forced into prostitution in order to survive. Widows – some of them still children – are often treated as non-persons (as a relic of ostracism for not submitting themselves to burning by suttee) and are not even given proper food lest it revives sexual desire.

The Ex-Dacoits' Story

At Baliapal, on Orissa's deltaic coast to the south of Calcutta, Oxfam began in 1979 to help a group of men who had lost all their possessions and livelihood in the floods. Evicted from their homes by moneylenders who customarily extort more than 15 per cent interest a month, they had been driven to become *dacoits* (as robbers are known in India).

In a textbook model of success – life is not always so simple – Oxfam lent them 7,000 rupees (£400) to form a fishing co-operative; in two years they earned 45,000 rupees, out of which they have repaid the bulk of the loan and also saved 5,000 rupees to purchase their boat and net. (The local banks had previously refused them any loans, because they could not pledge any security.) But this group have now achieved self-reliance in more than economic terms. Their village committee negotiates with government officials and the education and health authorities. They are also running their own literacy projects – which encompasses a knowledge of accountancy and natural history, as well as the traditional local songs. An important dimension of the teaching is that it encourages them to question superstition and traditions such as predestined untouchability.

When I asked the members at a village meeting – that started and ended with their music – why they thought they had hitherto suffered from underdevelopment, they gave these reasons: dire poverty, through lack of education and having no land; caste; swollen population; exploitation; no work; and a previous lack of any group consciousness. Development work can be easiest amongst groups like fishermen, who have to co-operate in order to succeed in their work and are drawn together by the common dangers they face. This particular group want to spread the ideas they have learnt to other destitute people. Their situation is not, however, cloudless: the success of the co-operative has affected and angered the extortionate local moneylenders, who now physically harass its members and are bribing the police to do likewise.

Fish-farming similarly could be one of the best hopes for the development of community consciousness throughout India, at the same time as producing more protein in impoverished inland areas. Of India's eight million hectares of village ponds, less than one-sixteenth are at present put to use in this way.

But the hardest people to help are those who possess nothing at all, except their labour. (As an example of how cheap labour in India is compared to food, a haircut costs 2 rupees – about 12 pence in UK money – which is roughly the same as the price for two Kashmiri-grown apples.) The 'poorest of the poor' are not organised to apply for grants. Most development work to date has, perhaps inescapably, been with those who have at least a few developable assets. Many community projects in fact continue to reflect the divisions caused by caste, religion, possessions, occupations, or morale. But as soon as an agency – and overseas ones are doubly suspect – begins to work with landless people, it inevitably starts to enter into areas of conflict with those who have a vested interest in the status quo. This is true whether it requests the implementation of the land reform laws or better education or unionisation in the hope of leading to improved conditions and wages. It is all too easy when giving development assistance in fact to widen the gap between the poor and the rich, because it is easier to assist those who can help themselves than the helpless or hopeless – those people used to no chance of work, or even if they were given it, are likely to have minimal 'productivity'. If the poorest sections of population do not receive some form of 'positive discrimination' by means of special development efforts, their predicament can only continue to deteriorate.

India has more people – some 350 million – classified as absolutely poor than form the whole population of black Africa. Poor people can be helped with solutions to some of their problems, but only by making available to them projects and tools that recognise the reality of their situation's circumstances – what Dr E. F. Schumacher called intermediate or appropriate technology. 'If the people cannot adapt themselves to the methods, then the methods must be adapted to the people. This is the whole crux of the matter', he pointed out in *Small is Beautiful* (Blond and Briggs, London, 1973).

> There are, moreover, many features of the rich man's economy which are so questionable in themselves and, in any case, so inappropriate for poor communities that successful adaptation of the people to these features would spell ruin . . . Unintentional neocolonialism is far more insidious and infinitely more difficult to combat than neocolonialism intentionally pursued. It results from the mere drift of things, supported by the best intentions. Methods of production, standards of consumption, criteria of success or failure, systems of values, and behaviour patterns establish themselves in poor countries which . . . fix the poor countries inescapably in a condition of utter dependence on the rich. The most obvious example and symptom is increasing indebtedness.

An approach involving small-scale appropriate projects is also much more realistic in view of the net amount of aid available, which totals overall less than £2 a head for people in developing countries.

The Rickshaw-pullers' Breakthrough

Madhu Gote, one of 5,550 rickshaw-pullers in the city of Nagpur, works hard for twelve hours a day to take home to his family – when he has a good day – 5 rupees (about 30p in UK money). He has to hire his bicycle-rickshaw from a fleet-owner for 4 rupees a day; on some days he has no customer at all and so earns nothing. Even on a good day his takings are scarcely adequate to feed himself enough for the physically exhausting work. Often, especially when he is ill, he has to borrow money from the fleet-owner, effectively falling further into debt-bondage. He is unable to pay to insure himself, or to save any money, and thus has no chance of buying his own rickshaw. Rickshawmen are among those at the bottom of the heap in Indian society – though an equivalent woman who does not wish to be married is, as Oxfam's Marcus Thompson points out, even worse off: there are no jobs for rickshaw-women. The average rickshawman, pedalling like an animal on a wheel in a cage, is thin and underfed, whereas the passengers he pulls weigh considerably more – since heaviness is a sign of status.

The solution Oxfam supports, through the Industrial Service Institute – a church-based organisation set up to help workers in Nagpur – is two-fold. The rickshaw-pullers are being helped to buy their own rickshaws; so far, over 2,030 now own their own vehicle. Secondly, their union is being assisted to convert their rickshaws from ones driven by bicycles – work that is officially condemned by the Maharashtra government as 'inhuman' – to scooterpowered ones. But the problem is that not only does each of the latter cost Rs12,000 (about £700), but it can have the effect of making ten bicycle ones redundant. The Nagpur rickshawmen are now visiting other cities to discuss with pullers elsewhere plans to unite to press for better conditions of work. (In January 1982, beggars in the northern Indian city of Jaipur formed their own federation – with the slogan 'Beggars of the world unite' – to try to share their alms more fairly, declaring 'Unless we unite we will not be able to fight those who are apathetic towards us.' Perhaps such a movement will eventually spread to all of Oxfam's clients?)

Vikas Bhai acts as an independent community development consultant to Oxfam from Varanasi (Benares). He pointed out, in confirmation of what was said in the last chapter about disasters, that 'India's regular natural catastrophes affect different classes differently – according to whether they can afford protection like savings or insurance. And only the more highly qualified or privileged refugees are for example able to transfer to jobs and a new life elsewhere. But such disasters can also be made the opportunity to begin longer-term programmes of social reform. With the help of the emotionally-generated appeal funds, these can lay foundations to offer more equal chances of opportunity, whereas – as we are continually finding – it is extremely hard to change class, caste or tradition in a non-disaster situation.'

A Lesson from the Untouchable Harijans

Vikas recounted an earlier episode that had taught both Oxfam and himself a crucial lesson: 'In a village called Sherpur not far from here, about 250 houses belonging to Harijans had been burnt to the ground by some landlords because they'd gone on strike; their families were left out in the open during the cold season. I managed to collect 2,000 rupees from people at the university in Varanasi and took the families a hundred blankets. Whereupon the Harijans held a meeting that lasted two days, and then came and told me that they would accept the 2,000 rupees only for legal fees so that they could take their case to the courts, but that they preferred to sleep in the cold. Later, ten of the landlords were tried as a result, convicted and imprisoned. *What we and Oxfam learnt from these Harijans is that people want justice, not charity.*'

Recently, several massacres of Harijans have gone unpunished in different parts of India. Children, not yet four years old, have been found working in unsafe conditions in firework and match factories in Tamil Nadu. Near Patna, police, at the instigation of local landlords, opened fire on rural workers who were asking for the minimum wage to be honoured as was their entitlement by law.

India has a number of benevolent laws, passed to help land reform and oppressed classes – laws which should be the envy of many other countries. 'But they are often never enforced, and the fellow at the bottom is probably even unaware of their existence,' is a typical Indian comment. India also has the benefit of an independent legal system, and a free press – better than that of many developed countries – which regularly reports injustices and corruption. What are needed are more of the courageous lawyers to connect the people to their rights, together with some effective pressure groups to try to see that the legislation is actually implemented. Here is where support from a body such as Oxfam can make a crucial impact for social justice. Yet it often has to keep a very low profile, not only for the sake of its own survival, but also since if the vested interests heard that outsiders are helping such troublemakers, this would damage their cause.

Wrongs and Rights in Bihar

But to be persuaded of the urgent need for such help, it is necessary to look no further than Bihar. This state of 70 million people is potentially rich in resources – it possesses two-fifths of India's mineral wealth, and two of the largest steel mills in Asia – but it has the lowest per capita income of any Indian state. It is cancerous to its roots with high-level corruption and violent intimidation. State ministers openly employ armed goonda thugs to control elections; one third of the state legislators are reported to be implicated in criminal cases; high-caste landlords and politicians use the police not to protect but to exploit and terrorise the poor and deprive them of their rights. J. P. Narayan and his Gandhian followers campaigned against these abuses, but the central government has conspicuously failed to intervene, despite Mrs Gandhi's motto that 'The needs of the many must prevail over those of the few'.

At the end of 1981, the Indian People's Union for Civil Liberties successfully filed a writ of habeas corpus on behalf of Ram Chandta, *who had been kept without trial for twenty-nine and a half years* in a Bihar gaol (despite a Supreme Court directive two years earlier ordering the release of all prisoners whose cases had been pending for more than six months). Other prisoners there have been awaiting trial for over six years on petty charges such as travelling on a bus without a ticket – for which the maximum penalty is seven days' jail – because they are ignorant of their legal rights. Bihar is the same state from where it has recently also been reported that Harijans have been burnt alive (at Parasbigha, in February 1980); tribal patients in hospitals were bayoneted to death (at Gua, in August 1980); and thirty-two unconvicted people in custody had their eyes gouged out by policemen with acid, needles and bicycle spokes (at Bhagalpur, at the end of 1980 – for which those responsible have not yet been punished; indeed one officer who exposed the crime has been suspended and another transferred).

Oxfam supports the Free Legal Aid Committee (FLAC) working at Jamshedpur in Bihar. The law governing charities prevents them giving any help for criminal cases, but the project (which also receives finance from Indians, so that it meets the require- ments of the UK Charity Commissioners) is able to press for speedier trials and penal reform, as well as to advise on civil matters such as land reform cases. FLAC, which is insistent that it shall be managed by ordinary lay people not lawyers, has been campaigning in particular about Bihar's jails. It has helped, for example, one 8-year-old boy who, though totally innocent, has spent his entire life in prison because his mother has been awaiting trial since before she gave birth to him. Other guiltless mothers and children have been incarcerated without hope for several years, not because they are charged with any offence, but because they may be required as witnesses in a case and are too poor to afford either bail or a necessary bribe. Such women and children have to live amongst hardcore criminals – 1,000 people crowded into jails built for 300: prison staff have a pecuniary interest in having the maximum number in their charge so that they can sell their medicines and rations. (Some honest police officers and prison staff are themselves so badly paid that they have to sleep in the corridors of where they work because they are unable to afford any home.) The Committee's work to try to remedy this appalling situation has been praised by Mr Justice Bhagwati, the highly respected Indian judge, and

Nani Palkhivala – perhaps India's most outstanding civil rights lawyer – has offered to take test cases on their behalf to the Supreme Court without fee.

India's original inhabitants: her Tribal People

Another Free Legal Aid Programme (FLAP) has been supported by Oxfam since 1977 as part of the integrated development work for Adivasis carried out by the Social Services Society at Rajpipla in Gujerat. India's 40 million tribal Adivasis – her original inhabitants – form about 7 per cent of her present population. Tony Vaux, Oxfam's Field Director in Gujerat 1977–80, who is one of many Oxfam staff who enjoys working overseas much more than at home, writes: 'I would say that legal aid is one of the very best forms of assistance which can be given to Adivasis. They have other problems . . . but illegal harassment and exploitation is perhaps the worst and theoretically the easiest to tackle.'

The Adivasis, who are not Hindus, have been pushed by successive invasions into the poorer and less fertile areas of the subcontinent (in a history with parallels to the invasions of America and Australia). Often unaware of their land rights, over the years they have been dispossessed of much of their ancestral land by unscrupulous neighbours. Because bribery is common, government officials too often turn a blind eye to violence, and villagers live in fear and distrust of the police and other authorities. Since Independence a number of Acts have been passed to 'uplift' the tribals; but the existence of these laws – or any means of claiming their rights under them – is unknown to the great majority of the tribal people themselves. Few Adivasis, even if they were aware, could afford the expense or the interminable delays involved in trying to pursue a claim through the courts. One example of the ploys by which unscrupulous large landlords circumvent the land reform laws is to register parts of their estates in the names not only of their cousins, but also their cows and dogs. FLAP is careful to investigate individual cases and only to take up genuine complaints; in its first twelve months of work, 80 land cases (involving over 2,000 acres, with land worth £60–£90 an acre) had been decided in favour of the Adivasis. This has had the effect of creating a new confidence in the judiciary and the rule of law, as well as to arouse concerted

Guatemala earthquake, 1976: Reggie Norton, the Oxfam Field Director, discussing with local leaders the priorities in the recovery programme. The town is Tekpan which was totally destroyed.

Xesuc, Guatemala: rebuilding the community centre after the earthquake.

In Cuzco, Peru: a typical Latin American shanty community. (See Chapter 4)

Amnesha community of Tsachopen, Pasco, Peru. Oxfam has funded the costs of a pottery and the potter's salary since 1977, to provide cash income for the community as well as to revive interest in this traditional craft.

Uganda 1980: children of a starving population. (*Mike Wells.*)

Somalia: *Above:* How water was obtained previously. *Below:* Oxfam-funded solar pumps working at La Dhure camp. (*Ben Whitaker.*)

antagonism – both legal and otherwise – from land-owners and money-lenders. But, as Michael Harris points out, 'Taking up even a few test cases can serve to deter those who would normally feel free to ignore the law with impunity.'

In 1979 Oxfam decided to support FLAP's programme for a further three years, and to fund a special loan scheme for training tribal lawyers. FLAP has already trained petition writers who help the largely illiterate people to present their cases. Few tribal people themselves have hitherto ever become lawyers, but one of them is now working with FLAP and encouraging others to train, since it is difficult for non-tribals to understand the tribal dialects and customs. Schumacher said, 'The best aid to give is intellectual aid, a gift of useful knowledge. The gift of material goods makes people dependent, but the gift of knowledge makes them free – provided it is the right kind of knowledge, of course – and also has far more lasting effects.' Teach a man not only to fish but to make his own fishing-tackle and you have helped him to become not just self-supporting, but also self-reliant and independent.

At a legal aid clinic and large irrigation scheme I visited, which is supported by Oxfam and run by Bhai Harivallabh Parikh in another tribal area south of Baroda in Gujerat, an Adivasi farmer smiled and said, 'Three years ago I was using a bow and arrow; today I use a spanner to mend the irrigation pump.' Not all projects are so successful. Guy Stringer recalls:

> In the guidelines which I send to any Field Director before I make a visit, I ask for the inclusion, if possible, of a programme which has gone wrong for some specific reason – to counterbalance the impression sometimes given by Oxfam literature that we have some magical key to human happiness. We should not attempt to hide these important experiences.
>
> For example, I'm thinking of one academic who was known to Oxfam as he worked in the Bengal disaster with a number of his students. On retirement four years ago, with his wife he founded 'The Society for the Advancement of Wisdom' – a marvellous Indian name and I only wish it had been applied more exactly to this particular affair. Encouraged by an enthusiastic government expert on chicken management, who based his arguments on 1972 figures, the Society persuaded 25 women, most of whom live in the rather grim village of Phansa in Gujerat, to take advantage of a government scheme requiring a member to commit herself to taking 150 birds and to build a chicken house to an established design. In return the Bank would loan 5,000 rupees, the government providing half as a grant, leaving 2,500 rupees to be repaid at 5 per cent over a number of years.

From the start everything went wrong. The chicken houses were delayed and so the chicks had to be handed over to another Co-operative to rear in the early stages and when they were returned there was some doubt whether the right birds came back as they were stunted in growth. The feeble birds, expected to come in lay by the 23rd week did not do so until the 27th, and meanwhile the price of chicken feed rocketed by 14 rupees a bag. Desperate for money, the Society appealed to us and in collaboration with Oxfam America we provided another 65,000 rupees [nearly £4,000] of which approximately half has been used. For a brief period, 85 per cent of the birds laid, but then instead of the production sticking at 90 per cent for 3 to 4 months, it declined and by June it was so uneconomic, together with a price decrease in eggs that the desperate little Committee of these women took the terrible decision (can you visualise the agony of the meeting) to sell all the birds without delay.

So the members are left with a huge empty chicken house, better built than their own cottages and a debt of 2,500 rupees to the Bank (approximately 2 years' earnings – translate that into your own salary!) and the poor organisers, so full of good intentions, are surprised and hurt that the members will not come to a meeting to discuss the matter, that the husbands have taken over the office and barricaded it, that the local political heavies are in on the act, and that the collector has conducted an enquiry into the matter. Anyhow, we persuaded them to see it as a responsibility and agreed that if necessary we would meet the whole or part of the women's loan as there is just about enough residual Oxfam money to do that, but that must be decided by the Co-operative who may or may not come to the meeting.

What kind of help does India want?

Since the official development aid of Western governments, including Britain, has lately become increasingly commercial (involving the supply of further steel-mills whose necessity many Indian and other experts question), the need for support for small, human-scale projects has increased. Oxfam has, for example, helped 'eye-camps' where the excruciatingly painful eye disease trachoma is treated and cataracts removed by a simple operation costing £10 a head (*thus transforming a person's life at the price of one restaurant meal in a rich country*). One 18-year-old wife who had been married for six years and been abandoned by her husband when she had become blind, was reunited with him after a successful operation during a two-day stay in the eye-camp.

A good development worker will feel a continuing need for contact with poor people, to renew his knowledge of the reality of what it is he is talking about. There is a temptation for all aid people coming from richer countries to slip into feeling godlike; Oxfam people remain humbler than most.

One individual person's case can be more meaningful and eloquent than the numbing effect of sheaves of statistics. Zabin Mehzabin, a Delhi girl aged 11, has been deaf and dumb since birth. Her father Mohabbat Ali, a vendor, supports a family of six on his income of Rs300 (about £18) a month; although Zabin is skilful and keen at dressmaking, the family is too poor to afford a sewing machine. In November 1981 her mother suffered a paralysis attack and was taken to hospital; the month before, her younger sister died of burns in a further tragic accident. Zabin is being given a sewing machine by Lok Kalyan Samiti ('People's Welfare Society', a local body running clinics and health projects in villages) which Oxfam supports in Delhi.

An Oxfam worker visited another project tackling similar problems in Calcutta. He reported: 'This is an incredible experience – Rehabilitation India occupies a tiny corner shop behind which are a handful of minute rooms just like a rabbit warren. Under the direction of the crippled manager, Mr Dhar, the rooms are packed with handicapped people – blind, deaf-and-dumb, and crippled – who, jammed together, make school chalks, joss sticks, pyjamas for hospitals and, with astonishing dexterity, hand-made envelopes. It's all hugger-mugger and cosy and rather too hot, and everybody shrieking and laughing. I can only hope that moving into the fine new special building being assisted by Oxfam will not destroy this very human, loving enterprise.' (A subsequent visit, after the move, made him think that some part of the original fervour and togetherness had indeed been lost.)

At the other end of the country, Oxfam also helps Sunderlal Bahaguna, a follower of Gandhi who started the vital 'Chipko' ('Embrace') popular movement to protect the remaining trees in the Himalayas – where 75 per cent of the forest has disappeared, with the result that Nepal alone is every year losing 240 million cubic metres of soil down the Ganges into the Bay of Bengal. Sunderlal teaches the local people a caring relationship with their natural resources, so that they plant and protect trees with the same close understanding that Swiss and Scandinavian mountain people show to their forests. Sunderlal denies there is any conflict between ecology and economics, urging that 'ecology is permanent economy'. Harford Thomas similarly argues, 'Social and economic development which raises standards of living and produces better educated citizens can reduce pressures on the environment in the Third World; there can hardly be a greater threat to wildlife than starving peasants . . . Development in its widest sense, with the opening up of social as well as economic opportunities, is the path to lower birth rates and sustainable use of environmental resources.'

Successful projects in India are frequently built round charismatic pathfinders such as Sunderlal or Bhai Harivallabh Parikh, who is the son of a family of Chief Ministers but has spent 30 years helping the Adivasis; or, occasionally, expatriates such as Mother Teresa or Dudley Gardiner, whom Stringer describes visiting in Calcutta in January 1981 not long before his death:

> We turned off the Lower Circular Road at 8 in the evening and walked up a narrow ill-lit muddy lane. At the end there was a large yard and at the top of it a green door. We banged on the door and behind it there arose a cacophony of barking as if the hounds of the Baskervilles were upon us. Eventually the door was opened, seven dogs were pushed out of the way by a man with a stick and we found ourselves in a huge kitchen. At the far end a corner was curtained off and walking through we came upon a huge fat man lying on a truckle bed. There were no possessions except a radio and a pile of empty cigar boxes . . . This was Major Dudley Gardiner. He was born in India, the son of a Quartermaster-Sergeant in the Royal Fusiliers, and joining up as a Boy Soldier at the age of 12 he was educated in the Army School – a grim experience. All his life was spent in the same Regiment as his father and he eventually rose to be a Major Quartermaster. Twenty-three years ago he came to Calcutta, after retirement from the Army and he started feeding 50 people using his own money. Since then he continued this private struggle against hunger, and distributed food with his own hand to 6,300 people every day of the week. During the day long lines of families came with their ration cards to the YMCA Centre where he lived and each evening he travelled in a battered Land Rover, given him long years ago by Leslie Kirkley and Jim Howard, to distribute food directly to families in the poorest parts of the city. In the whole period of the 23 years he only failed his people for one fortnight. He tried to train some young men to follow him, but it was a failure.

The next month, Stringer wrote from Nagpur: 'Personally I am disappointed that we have not moved more authority for grants and management into India as this I certainly understood was our general plan. In the 1980s in this huge land, now the tenth biggest industrial producer on earth, it seems astonishing to me that we should continue to direct so much of the programme

from a concrete building over a laundry in the Banbury Road . . .
If Oxfam is really a partnership of people then our present policy
seems to me to deny that, and in the long term strategically it
must be mistaken, as I am pretty confident that this great country
will not continue to allow expatriate voluntary Agencies to work
in the way that they currently do.'

There were some difficult hurdles to overcome in tackling this
problem. One was that with Oxfam rightly paying its Indian staff
at the same not over-generous rates it paid its British employees,
some of them were receiving higher salaries than government
ministers in India. A proposal to move more authority for grants
and management to India was rejected by Oxfam's Trustees. But
some progress has recently been made to Indianise Oxfam's
work in India. Half the senior field staff are now Indians. And
funding has been provided for Search, an organisation with its
headquarters at Bangalore in southern India, whose object is to
recruit and train Indian development workers, and which was
founded as a result of John Staley's increasing conviction when
working as a Field Director for Oxfam that progress in social
welfare must eventually come from within a country and not be
imposed from outside.

In some parts of India, it is not easy to find good projects to
support. It is easier in Kerala (the only Indian state with a
minimal increase in population, due to the status of women
there and an enlightened policy of family planning education),
Gujerat, and West Bengal. It is hardest in Bihar and in Uttar
Pradesh – which are precisely the states where nongovernmental
programmes are most needed. But some areas – as in communist
societies and in parts of Africa – have no tradition of voluntary
social organisation (as distinct from Hindu or Muslim concepts
of personal alms).

Oxfam has always preferred not to initiate projects itself, both
because it is reluctant to shoulder their administration, and – as
Staley argued – because it is better to help local initiatives.
(Other Oxfam employees see a danger that the people they are
trying to help might become dependent on local organisations,
instead of spreading and sharing their ideas and benefits. They
argue that Oxfam should therefore link more with poor people
directly, rather than with local organisations.) But anything
known to be foreign-funded is suspect to many Indians.

Consequently in 1981–82 the Oxfam (India) Trust pioneered a new idea: seminars and training programmes about fundraising for small humanitarian Indian organisations, which had traditionally drawn support from Oxfam but which Oxfam wanted to develop secure base-roots in their own society. Stringer suggested to the first seminar's audience some points of advice which might benefit other charities as well:

1. Your society should be an effective and efficient medium between donor and the beneficiary. Play your part in that – it is a partnership both ways;
2. When you accept a donor's money, you automatically inherit a further obligation to him or her, in ensuring the proper use of that money and keeping the donor informed;
3. Commitment first, technique second;
4. Always check every suitable occasion and communication that you have provided 'The opportunity to give';
5. Tell the truth: if things go wrong, say so;
6. Be open to review: there may come a time when it would pay you to have a full time salaried professional fund raiser;
7. The press have need of you and you of them – study their needs and set out to make a friend of them;
8. Editorial is better than paid advertising;
9. Businessmen are people and are like sheep – find the shepherd;
10. Plan interviews and presentations with great care – and keep them short;
11. Look after the donor – he or she are priceless assets – make them your friends.
12. When you write a letter – let it be a letter from you and don't use the words written by government officers.

Finlay Craig, a senior organiser for Oxfam in Scotland, added these suggestions:

1. What can go wrong – will go wrong. So plan to cover every eventuality;
2. Prepare a clear fundraising plan and budget – it's not chance;

3. All fundraising events should further the cause – in the long run the policy of the educated rupee will always pay;
4. Consider *all* new ideas; but assess their potential carefully;
5. Where there's people, there's money – cash in on other people's activities;
6. Large numbers of small regular donations have special value: start a Pledged Gifts scheme today;
7. An 'open door' policy: welcome people and what they have to offer;
8. The volunteer and the organisation should be clear about and agree their roles and mutual responsibilities;
9. Allocate time and training to helpers – they are your most important asset;
10. Learn from mistakes – yours and other people's;
11. The midget clown may succeed better than the governor: avoid stereotypes – try to be novel;
12. There's no better expression than 'Thank you' – you cannot say it enough.

How do Indians view Oxfam?

Vikas's judgment is that, 'In the last 15 years, Oxfam has become much more approachable and decentralised while it has grown bigger – it can respond faster than other agencies. One of its greatest virtues is that is has no ironcast policy; instead it believes in individuality and flexibility.'

But at the same time he asked pointedly: 'How many Asians are there on the Asia Committee in Oxford?' A colleague of his added: 'The knowledge most retired diplomats, ex-Indian Service and academics have of India is so often 10 or even 20 years out of date. The effect of having so many tiers of vetting in Oxford means that often only the safest projects go forward.' Vikas would also like to see more inter-regional exchange of ideas: 'It's quite possible that lessons learnt about irrigation or community development in, say, Indonesia could be of value in Sri Lanka. But it's still more likely that an Indian development worker will visit London than anywhere else in Asia – unless he's a UN employee, when his salary-scale cuts him off from the problems of ordinary people. Even most intermediate technology concepts are still far too often Western concepts.'

Other Indians working for British private aid agencies said they were embarrassed – and to some extent compromised in their work – by simplistic advertising in the United Kingdom about pathetic, starving Indians (one particular advertisement featuring rats has been sent to Mrs Gandhi by Indian MPs in protest): 'These agencies are promoting an image of India that is simply not acceptable.' The implications of this issue are discussed in Chapter 10; but if Indian resentment and sensitivity against what they perceive as paternalism gathers strength, it is possible that the Indian government will require specific prior permission to be obtained for each project by an outside agency (although that constraint would be no worse than that under which Oxfam operates in, for example, Vietnam). The Indian central government, however, could scarcely in logic object to projects aiming at the implementation of its own anti-discrimination, pay and land laws.

One policy change which might benefit the situation, as well as being worthwhile in its own right, *would be if development help were made a two-way flow*. Indian people could participate in some Oxfam-funded projects in Britain: for example helping co-operatives, craft industries or community development (the subcontinent's experience in trying to defuse community tensions could be of benefit to urban areas in the United Kingdom which suffer from communal divisions).

The scale of both the needs and the problems of India (Pakistan by comparison is often unfairly neglected) can at times be daunting. But the perspective is set in clearer context when one remembers that India has a population roughly twice that of the whole of Europe, informed by (unlike many other developing countries) a lively press which is continually reporting the country's problems. Lately there have been hopeful indications. India's agriculture has been steadily improving for 30 years. Whereas during the last 50 years of the British Raj, food production increased by only 0.3 per cent a year, since 1950 it has risen by 3 per cent annually: as a result, India has recently scarcely needed to import any grain, even when the monsoon failed badly as in 1979–80. In 1981 India's industrial growth rose by 8 per cent – double the rate of the previous year. There is renewed support for family planning (stimulated by the shock of the most recent census's revelation that the country's population is 50 million people higher than the assumed and planned-for 630 million). Not enough is heard about India's success stories: the growing co-operative movement, its technological achievements. And British people in particular should show a little humility in face of the fact that, whereas there are 120 out of 542 members of the Indian parliament who belong to the scheduled castes and tribes, there is not a single black or Asian member of the British House of Commons. Brian Walker doubts whether India will continue to be one of Oxfam's priority countries for very much longer. Meanwhile, an Indian development worker in Calcutta advised: 'Oxfam's best course is to give help to women, bonded labourers, the scheduled castes, tribals, the rural poor. A good pioneering project causes ripples elsewhere, and so has a doubled value . . . *Perfection however can be the enemy of the good: we must never use that as an excuse for not continuing to try.'*

PART III

'A Peculiarly British Body'

When planning for a year – sow corn; when planning for a decade –
plant trees; when planning for a lifetime – train and educate men.
Kuan Tzu (Chinese philosopher, 3rd century B.C.)

You are not making a gift of your possessions to the poor person.
You are handing over to him what is his. For what has been given in
common for the use of all, you have arrogated to yourself. The world
is given to all, and not only to the rich.
St Ambrose (c. 390 A.D.)

It will soon be dark – get on with some decisions.
(Contemporary Tamil saying)

We know incomparably more than any human beings before us
about what is going on in other cities, in other countries. Particularly
the immediate prospect of human suffering. We see people starving
before they have died: we know that they are going to die . . . it is
going to need great sacrifices. Including one of the most difficult
sacrifices of all, the sacrifice of our rigidities . . . Despair is a sin. Or,
if you talk in secular terms as I do, it prevents one taking such action
as one might, however small it is.
C. P. Snow

The international community acts more readily to alleviate human
suffering when it is already caused than to eliminate the causes
leading to it . . . Now, more than ever, it is essential that Non-
Governmental Organisations should strive to place the issues
squarely in the arena at every level of contemporary society.
Sadruddin Aga Khan,
Gilbert Murray Memorial Lecture, 1983

9

'Faith, Hope, but not Charity': Human and Financial Accounts

Whosoever has a surplus has stolen it from his brother.
St Francis of Assisi

I am of the opinion that my life belongs to the whole community, and as long as I live, it is my privilege to do for it whatever I can
George Bernard Shaw

We are all generally agreed that we should take care of our family . . . the real question is where does our family end?
Wendy Harpe

The continuation of Oxfam's work cannot rely on the chance of emotional donations being triggered by caprices such as the media's haphazard treatment of dramatic disasters. It depends on the – often unnoticed – labour of thousands of volunteer women and men, on clear-headed financial planning, and on Sisyphean fundraising. Just as Oxfam's 133 overseas staff receive the advice and backing of experts who give their time unpaid, so volunteers form more than 97 per cent of the total number of Oxfam workers at home: 3,000 collectors, 20,000 women and men who work unpaid in the shops, the people of the 650 Oxfam groups which maintain links with the 300,000 donors (including 43,000 covenant donors, and 12,000 who give reguarly by banker's order).

In the financial year ending 30 April 1982, Oxfam had an income of £16,214,000 (compared to £15,800,000 the previous year). It was raised by:

Cash donations (including banker's orders,
  covenants, and legacies) raised through
  press advertising, mail appeals, and
  special events: £6,658,962

125

Gift-shops' sales, net after costs such as
rent and rates: 5,552,839
Trading profits of Oxfam Activities Ltd.,
covenanted to Oxfam: 1,023,103
Blankets and clothing for shipment overseas: 56,171
Contributions from the UK Government and EEC: 1,752,919
Contributions from other Agencies: 880,520
Investment income and deposit interest: 276,189
Surplus on disposal of fixed assets and
miscellaneous income: 12,848

It was spent in the following way:

Allocated to *overseas programmes:*	£11,327,005	(69.9%)
Fundraising costs:	2,659,903	(16.4%)
Capital *reserve* fund for development of shops, etc:	750,000	(4.6%)
Kept to be available for future grants:	114,530	(0.7%)
Educational work:	711,999	(4.4%)
Administrative costs:	530,114	(3.3%)
Irrecoverable *VAT:*	120,000	(0.7%)

Unlike some other charities – both large and small – who decline to tell the public or the Charities Aid Foundation how much they spend on overheads, Oxfam is willing to open its books and disclose its figures, including salaries. It also publishes each year an itemised list of all the grants it makes. Indeed at the start of 1981 it spent £5,000 of its £250,000 advertising budget on large display advertisements to inform readers of *The Economist* and *Sunday Times* just how it raised and disposed of its annual balance. The text stated plainly – to pre-empt one of the main excuses with which people rationalise their failure to contribute – how much out of every £1 Oxfam spends on administration and on fundraising. This corporate advertisement was a special initiative by Oxfam, planned to impress a selected readership that Oxfam is a businesslike concern, and also – according to Sam Clarke, its Appeals manager – as a marketing strategy to try to enlist companies to support Oxfam. British commercial and industrial undertakings give far less to charities than their

Geographical breakdown of aid

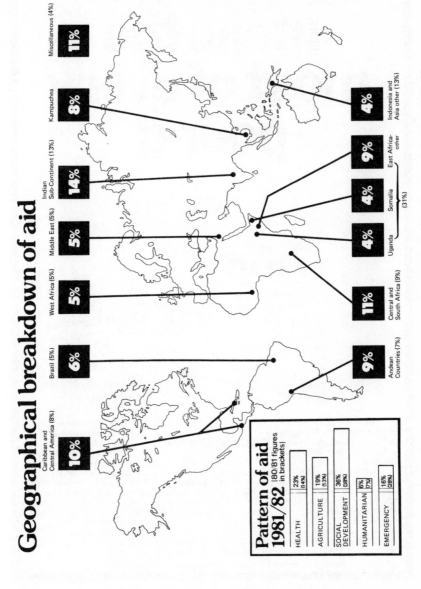

Caribbean and Central America (8%) — 10%

Brazil (5%) — 6%

West Africa (5%) — 5%

Middle East (5%) — 5%

Indian Sub-Continent (13%) — 14%

Kampuchea — 8%

Miscellaneous (4%) — 11%

Indonesia and Asia other (13%) — 4%

East Africa-other — 9%

Somalia (31%) — 4%

Uganda — 4%

Central and South Africa (9%) — 11%

Andean Countries (7%) — 9%

Pattern of aid 1981/82 (80/81 figures in brackets)

	1981/82	(80/81)
HEALTH	23%	(14%)
AGRICULTURE	19%	(13%)
SOCIAL DEVELOPMENT	36%	(38%)
HUMANITARIAN	6%	(7%)
EMERGENCY	16%	(28%)

Oxfam's analysis of where its aid goes, published in its *Review of the Year 1981–82.*

How Oxfam make the most of every pound

76½p Overseas Aid and Education

15p Fundraising

5p Capital Expenditure

3½p Administration

The most important consideration when advising on a legacy to charity is how effectively the money is to be used.

Oxfam can promise — and you can promise your clients that every pound given to them will be put to the best possible use.

Oxfam gets to the root causes of poverty, and teaches people to help themselves, so the help is perma-

Total Income 1980–1 £15·7m

nent and gets passed on from generation to generation.

More people entrust Oxfam with their help than almost any other charity - our income in 1980-1 was £15·7m.

Every project is visited personally, by highly trained Oxfam staff on the spot who

see that the money goes direct to the purpose for which it is intended.

If you would like further information about how Oxfam put their funds to the best possible use and their helpful leaflets on how to make a will; please contact Patrick Wise on Oxford (0865) 56777.

Oxfam, Room WC01. 274 Banbury Road, Oxford, OX2 7BR.

In addition Oxfam handled a further £7 million for the Kampuchea programme.

'How Oxfam make the most of every pound'
A special advertisement on the effective use of the charity's money designed for papers such as *The Economist* and *The Sunday Times*.

equivalents in other countries do. In 1980 Oxfam received only £112,000 from companies out of a total of £4.8 million donations, and in the first eight months of 1981 a mere £15,000.

Oxfam may have outpaced other charities since the rocket-like trajectory of Shelter's rise in its heyday, but in real terms its income in the face of inflation has – aside from the special appeal for Cambodia – remained more constant. Meanwhile its number of paid staff has had to double to administer grants for the ever expanding number of projects it helps in more countries abroad. To generate regularly the level of income required is like 'running on a treadmill weighted with collecting boxes'. Clarke, a 34-year-old former IBM systems engineer, has had most success in developing Oxfam's computerised list of regular donors. Research has shown that people who had given in the past are the ones most likely to give again: Clarke's strategy is to try to coax them 'up to the next stage of giving'. People who send a donation are liable to receive personal chatty letters from a worker or volunteer. Mail shots go out three times a year in addition to Christmas, in what has been described as one of the most effective and sophisticated of such operations anywhere in Europe. A donor's file can within three seconds be traced and selected for a particular mailing from a permutation of over 150 attributes (so that, for example, those people who contributed for a flood previously can be pinpointed and asked to donate again when another flood disaster occurs).

The 1982 Christmas mailing, focused on the subject of hunger, produced £500,617 – a 1 per cent increase on the previous year – from 31,200 respondents out of a circulated total of 288,000. In March 1981, a special letter was sent to a bought list of academics. All are signed 'A. Guy Stringer – Deputy Director'. One recipient replied 'Who is this guy Stringer who keeps on asking for cash? Is he in a specially bad way?' (Another hopeful reply from abroad enquired, unsuccessfully, if Oxfam gave out video recorders.) All the appeal letters are written as personally as possible, citing practical examples of what a specific sum could pay for. ('*2p buys the vaccine to immunise a child in Haiti against polio. £1.10 a day is the cost of feeding ten children in a small orphanage in Orissa. £110 pays for one month's salary for a nutrition expert working with women's groups in the Dominican Republic.*') And on the back of every letter sent out from Oxfam is printed a blank Bankers Order form.

It is disagreeable, embarrassing to have to raise funds. It is even less comfortable to have to starve. It is in fact a luxury to be able just to try to raise funds. 'Oxfam pioneered', Harold Sumption says, 'the application of direct response promotion as a means of fundraising. Press ads and direct mail had a dual function: to evoke a modicum of understanding of the needs of developing countries and refugees, and to produce contributions as a consequence (what Oxfam calls "the educated pound"). And then to develop that understanding once support was won. It thus began to change the voluntary organisation scene from the patronising lady bountifuls of the 'twenties and 'thirties to the active involvement of our time. It became a movement, as well as a charity: uniquely in the 1960s Oxfam managed to combine support from the "lavender and old lace" ladies of Cheltenham to the radicals of Third World First and student groups. Oxfam also pioneered charity trading through shops and, by importing Third World (Bridge) products, made a significant part of its trading directly relevant to its work.'

Not all respondents are positive:

I sincerely hope you will fail in your objectives. It has become so apparent that money and other assistance keeps worthless dictators in luxury and power . . . How right the public are to adopt an attitude of apathy towards the schemes which allege to give aid to developing countries.

This lady received a polite personal reply:

You mention that it has become apparent to you that money and aid does not reach those people in need – to which I can only reply that we take great care to make sure that ours does. Oxfam is now almost forty years old. In that time we have made mistakes, but we have learnt from them and now have a very experienced team of Field Staff who constantly check what happens to money we spend. I will send you some of our latest bulletins, which list how some of the money entrusted to us is spent. I hope you do not feel that it is going into the pockets of 'worthless dictators'. I'm sorry that you hope we will fail. As you say, the answer rests with the public. Whatever happens, we appreciate your interest.

Another 1981 correspondent was more sympathetic but asked how she could answer people who criticise that goods do not reach the people for whom they are intended. Patrick Wise at Banbury Road patiently replies again:

Many people, myself included until I came to work here, have this view of Oxfam shipping out vast quantities of goods to poor parts of the world – and they all have a 'horror' story of it falling into the hands of local black-markets. Maybe this did happen a few times long ago, but we try not to make the same mistake twice. Nowadays we have very experienced field staff who make sure that anything we send gets through. I could go on, but you asked me to be brief, so suffice it to say the following. Much of what we supply is expertise and experience. That can't be stolen. Our salaries are the minimum. For instance, much overtime is done but none is paid.

The next letter received was from a man in prison who wrote:

I wish I could help the work you do to relieve the suffering of the poorer people in the world. Unfortunately I only receive £2 per week here and what with the price of sugar, milk, etc., I may not be in a position to forward monthly payments to help your work, as I have no money whatsoever outside of these four walls. I am not due for Release till March 1985. I believe by that time I will be too old to be of any practical use to anyone. I wish you God's Blessing.

The reply went back:

Thank you for your interesting letter. We quite understand that your situation does prevent you from actively helping us in many ways. However, there are ways that you can help us. The main one that comes to mind is what might be called 'spreading the word'. I will enclose with this note some literature about our work. When you read it you can speak to others about it – try and get them interested. I know that might be difficult, but someone might listen. Do you have any kind of notice-board where you could pin up an Oxfam leaflet? Are there any groups or classes in your prison who might be interested in learning more about Oxfam and its work? We have plenty of leaflets for them (see enclosed list). Is there a workshop in prison where items could be produced for sale in Oxfam shops? . . .

Other people sent in the money they'd saved up for their holiday. Two collections of £150 and £310 for Cambodia were given by Arab refugees in a camp near Amman with a letter: 'We are sorry it is a small amount, but it still remains a donation, from Palestinian refugees who know very well what it means to be a refugee and hungry.'

Cathy, aged 8, sent £10 with a note:

Dear Oxfam, I and my friend got a tub of water out of the pond and we were going to put a frog in it but when we looked close we could see lots of little animals so we got slugs, snails, and all sorts and we made a zoo and people had to pay to look, they could pay as much as they wanted and that was how we got some money for Oxfam. Love.

Two old age pensioners sent £3, having gone without meat to save this. Recently, the first donation was received from a person in the Soviet Union (£5). Another man wrote anonymously:

> Please accept £100 from a Remorseful Sinner who has just won the Pools. I hit my girl friend, who is more beautiful than Lady Diana, and told her she was not good enough for me now that I'm rich. Then I met my old Sunday School teacher on a bus. I confessed to him what I had done, and showed him this 100 quid which I was going to pay a prostitute in a sauna bath place I used to visit. He showed the photos of what was happening in Somalia to those poor starving people . . . I am back with my girl friend now.

Other fundraising work ranges from organising sponsored Marathons and – appropriately – sponsored slimming (£1 for each pound lost, though a 'Hungry for Peace' fasting campaign in 1981 had to be called off because of the Northern Ireland hunger strikes). Oxfam America, which does not have the network of shops there are in Britain, builds its main annual fundraising drive on fasting each autumn.

In the UK, personal visits are made to bank managers and solicitors up and down the country by 40 volunteers – retired professional men and women – who explain Oxfam would like to be remembered in covenants and in legacies. ('Can I give you the facts, Ted?' 'Is it true Oxfam's administrative costs are 50 per cent?' 'No, 3 per cent, here are the accounts.') The legacy team's overheads are very low, and its cost-effectiveness is estimated to be around £100 for each £1 spent. These legacies should ensure an increasingly strong financial base for Oxfam in the future.

Outlaying funds to raise more money has always been a difficult decision for charities to make – although any commercial concern is expected to risk capital for the sake of future profits. Oxfam's overall fundraising target is 1 to 5 (it used to be 10): £1 will not be expended unless at least £5 is reasonably expected to be raised as a result. Merely doubling a sum of money is not good enough, because critics will carp that 50 per cent has been spent fundraising. In fact, because Oxfam is able to finance more than the cost of all its administration and fundraising out of the profits from its shops, it could be said that it is able to use 100 per cent of all money donated for its overseas work.

Special leaflets exhort people to send Oxfam your holiday change, or to knit a blanket for Oxfam. The Stamp and Coin Unit at Bicester has been expanded successively to sort and sell post-cards, cigarette coupons, trading stamps, medals and badges. Volunteers spend days on end sticking trading stamps into books so that they can be redeemed, or fill their baths full of postage stamps soaking off envelopes. Recently Y. C. Patel, a supporter of Oxfam in Gujerat, sent 30,000 stamps. The Unit now produces over £100,000 a year. A special newspaper has been produced by Sue Greig to be sent to trade unionists. The *Crack-a-Joke* book, compiled by Richard Stanley – formerly Oxfam's press officer – of groan-inducing favourites ('Why was the cricket team given cigarette lighters?' 'Because they lost all their matches.') was the fastest-selling title in Puffin's history, and brought the royalties on over half a million copies to Oxfam.

Some charities' fundraising schemes can degenerate into highly uncharitable competitiveness or a desperate search for a fresh gimmick. But in the past, one of Oxfam's most reliable sources has been the 'pledged gift' scheme, which has steadily raised nearly £3.5 million for Oxfam since it began in 1959. Three thousand collectors, all volunteers, collect £150,000 a year from their neighbours in small regular amounts – often only 10p to 50p a month. Each collector receives a copy of the monthly newspaper *Oxfam News*. But the total raised in this way has not kept pace with inflation, and it is increasingly difficult to find new collectors: at present Oxfam is losing twice as many as it gains each month. The growth in income instead has come from the shops – which some saw as an idea of the past – and from Oxfam Activities' trading: Oxfam is now Britain's biggest importer of developing countries' handicrafts. Stringer is also determined to treble Oxfam's £2.5 million income from covenants before he retires.

The organisation has always rejected dependence on investment income, and intentionally spends approximately the same amount of money as it raises each year. Until four years ago Oxfam kept virtually no cash reserves, and for the final quarter of each year often had to overdraw at the bank. Falls of sterling play havoc with the budget; in 1978 an urgent telex had to be sent ordering a cut of 15 per cent in all projects due to the unexpected deficit. The next year it was decided to plan a reserve of £1 million. Sir Geoffrey Wilson, Oxfam's Chairman, spelt out the reasons why this was necessary:

Firstly, such an increase would effectively reduce interest payments on potential borrowing during the month of low income. Secondly, if future income falls below budget allocations, increased reserves would allow the overseas programme to remain secure, thus permitting longer term commitments. Thirdly, the growth of the Trading Company really requires us to keep adequate reserves in order to provide working capital to finance increased stock holdings.

In August 1980, at the time of the East African refugee crisis, a man in the City of London – unsolicited, but moved by a television programme – rang Oxfam up and asked how he could best help. Stringer suggested that he gave £20,000 to launch a national press appeal for funds to support refugee relief, and guaranteed that this would produce an amount quadruple the outlay. In the result within a few weeks it raised £140,000. The 7:1 success of this investment encouraged Oxfam to try to coax further sums from business and industry.

British firms are notoriously only one-third as generous in giving to charity as United States ones, donating overall less than 0.3 per cent of their annual pre-tax profits. Venezuela since 1965 has had 500 companies pledged to give a 'Voluntary Dividend for the Community' of between 2 and 5 per cent of their annual net earnings. Oxfam America was recently given $2 million by Burroughs from assets it had which were blocked in Zimbabwe; the United Kingdom Oxfam has never been so fortunate, although one British paper-maker gave £10,000 blocked in Ghana, and Jardine Matheson £10,000 for use in India. Another well-known purveyor of tinned food used to send a great number of tins of potatoes in mayonnaise (a somewhat specialised taste, and heavy to freight): Oxfam prefers not to be offered gifts in kind, except for its shops, because of the difficulties they may cause.

'Straightforward appeals remain uncontroversial,' comments Diane Fisher in *Marketing*, 'but the more a charity campaigns, the greater its image problem, especially in the eyes of big business.' Some Oxfam campaigns in the 1970s stated that the goods marketed by certain household-name companies were the products of sweated labour and in fact were part of the cause of grinding poverty in their countries of origin.

Many staff at Banbury Road support the idea that Oxfam should take more such moral stands: 'If income fell by half a million pounds as a result, that wouldn't be the be all or end all.'

'What's it got to do with us?'

This was the successful disaster advertisement raising £7 for every £1 of cost: the total costs of £20,000 were borne by an imaginative and committed businessman.

Others, faced by the unfulfilled needs abroad, advocate that primacy should be given to the growth of Oxfam's work. A third group suggested scrutinising each potential donor company on its merits: arms profits, for example, would be particularly unacceptable to Oxfam's high number of Quaker or pacifist supporters and staff. Debates ensued about whether the makers of baby-foods, drugs, lipstick, alcohol, furs, whalemeat and pet food could pass through the eye of the needle. . . Rothmans once offered Oxfam £5,000 for a promotion campaign without strings: to the chagrin of those who had set the deal up, this was refused – on the double grounds of both being profits from tobacco and being South African owned. Henley Forecasting gave free computer help in planning Oxfam's shops, but when this unit was bought by RTZ, the help was declined despite the six months' setback that resulted. But Patons wool, however, ran a successful joint scheme so that Oxfam profited from each of their patterns that was knitted. One Oxfam man ruefully commented: 'We make moral conditions, but in fact it often boils down to whether we would get good publicity or bad out of it.'

Concentration was sharpened by the discovery towards the end of 1981 that Oxfam was running £1 million below its hoped-for budget. Due to the national economic recession (with people perhaps wearing their potential gifts of secondhand clothing themselves for a year or two longer), income was increasing barely ahead of inflation, instead of by the previous 25 per cent annual rise. No dramatic disaster appeal was possible. (The great success of Cambodia, even though it owed much to *Blue Peter*, was especially impressive considering that many of the recipients were 'commies' and in a far-away country of which little was known – unlike, say, Italy's earthquake victims.) Oxfam does not believe in using professional fundraising firms, but prefers to draw on its own skills and ideas. Geoffrey Busby (a former Proctor and Gamble marketing man) set out to call on company directors, inviting them to sponsor either Oxfam projects abroad or to advertise home or fundraising events. It was hoped that the Brandt Report's and Edward Heath's advocacy of the co-interest between our industry and the Third World's economic health would help persuade some boardrooms. Unfortunately this hope has not been fulfilled to date.

The Volunteer Army

Perhaps the two most frequently quoted saws amongst those who work for Oxfam are *'Oxfam is people'* and *'The volunteers are our hidden strength'*.

For different causes and in various ways, more than 5 million people in Britain give up several hours a week to help others voluntarily: collectively their work amounts to double that of all the social service professionals combined. Oxfam is a voluntary society: its policies are ultimately decided by volunteer Trustees; and it is voluntary committees, not the staff, who allocate the money. The 'volunteers' room' at the headquarters in Banbury Road is continually manned for administrative tasks. Working in permanent posts in several parts of the organisation are volunteer men and women: in charge of Trust appeals, running the administration of the legacy programme, or providing the administrative backup for industrial appeals. Guy Stringer says,

> There seem to me certain things that a volunteer should expect of Oxfam – firstly that they are readily accepted, not as second-class citizens but as full participants in Oxfam's affairs and that their particular skills should be efficiently used as best may be. That training should be provided to improve their performance; and finally, that they should be fully informed of the aspirations, achievements and disappointments of Oxfam.

In the other direction, any charity has the right to expect from its volunteers loyalty, commitment, and certain minimum standards. Nobody is welcome who thinks that because their work is unpaid, it does not matter if they do turn up or if they let their colleagues down in a crisis. In 1980 Oxfam appointed its first Volunteer Co-ordinator to help find the right jobs to fit the abilities on offer, and training schools are now run for them at Oxford. Volunteers of every type are attracted to Oxfam: religious people and humanists; women and men of all politics and of none; socialists who have worked abroad with the poor, and readers of the *Daily Telegraph* who 'want to improve the lives of the blacks out there so they don't want to come over here'.

'Oxfam is a peculiarly British body, with all the liberal virtues and vices,' a woman who works for it reflected. 'We may over-estimate our supporters' traditionalism: they're changing all the time as they are affected by the feedback from our work abroad . . . What's our psychology: why do we do this work?

Partly probably the guilt of a former colonial superpower. A bit of the missionary. Partly perhaps to learn more ourselves, partly to teach at the same time.'

Many others commented on the effect that working for Oxfam has on people, whatever the type of job. 'People work for Oxfam because they like to feel they're wanted,' said Stephanie Ross. This is reiterated in a film that has been made for Oxfam by Geoffrey Petts, a senior member of Oxfam's regional team. The most satisfied emotionally appear to be those who work as 'people to people' – just as many MPs and local councillors in their jobs get the most satisfaction from the amateur casework that they do. A few of the people who volunteer for charities have so many personal problems of their own, or can be so authoritarian or patronising, that the difficulties they generate outweigh any contribution they make. The motivation of charity helpers can range from a real sense of generosity and genuine compassion to – or co-existent with – an itch to exert power over others, or a desire to impose values and attitudes in which the volunteer believes. (But if a donor gives only out of a desire for status or to avoid being thought selfish and stingy, does that in fact matter to the fishermen who may receive a net as the result?)

Over and over again people speak of the meaning and fulfil-ment, as well as interest, working for Oxfam gives them. Ms Ida Ganswick, who said that she enjoys the work of a volunteer very much and hopes to go on working for Oxfam for many more years, is 92 years old. Ms Hilda Hewitt of Birmingham says, 'We have a happy working relationship and we enjoy our work, which we do well. But I'd ask you to stress – besides the humour and the pathos we see – that Oxfam shops, in addition to sending money to help the poorer developing countries (please don't call it the "Third World" – we all live in one world), help the poor and needy of this country, of which there are many in a large industrial city. However,' she warns, 'Oxfam is not popular with the general public.'

Oxfam has 20 Area Offices in Britain, besides ones in Belfast and Dublin. (Ireland, North and South, are two of the most generously donating areas of all.) These are at Edinburgh, Glasgow, Newcastle-on-Tyne, Colne, Shipley, Chester, Worcester, Cardiff, Bristol, Exeter, Southampton, Guildford, Maidstone, Brighton, Reading, Nottingham, St. Albans, Maldon, Sheffield and London.

There are also District Offices at Dundee, Aberdeen, Darlington, Whitehaven, Manchester, Blackburn, York, Leamington, Northampton, Cambridge, Norwich, Lincoln and London.

Gordon Macmillan is one Area Organiser, looking after 31 shops, 8 full-time staff and a thousand regular volunteers in the south Midlands. (When he began his work Leslie Kirkley asked him 'Could you please take on the south of Britain?', and he kept the collecting-tins under his bed at home.) He prefers this job to being 'a cog in the hierarchy at headquarters – you're more responsible here to those you work with' – though he was also very interested to visit Zaire, Jordan and the Yemen to see some of the people and problems he talks about. Some of his helpers come because 'husbands, who won't let their wives go out and take a job, allow them to work unpaid in an Oxfam shop. Another woman, who's 86 years old, has the mental and physical output of a 26-year old – it's all a question of attitude.' Macmillan sees young people today as increasingly generous and international in their views. Oxfam's Cambodia campaign 'brought the whole community together. It was the best thing that happened for our village's life since the war – for its own benefit, quite apart from helping others. The vicar, the doctor and the chairman of the parish council were all up the church tower together, fasting!'

Other regional helpers describe how their house-to-house collections for objects to sell in the shops raise on average about three pounds' worth a call, whereas visits collecting money 'average 20p a house if you're lucky.' 'The secret of street flag collecting depends on having enough collectors to saturate an area, and then something like a band or a barrel-organ to help put people in a good mood. The happier they are, the more generous they'll be.' Raymond Mine, an Oxfam supporter in Swindon for the past seven years, wants to have more than the present one flag day: 'I am going to try and right the law which tells us we're only allowed to collect once a year.' W. M. Hobson in Sheffield unsuccessfully tried to get local industrial workers to agree to 5p being deducted from their wages each week ('When I put this to some local companies, they said that with deductions already being made for sports, superannuation, unions, etc, in this age of computers it would be far too difficult to introduce something else!') Instead he put collecting tins in eight wine-shops and hairdressers. ('These are very slowly filled – in fact, actually to *fill* a tin would take several years – however I collect the tin when it seems to be getting heavy enough to be holding a pound or two, and it must all help.')

In 1982 Stephanie Ross, Bill Yates, Bernie McDermott and Sally Coles organised a Village Fair in Battersea Park in conjunction with *Sunday* magazine, to which 75,000 people came. A *Blue Peter* programme produced £148,000 from stamps and coins sent in by children for water programmes in Indonesia. Rosemary Schlee of north London has raised £1,000 by organising Bread and Cheese lunches at £1.50 a head. A group at Southampton collected over £3,000 from a Fashion Show when 13 amateurs modelled 500 garments for auction. A quite different appeal with considerable potential was pioneered by 11-year-old Guy Walker and his friends at Edenhurst School, Newcastle, who raised £433 for East African refugees by a Sponsored Silence.

Transnational Shop-keepers

Oxfam's chain of 620 shops is now one of the ten biggest in Britain – a greater number than Marks & Spencer. Their success in this field is increasingly being copied by other charities, such as the Spastics Society, Help the Aged, and MIND. The replicated competition convinced several others, such as the R.S.P.C.A. and the National Society for Mentally Handicapped Children, to stay out of the shop market. Oxfam, after hesitating because of the recession ('People may be buying more secondhand, but inflow of good stock to sell is essential, and folk are wearing out their clothes more'), took the decision in 1981 to open 150 more shops in areas not previously tapped.

Some shops make only a little net profit, but have other values. They act not just as a window for Oxfam's work and as a reminder to High Street shoppers of overseas needs, but also as a channel for people to express their wish to give, in the same way as Titmuss described the phenomenon of blood-donors. It is not the most affluent areas or streets that are the ones which raise the most funds. 'I have long held the view,' Brian Walker says, 'that historically the contribution which Oxfam makes to keeping alive the charitable spirit here at home, is at least as important as the work we do in our projects overseas. A nation with the fires of compassion, of caring and considerate people – that is a nation fit to live in, and one in which it is a joy to bring up one's family. . . We should not think of an Oxfam shop simply as a means of raising money. Many Oxfam shops are able to develop a web of social therapy, which is integral to Oxfam's presence in a particular community. The friendships which are sparked off within a team of shop volunteers and their own regular customers, especially when those customers are elderly or infirm, the special bits of social engineering which some of our groups develop when they support good causes within their own community and which in no way conflict with their primary responsibility for raising money, all add an extra dimension to our work. One shop, for example, has agreed with the local mental hospital that patients there may visit the shop from time to time to receive the warmth and sympathy which would not be possible in an ordinary commercial shop. There are all kinds of examples like that – of social therapy on top of, or beyond the task of selling donated gifts to raise money. I believe that the money we raise in this kind of environment is enhanced, improved, enriched in a way that cannot be shown on the profit and loss account. In a word, a neighbourhood should be richer and fuller *because* of the presence of an Oxfam shop.'

Mrs Cole of Glamorgan describes a typical day in an Oxfam shop:

Second-hand clothes shops are nothing new to this market town of Pontypridd in the Rhondda valley, still bearing the scars of the '30s depression. So, although clothes are a main source of our income, we do a brisk trade with some of our Oxfam Trading handicrafts. Bead curtains, hanging-baskets and plant pot-holders are all in demand from some of the new married couples on the housing estates in and around Pontypridd. Our regulars greet us like long lost friends, and I often feel we should serve them a cuppa, as all have made long bus journeys to do their weekly shopping. One old chap, spruce and as bright as a button, has walked 3 miles from the top of the Rhondda valley and will walk back. He never buys anything, but always puts a coin in our box. Then in comes an old lady asking for any oddments of wool to knit some baby clothes for sale in the shop. She also dresses any dolls that we give her. Some of the dolls are very dilapidated when they are handed in at the shop, but she returns them washed, brushed and always exquisitely dressed. Now comes our star turn of the day. Two young men from the local fancy dress shop, on the look-out for bracelets, bangles, scarves, and hats. In fact, anything that they might turn into fancy costumes. They amuse themselves and us by trying on some waistcoats and bowlers. We expect them to break out into a song and dance routine. Today we do a brisk trade in winter coats, all at a very low price, being the end of the season. Some of the larger ladies require some assistance, mostly reassurance, on fit and suitability. Lunch is brief, mostly coffee and a sandwich, as we see the carrier van parked outside the shop. They collect weekly, bags of unsaleable clothing, which goes to the Oxfam Wastesaver Centre to be sorted, then repulped and sold. We struggle with the usual 20 or 30 bags, bringing them from the storeroom above the shop. During the week, helpers have sorted and packed these bags, also marked for size and priced the many garments that are on sale in the shop, so our main job in the shop is serving. My assistant then empties the payphone. Besides being a source of income for Oxfam, it also provides us with potential customers, even if they only put a coin in the box. Towards the end of the day, she also banks the day's takings.

We sell a good many books in the afternoon, mostly to students from the local Poly. Since one student told me she bought a J. B. Priestley First Edition for 10p some weeks ago, and it is now worth £25, I cast a quick glance for any possible finds, noting leather bindings, rare or specialist subjects. Pontypridd being a chapel-going community, bibles and hymn books are in constant demand. Dictionaries too are always a good sell. I answer the phone to a lady asking if we can collect a house clearance. I refer her to the Salvation Army, but say we will be glad of the clothes and any bric-a-brac if she can bring it into the shop. Children come in now from school, with stamps and coins in response to the Blue Peter Appeal for clean water in Java. Then comes a teacher with a donation from her class of small children – £5 in small change. I write out the donation receipt which she will show to her class tomorrow. We hastily tidy the shop in readiness for a busy day tomorrow, market day; I put the closed sign on the door, confident that my day's work has not been in vain.

Most helpers give a couple of hours once or twice a week, but others devote whole days. Several shop helpers are anxious that no war-toys should be sold in their Oxfam shops, as part of its disarmament campaign. Life is rarely the same two days running in a shop. One morning a distressed man appeared at the door of the Dublin shop, and with some difficulty explained he had dropped his teeth down the grating of the shop the night before. Reunited with them, the owner, restored to his usual eloquence, gave Oxfam £5 and a grateful smile. On another day the Dublin shop's helpers were working feverishly behind closed doors to finish some sorting for Christmas, when a man knocked. Thinking him a nuisance, the door was opened with a degree of reluctance. 'I just want to give you some money,' he said, handing over £400.

A new shop opened at Crieff in Scotland raised £24,441 in its first year. One of the latest shops, in St. John's Wood High Street, is one of the few open on Sundays; sometimes Rolls Royces are double-parked outside it. From cast-off Dior and Cardin clothes in St. John's Wood to the end result of a new waterpipe in Bangladesh is a long way.

Oxfam provides an opportunity for its long-term workers at their own expense to visit a developing country to see for themselves some of the results of their labour. Brian Walker himself worked for a week in the Newbury shop, and was disappointed to find 'that an Oxfam shop offers little real opportunity for Third World education. I never once saw a customer looking at the posters or educational material displayed in the shops. Customers were there, naturally, to buy and, if possible, to secure a bargain.' Helpers at Henley, however, wish to make a plea to those who give goods:

> *Kindly Reader, ere you drop*
> *Your bundles at the Oxfam Shop,*
> *Spare a thought for those within*
> *Who soldier on, through thick and thin*
> *To sort and price, or put in sacks*
> *Items not welcome on our racks –*
> *The worn out shoes, the heel-less socks,*
> *The suitcases with broken locks,*
> *Electric blankets we mayn't sell –*
> *That goes for children's shoes as well –*
> *The magazines of massive weight*
> *With information out of date,*
> *The toys with vital pieces gone –*
> *The sorry list goes on and on.*
> *We beg you, sort the gifts you bring*
> *And, if in doubt, just ditch the thing!*
> *We like to have, upon our shelves,*
> *Goods which you'd want to buy yourselves.*

A few rival retailers grudge the competitive advantage that half rate relief and unpaid staff provide. Birmingham City Council successfully challenged in the courts the right of charity shops to rate relief, until a lobby led by Oxfam persuaded the government to rectify the situation in 1976 with the Rating (Charity Shops) Act, which permitted the 50 per cent rate concession for shops 'used wholly or mainly for the sale of goods donated to a charity where the proceeds of the sale . . . are applied for the purposes of the charity.' To qualify, this means a 50 per cent limit on new goods. Oxfam has recently taken the lead in the more professional development of charity shops, and besides employing a specialist property management team of four, can call on the voluntary help of 150 chartered surveyors.

In the year 1980–81 Oxfam's shops generated a net profit of £5.5 million on sales of approximately £10.5 million. 'Recently,' Brian Walker said, 'quite a number of other charities have been trying to emulate the success of our shops operation. Of course, there is plenty of room for other charity shops, but our loyalty is to Oxfam, and that is why we have to keep abreast of developments in charitable shop-keeping. We originated the idea, have more shops than anyone else, and should continue to be the leader. Anything we can do to improve the quality of our shop work, to keep abreast of modern retailing skills and opportunities, is bound to be an advantage in the long run. I cannot accept the suggestion which some people make that there is a contradiction between high professional standards and a compassionate, caring organisation. My point is that just as in medicine, nursing, teaching or the church, we assume that a caring approach is consistent with high professional standards – so it should be in Oxfam.'

A major programme has been under way since 1978 to put more capital into developing the shops: 'trading up' many of them from being transient venues for junk and jumble to becoming permanent Main Street gift-shops. A plan to open a prestige shop with high-grade overseas handicrafts in the West End of London, however, has had to be dropped – one hopes only temporarily.

Trading Schemes

Charities are by law not allowed to trade, so in 1965 Oxfam Activities was set up as a company which covenants all its profits (£1,023,103 in 1981/2) back to Oxfam. Its prime purpose is to create job opportunities in the developing world by marketing their products. It has a volunteer chairman who comes from Marks & Spencer, an overseas director from Unilever, and a managing director – John Pirie – recruited from Pringle. To try to stimulate shop sales during the 1981 recession, for the first time

Oxfam fieldworker Pat Diskett weighs a Somali refugee. (See Chapter 7) (*Andy Hosie*.)

India, June 1973: Oxfam's then Director Leslie Kirkley (now Sir Leslie) talks to Indian farmers at a village near Wadala mission, a centre of Oxfam-supported child feeding and agricultural extension work.

India: Oxfam lent the money to set up this fishing co-operative south of Calcutta which can now purchase a boat and net as well as support education and health in its community. (See Chapter 8)

India: Oxfam's Director-General, Brian Walker (left), in conversation with Mother Teresa and David de Pury, then Oxfam's Field Director for eastern India.

New Delhi, India: *Above:* Rajasthani migrant labourers working on a building site. These women earn around Rs 6.75 (45p) per day mixing and carrying cement. Behind are half-finished new apartments of a housing scheme at Mandangit, contrasting with huts thrown together from waste bricks in which families exist around the site. (*Mike Wells.*) *Below:* Elementary lessons in a half-finished apartment: a creche for the migrant labourers' children. Delhi Mobile Creches use any rooms contractors will lend them, to bring health care, meals, and education to New Delhi's poorest immigrants. (*Mike Wells.*)

Bangladesh, 1975: *Above* – in a ruthless operation to clean up Dacca, the government began to clear people from the bustee slums, and to move families – many of whom were refugees from famine – to camps outside foreign visitors' view. *Below* – an Oxfam-funded sanitation unit being assembled. (See Chapter 2)

an advertisement on television was tried, in the Southern region: John Le Mesurier, Judy Geeson, Rosemary Leach and Martin Jarvis gave their services free, but the effect did not justify further outlay. A more successful innovation has been Oxfam parties in peoples' homes, at which hostesses have boosted sales from the mail-order catalogue by nearly £10,000.

A survey of the shops in northwest England, by Catherine Conway of the Manchester Business Administration School in 1980, found that a number of the volunteers were happy for their shops to serve the needs of local poor and elderly people rather than to raise more money for overseas, and were worried lest adopting a more professional marketing approach might destroy the friendly chatty atmosphere. The majority of shop helpers are older women, although the *Blue Peter* campaign recently brought in more younger people. Of the shop volunteers Conway interviewed, 77 per cent were over 50 years old, and only 2 per cent were male; 41 per cent of them did other forms of voluntary work as well, including two-fifths of the shop leaders. Only 8 per cent had never worked in paid employment; 40 per cent had previous experience of retailing. Almost a quarter had worked for Oxfam for more than ten years, and 95 per cent had worked for more than one year.

Similar tension is occasionally perceptible in a few shops against replacing too much of the secondhand clothes' space by goods which have been imported from developing countries. The Oxfam trading company markets these under its 'Bridge' scheme, and also a 'Good Neighbour' programme selling the products of handicapped and other groups in Britain, through its mail-order catalogue at Christmas, as well as in the shops. Oxfam's trading sales have expanded from £2.1 million in the year ending April 1979 to £3.7 million for that ending April 1982. Terry Simpson reorganised its 38,000 square-foot warehouse at Bicester on ergonometric lines (with advice from Freemans, the mail order giant) so that it resembles a supermarket, and has a computer for stock control. The idea of Bridge was started in 1964 by Roy Scott when Oxfam workers, visiting the scenes of disasters abroad, were shown some goods people had made and wanted to sell to regain their self-respect, and suggested that these could be tried in Oxfam shops. Now it is supplying retail chain stores and Habitat as well. A design expert employed by Bridge travels abroad for 20 months in every two years, advising craftsmen and women in India, the Philippines and elsewhere – some of them working on the pavement – about marketing, tools, packaging, accountancy, costing and shipping. Recently Africafe, an excellent strong instant coffee from co-operatives near Lake Victoria in Tanzania, and also tea from co-operatives in India, have been marketed in Britain.

John Pirie, Oxfam Activities' managing director, describes the company as a 'self-financing aid programme', and being as important and useful as much of the direct aid that Oxfam provides. Bridge gives a 'Producer Dividend' of 25 per cent of annual profits to the makers of its products in the form of grants for projects which benefit their local community; 70 per cent is used as an 'Expansion Dividend', and 5 per cent is used for educational work. This makes some of Oxfam's prices higher than those of cut-throat commercial competitors; as also does Oxfam's insistence on only buying from suppliers whose wages, rates, and safety-at-work conditions it has investigated and approved, whereas other traders buy from any bucket-shop of exploitation. Another problem is that many overseas craftsmen prefer to make each of their products different: the Indian makers of the beautiful durries do not feel they are artists if they standardise – whereas most home buyers who order from a catalogue wish to be sure of a consistent design.

It requires exceedingly careful judgment for Oxfam's Julian Francis in India to forecast the likely Christmas demand in Britain many months in advance. A frighteningly irrational amount may hinge on the fleeting whim of fashion, the way an item is lit in the catalogue photograph – or if the model being photographed happens to smile that day. When one excellent article was captioned as having been made in a leprosy rehabilitation project, its sales fell like a stone. A swing in fashion's whirligig can spell tragedy for a small producer who has become dependent on the Oxfam bulk order. Stocks which have piled up because of a change of taste – or possibly a sudden groundswell of political mood against the policies of a country's leaders – can hardly be returned to the makers, who could face starvation if that happened. In most cases orders have to be up to 50 per cent prepaid to enable the supplier to be able to buy his raw materials. And exporters from India, until recently, needed to complete

45 different forms for the Indian authorities (some requiring over 20 copies of each, which are too many for carbon paper and necessitate cyclostyling). A governmental committee deliberated for thirty months and then reduced the number of documents required to 36 – still beyond most small craft co-operatives unaided: besides being a millstone for India itself which needs foreign exchange earnings.

Oxfam's experience with Bridge is being offered to help other charities such as Action Aid. Its Good Neighbour project is of increasing benefit to Britain as the recession widens (though there were occasional hiccups in supply here too, as when almost all the members of the Bristol black workshop making oven-gloves were locked up after a riot). At Yateley in Hampshire, sixty disabled people work at hand-block printing fabric by a method learned in India, and can now offer 4,000 designs. In Camphill Villages mentally handicapped people produce goods ranging from glassware to toys and candles. The Burnbake Trust project gives craft training to ex-prisoners.

The Bicester warehouse gives work to several local disabled people as well as to licensed inmates from Grendon Underwood. It also maintains Oxfam's emergencies and disasters stores: many more secondhand blankets are recently being donated as families switch to duvets. When news of the Algerian earthquake was received by telephone one midnight, 5,000 blankets were loaded aboard aircraft in less than 12 hours. Ironically, on 21 September 1982 the Bicester warehouse itself was struck by a freak whirlwind – on the eve of the busiest Christmas order period. The insurers agreed to repair the considerable damage immediately, and (with the help of rapid work by Bovis) the orders were able to be dispatched in time.

Waste Saving

Another project of Oxfam's which offers a practical benefit at the same time as producing funds is the Wastesaver Centre at Colne Road, Huddersfield. This recycles clothing, textiles and aluminium sent by Oxfam shops, who are paid by the Centre for their consignments. They – and other charities' shops as well – sort and forward to the Centre clothing and waste textiles which are not saleable: this enables them to dispose of damaged or threadbare items, and to avoid being over-cluttered with slow-moving stock. Seventy tonnes of material sent to the Centre are sorted and graded each week. White wool, for example, can be dyed; other wool, cotton or synthetic fibres are converted into underfelt or roofing felt. Disabled people help at the Centre, and recycled raw material is sold as far afield as Poland and Nepal. About six tonnes of aluminium are collected by supporters throughout the country each month in the form of bottle tops, foil containers or ring pulls: 20 tonnes of baled ingots of aluminium can be recycled for the same amount of energy required to make one ton of new metal from bauxite.

British householders throw away more than 19 million tonnes every year. Approximately half of this mountain of material consists of glass, metals, rags, paper and other recyclable items – only about 4 per cent of which is rescued by local authority recycling schemes. The obvious wastefulness of our throwaway society is a striking contrast to the struggles of poor people in many countries who lack even minimum of basic material needs; the Wastesaver idea was conceived as a practical symbol to reduce the unnecessary and conspicuous consumption of finite resources in a world of want. When Oxfam began the project at its first Wastesaver Centre at Albion Mill (in a Victorian spinning mill in Milford Street) during 1975, its aim was to pioneer a comprehensive waste collection and recycling business, testing the feasibility of recycling a number of items, in order to make a modest income for overseas work. It was set up with support from local and central government and commercial interests. At first it handled glass, plastics, tin, paper, aluminium and rags for sale to industry; and clothing, books, furniture, electrical goods and bric-a-brac which were sorted, cleaned and repaired for sale in a shop housed in part of the mill. Initially a house-to-house collection was operated serving 5,000 households in Huddersfield who sorted their waste into special sacks fixed on a stand. The local market provided paper and cardboard, and local youth groups and others made special collections.

Unfortunately, the economics of such a large and varied enterprise soon proved unsatisfactory. Original working estimates drawn up before the massive oil price rises at the end of 1973 became meaningless. Transport costs rose sharply; in the economy at large, demand was slack. A glut of waste paper cut off that market for some time. Ironically, Wastesaver experienced the same problems of fixed or rising costs with fluctuating prices and uneven demand which confront Third World producers of raw materials: the price of aluminium in 1982 dropped to £180 a ton from £460 three years previously. By 1977 the decision had to be taken to stop house-to-house collection, and to cut out the uneconomic items. Further streamlining followed, with a move to smaller but more suitable premises in March 1979. But by concentrating on just two items – textiles and aluminium – John Fitch-Peyton has been able to expand the textile sorting into further categories to obtain the best possible prices, and has recently begun to collect shoes as well. Jon Vogler, who originally pioneered the project, is now researching for Oxfam waste reclamation possibilities in the developing countries, so as to help them economise their resources at the same times as creating additional jobs. (A fuller account is given in *Muck and Brass*, published by Oxfam's Public Affairs Unit.)

Working for Oxfam

In 1979 a Working Party on Fundraising under the volunteer Jack Wood proposed that Oxfam should recruit Honorary Executives, as 'a new style of volunteer: the man or woman with professional, business or trade union background or the graduate/ex-professional woman who no longer has home ties . . . either recently retired or working people who might be prepared to give some hours per week.'

The personal commitment of Oxfam's paid staff is evidenced by the fact that many of them are highly able people who could be earning substantially more were they not working for charity. (Brian Walker, who himself took a 60 per cent cut in salary when he moved to Oxfam, however, says that this commitment, although it 'gives us our strength', can also be a source of weakness: 'To apply lateral thinking to something which is sacred and holy is a dangerous exercise.' 'Most of the staff believe they have a private hot-line to eternal verities,' said another employee.) At the beginning of 1981 Oxfam discovered that more than 20 of its full-time employees were earning below the National Assistance level; pay had fallen so far behind inflation that a 30 per cent increase was independently judged to be justified. When Michael

Harris several years ago first went to Malawi, he was asked what was the minimum he and his family could exist on: he answered '£1,200 a year', and was given £1,000.

Oxfam still pays a lower scale-rate than some other comparable charities, though they are reluctant to publicise these figures since 'with so many volunteers in the organisation anything looks like too much.' Ken Duncan, who unsuccessfully tried for a year to unionise the staff with ASTMS, urged that employees should be paid a proper salary, but that those who wished to do so, could give or covenant part of it back to Oxfam. He argued that the pay-scale was the reason why so few able 30- to 45-year-olds were able to remain with Oxfam, which consequently became overweighted with either young or retired workers. Approximately one-fifth of the staff still leave every year (compared with a third six years ago), despite the fact that Walker and Stringer backed the principle of realistic – if not generous – pay. The scales now range from £3,125 to a maximum of £16,500 a year, and a significant amount is covenanted back to Oxfam by some staff from their salaries. Employees overseas are paid under half of what the World Bank or UN Agencies' employees receive (almost every voluntary agency worker has a fund of scornful stories about the latter's life in Intercontinental Hotels). A number of European aid agencies pay their employees on the scale of civil servants' rates.

It is a false economy (if not downright expensive in the long term) to try to staff any concern too much on the cheap: the real cost to a charity of incompetent or inert employees can be far greater than the money saved. Some of Oxfam's staff work a 24-hour day – most recently to help with the installation of its new computer. Oxfam's headquarters had become so overcrowded by the growth of its activities that in the spring of 1983 a new extension of 11,600 square feet had to be opened, financed by a special appeal so that no money for overseas work would be diverted.

It is usually agreed that salaries should take account of job satisfaction: but should this be measured subjectively or objectively? More than almost any other organisation, Oxfam is a body of determined individualists. Charles Skinner and David de Pury who were both diplomats previously, say they have few regrets at their change of career. 'For many of us, the development of ourselves – our "conscientisation" – has been even more marked and noticeable than any effect on our clients,' said another colleague. 'It's the best job one could possibly have,' said Stringer who, it is universally thought, could – like Walker and some others – have made a fortune if he had been ambitious for himself. 'Where else could one do such worthwhile work while having so much responsibility and freedom?' The overseas staff almost invariably become the most radical, both as a result of their experiences, and because such postings tend to attract people with the strongest commitment. A few such as Reggie Norton have been transformed by finding a new vocation in working for Oxfam.

Oxfam's finances unfortunately are not immune to the effects of the recent recession. The income of £5.5 million from shops in 1982 was the same as the previous year's. Traditional types of fundraising held up well (Christian Aid's income, collected by similar methods, was a record £8.9 million in the year ending in March 1981).

A certain amount can be saved from the deferment and re-phasing of financing; all new staff appointments were frozen for a period; painful cuts had to be made in educational work and shop budgets. In March 1982 Oxfam launched a special appeal for the 500,000 victims of the prolonged civil war in El Salvador – where at least 19 Salvadorians working on Oxfam-supported projects were known to have been killed by the government-controlled paramilitary forces in the previous 18 months. But this failed to capture the interest of the British public in the way that Cambodia or the East Africa refugees had, and the Falklands crisis soon put a further veil over most people's view of Latin America. The continuing disaster in Uganda suffered from another type of indifference: by being so prolonged, it came to be regarded as insoluble, whereas impulsively compassionate people like to feel that their contributions achieve tangible results.

The overall average rate of charitable giving in the United States is just over an annual £45 per capita, compared with about £14 in Canada and less than £7 in Britain. There are now over 137,000 different charities in Britain, with a total overall income of some £3 billion a year. A survey by *Which?* magazine showed that the most popular ones with the public are those for medical research, children, handicapped people, famine relief and animals. Any rumour, for example, about a particular charity's overheads, is liable to be seized upon as an excuse by those who don't want to give.

In the USA, by contrast to Britain, contributions to charity of up to half one's annual income may be deducted from a person's gross income before it is taxed. Between 1970 and 1980, donations to charities from all British companies declined by 64 per cent in real terms: falling, as a proportion of pre-tax profits, from 0.70 per cent to a mere 0.23 per cent. Even after death the British seem more tightfisted, giving about 30 per cent less in bequests than Americans do. Although their response to emergency appeals such as Aberfan and Penlee – as well as Cambodia – is often emotional and warm, British people seem less generous than many other countries in responding to the less dramatic but continuing needs of charities in the longer term.

The financial rise of even successful charities such as Oxfam over recent years is, in real terms, continually being eroded by inflation. But is growth so important? Some employees worry lest they become ever more donor-oriented than recipient-oriented. Walker, in his first speech in 1974 as Director, said: 'I give you a new Oxfam slogan: not "Bigger and Better" but "Smaller and Better".' And Russell Richards, its regional organiser in Cumbria, points out: 'Experience shows that you do not need vast sums of money to run successful projects. The World Bank and various UN agencies prove this.' Ken Bennett, the previous Overseas Director, believes:

> Achievements in growth of income and fundraising, particularly in more recent years, are little short of spectacular. I have had, however, for many years – and have expressed these views in Committees – a niggling doubt whether it is a valid assumption for an organisation like Oxfam that whatever amounts can be raised can also be responsibly spent. A variant on this: do you go all out for maximising and constantly increasing income and then decide how you are going to spend it? Or do you first assess the scale of needs *in terms of Oxfam's philosophy and priorities*, and then set about raising the money? It is possible, I think, that with increasing income, philosophy and priorities are adjusted to encompass the increase. I am well aware of the argument that the needs of the Third World are so vast that there can be no limit to what Oxfam can properly and usefully spend. But I would have some hesitation in accepting that argument 'ad. inf.'.

These different arguments regarding which direction Oxfam should take in the future are discussed below in Chapter 12.

10

'Only Connect . . .'

The biggest disease today is not leprosy, or tuberculosis, but rather
the feeling of being unwanted, uncared for, and deserted by everybody. The greatest evil is the lack of love and charity, the terrible
indifference towards one's neighbour who lives at the roadside
assaulted by exploitation, corruption, poverty and disease.

Mother Teresa

But what if I should discover that the very enemy himself is within
me, that I myself am the enemy who must be loved – what then?

C. G. Jung

As we became more affluent, we became less politically and socially
conscious: ironically, now that we could afford to contribute
regularly to Oxfam, we did not do so.

Giles Gordon, 'About a Marriage'

British charities – of every kind – spend £4.3 million annually on
advertising for funds. (If this seems a large amount, by comparison the United Kingdom's outlay on slimming foods is more
than £200 million a year, together with a further £3.3 million on
advertising aids to slimming.)

'Children and animals remain the most emotive ads and get
the biggest response,' comments Oxfam's former professional
advertising agent, Dan Colman, who sent a copywriter and a
design artist to live in Bangladesh for a month to get a better
sense of what Oxfam does. (All charities' administrators would
do well to spend days every year sharing the life of their clients,
to help them remember what it is all about.)

But many members of the liberal middle classes have recently
become less concerned – except when stirred by a new dramatic
disaster – with the continuing problem of distended brown
bellies, in favour of their own economic preoccupations nearer
home. Overseas aid organisations' advertising today produces
about £5 for every £1 of cost in the case of disaster appeals,

but only a marginally profitable £1.40 for each £1 outlaid for advertisements about development and similar issues.

Oxfam's ads have often been pace-setters in their field. A recent letter to *The Guardian* – the charitable tribes' noticeboard, and still the best forum for charity advertisements – demanded: 'CND . . . must go professional and find more funds to attack public complacency and ignorance with the same gall that Oxfam uses on its street hoardings.' But as campaigns by other active overseas development agencies like War on Want and Christian Aid – as well as by home bodies like the Salvation Army – have followed suit, some people now fear the danger of satiation from the competitive bidding of leap-frogging shock/horror publicity or hard-hitting copy about poverty, ending with a heart-tugging appeal to 'Give until you are proud of yourself!'. Harold Sumption, who has influenced Oxfam's advertising for most of its life, says, 'it has had to aim at a constant balance between the primary need to raise money and, on the other hand, the need to explain Oxfam and "educate" the reader. Unfortunately, the hard figures show that the results in cash fall off the more in-formative one gets.'

In 1970 Oxfam drew up a charter for its Public Relations:

Oxfam is incidental to its raison d'être. The *cause* for which Oxfam exists has always to predominate over the organisation and its methods. Emphasise that Oxfam is a *means* to an end. A means used by a great number of people from all walks of life as a channel for their compassion. Play down fund-*raising*. Play up fund-*giving*. Highlight *the widespread voluntary element of Oxfam* which outnumbers many times over its paid staff. Use every opportunity to accen-tuate the *freedom* which Oxfam has always worked to retain for itself. It is unfettered. It is not bound by affiliation to any other organisation or to any particular section of the community whether at home or overseas. It is free from red tape and can act quickly and flexibly when the need arises. Show how Oxfam represents real *catholicity of support*, bringing together in a common purpose people of all ages, professions, politics and belief. Above all keep Oxfam singular. It is a mechanism, a movement, an all-embracing undertaking. Hopefully it will one day come to represent an attitude of mind. Oxfam *is*. Oxfam's purpose is positive. It is 'for' not 'against'. On those occasions when Oxfam has to deplore some action or inaction its statements should always conclude by spelling out *what it wants to see done*. What it is working *for*. To be 'anti' is to risk appearing to know only what one does *not* want. Oxfam's policies are purposeful. We seek to build, not demolish. And we get on and *do* something. Whatever we can. Oxfam *acts*. Oxfam is *a little impatient* for it is in touch with crying need. When there is so much we can *do now* we don't intend sitting around talking about it. Realism and a sense of urgency should permeate

'Your crash diet is a lot more than my ordinary diet.'

If you went on a slimming diet in this country, you would probably make a great effort to get your intake down to 1,600 calories a day. For a short period.

If you were an average Bangladeshi, you'd be lucky to get 1,300 calories a day. Over the whole year. And you would live in permanent danger of contracting a whole range of appalling wasting diseases. This poignant contrast is what the continuing food crisis is about. Not just an occasional disaster or famine. But a continual tragedy, in which one half of the world overeats, while the other starves.

Oxfam's aim is to help some of the other half of the human family to increase their food production for the future. You can contribute to constructive development on a regular basis by filling in the banker's order form below. Giving just 1% of your income (£2 a month if you earn £2,400 a year) wouldn't change your life at all. But it could save a life in a hungry corner of the world.

Feed all the family.

This form is simply an instruction to your bank to pay regularly whatever sum you choose to Oxfam's work. You can of course cancel it at any time by contacting your bank.

To: The Manager   Date _____ 19 ___

Bank Name _____

Bank Address _____

Please pay Oxfam £_____ every month/year* starting on _____

_____ (date) until further notice.

Name (Block letters please) _____

Address _____

_____

Signature _____

P.O. GIRO 2002000

*Delete where applicable

When completed this form should be sent not to your bank but to: Room XX, Oxfam, Freepost, OX2 7BR. (No stamp is needed.)

OXFAM

'Your Crash Diet is a lot more than my ordinary diet'
This was a very successful advertisement which also pioneered the idea of encouraging Banker's Orders rather that single individual donations direct from 'off the page'.

all that we do. There is so much talk about the world's needs. There are so many critics of what is being done: if Oxfam is sometimes constructively critical it is from the centre of the arena. Oxfam has been in there fighting since 1942. Its views derive such authority as they have from this first-hand experience. From doing.

Oxfam is a *pioneering role*. We are blazing a trail for the hungry and those caught in the vicious spiral of poverty. We are working for the oppressed, the helpless and the neglected. Campaigning for the basic rights of humanity. Hunger and poverty are *unjust*. Inevitably we are *prepared to take risks*, considered risks, in the hope of catalysing others. Accentuate Oxfam's *effectiveness as a catalyst* – a function which multiplies many times the value of Oxfam's aid. Traditionally the British people – our constituency – have a liking for pioneers and innovators. They also side naturally with the weak. We do well to take advantage of this heritage. We ignore it at our peril. There is arrogance and danger in every reference to the bigness of Oxfam. The 'big-heartedness' of Oxfam – yes. Goliath Oxfam – no! *Oxfam is David*. Oxfam must be seen to sustain a personal touch about all its affairs for we are wholly concerned with people. Nothing should appear to be too small to be considered or welcomed. We need to make the job Oxfam does more tangible. Show how it *applies* to people. Take every opportunity to *humanise* Oxfam, especially its figures and statistics.

Many Oxfam ads have been designed to shock people out of regarding Oxfam as a familiar piece of the British furniture:

'HER LIFE IS RUBBISH.'

'WOULD YOU LET YOUR DAUGHTER . . .?'

'HELP STAMP OUT OXFAM'

'THE LAST THING OXFAM WANTS TO DO IS FEED THE HUNGRY'

'OXFAM HATES STARVING CHILDREN' – are coupled with a coupon which the reader whose eye has been caught can send in to learn more.

'GIVE AND LET LIVE', and 'THE POOR CAN'T MAKE ENDS MEET, WHILE THE RICH MAKE ENDS OVERLAP' are captions designed to appeal to two major but differing emotions: the first, to make or reinforce the reader's feelings of being godlike – so that he or she is flattered into giving; the second one, to touch the reader's puritan guilt – so that he or she is shamed into giving. It is interesting that in a similar way the Christian Gospels offer both carrot and stick in their encouragement of charity: 'Let your Light so shine before men, that they may see your good works' (St. Matthew, v, 16) cf. 'For it is easier for a camel to go through a needle's eye, than for a rich man to enter into the Kingdom of God' (St. Luke, xviii, 25).

What are the motives of those who give? Harkhuf, an Egyptian living twenty-three centuries before Christ, took care to have his charitable donations recorded on his tomb with the inscription that he 'desired that it might be well with me in the great God's presence'. The idea of insuring a place in heaven – or purchasing a fire-escape from the alternative – is also echoed in other religions. The Khuddaka Patha, the scripture of Theravada Buddhism advises: 'By charity . . . man and woman alike can store up a well-hidden treasure.' The words for 'justice' in both Arabic and Hebrew came to be used for 'alms'. While the Koran emphasises what a kindness it is to relieve the rich of their burden – 'Of their good take alms, so that you may thereby purify and sanctify them' (ix, 103) – Mohammed added the timely warning that 'A man giving in alms one piece of silver in his lifetime is better for him than giving one hundred when about to die.'

Some psychologists such as Karl Abraham allege that altruism is sometimes the action of benefactors who do not find it easy to love people in their personal lives, and who prefer to give pity instead to impersonal recipients with whom they need not form a relationship. For Trobriand Islanders, possession automatically involves an obligation to give – whereas among the Goodenough Islanders, gifts are a ritualised expression of hostility, since the ability to dispense largesse is the ultimate proof of superiority. All in all, it is not perhaps surprising that Anna Freud concluded, 'It remains an open question whether there is such a thing as a genuinely altruistic reaction to one's fellow-men, in which the gratification of one's own instinct plays no part at all, even in some displaced and sublimated form.'

In almost all their advertising, the voluntary agencies (often competing with each other) are – implicitly or explicitly – implying that the reader has the opportunity to do something which will have a tangible and beneficial effect upon the poverty of developing countries. Cheerful advertisements are especially welcomed by readers today – but unfortunately they have been found to produce less money, at least in this particular field. Personalised accounts about families or individuals are almost always more eloquent than the numbing effect of statistics (of which there may be all too many in this book). As Gerald Priestland has said, 'The only way a relief and development worker or donor can make sense of what he is doing – and to my mind the only reason he ought to be working or giving is by *thinking* small, thinking not of the vast hopeless statistics that make up a national problem, and before which his resources seem futile, but of the known child saved from starvation, the named village that has got water because one particular town in Britain raised the money for a pump.'

Other agencies have also run highly successful ads: Christian Aid's *'Soak the poor'* campaign for providing water; *'Ignore the hungry and they'll go away'* on its poster showing rows of graves; and *'You won't be the only ones with tummy trouble this Christmas . . . Well, we know a few million people who wouldn't mind being sick on a full stomach. It'll make a nice change from being sick on an empty one'*; War on Want's *'The real disaster of the poor world isn't so much tidal waves and earthquakes. The real disaster is our refusal to help develop the countries of the poor world into nations strong enough to withstand tidal waves and earthquakes'*; or the Peace Advertising Campaign's *'The money required to provide adequate food, water, education, health and housing for everyone in the world has been estimated at $17 billion a year. It is a huge sum . . . about as much as the world spends on arms every two weeks.'*

The inhabitants of developing countries, understandably, do not enjoy being represented so often in a pathetic light in the Western media, frequently in strikingly emotive and memorable pictures. Sometimes this is the only attention their country ever receives. A recent well-intentioned article in *Newsweek* began, 'They have become the disturbing icons of Africa's agony: spindly black children, bellies distended, waiting for a dollop of aid-station gruel – "their mouths", said one heartsick United Nations relief worker, "open for food like baby sparrows" . . . desperate Karamojong tribesmen have reverted to cannibalism to survive.'

But unfortunately, advertisements of success stories in development generate few contributions from readers. 'Advertisements need to strike,' is the professional wisdom. And it is the public's complacent apathy about poverty overseas that seems so obviously the target problem to attack. Surely, the well-intentioned urge with moral – and often not unjustified – impatience, all we have to do is get the truth over that Britain spent £4,279 million self-destructively on tobacco, compared with only £794 million on overseas aid . . . that the USA puts more fertiliser on its cemeteries, golf-courses and gardens than the whole of India has to help provide sufficient food . . . that some mine-owners spend as much on a dinner as their miners, risking their lives, can earn in a year . . . that the average annual income in Bangladesh is less than a theatre ticket in New York . . . that in California, where supermarkets' racks of 'slimming foods' have failed, surgeons are increasingly being asked to staple or short-circuit people's intestines so that they can continue to overeat without their bodies showing their surplus calorie intake count.

But is it as simple as that? And problems can beset campaigns both at home and overseas. When Leslie Kirkley and a professional agency wanted Oxfam to mount an advertising campaign in 1972 about a 'battle' against leprosy and 'campaigns' for clean water, Oxfam's pacifist trustees vetoed this. And when Oxfam subsequently ran campaigning ads concerning chocolate and how little of its purchasers' price went to the growers, some of its most powerful supporters were resentful (major chocolate firms are great Quaker satrapies). Different criticisms have been aroused in some developing countries which have been specifically featured in some ads. In May 1981 an indignant Indian MP denounced in the Lok Sabha Oxfam's advertisement which featured a rat with the wording *'PEOPLE EAT WHAT HE LEAVES . . . They take the rat's food from the nest. Then they and their families eat it. Such is the desperate poverty in one village near Gazipur, India'*.

Jorgen Lissner in the *New Internationalist* described some agencies' pictures of starving children as being 'dangerously close to being pornographic', by degradingly exposing private suffering to public view without any proper respect for the person involved. The highly talented and committed news photographer Romano Cagnoni is loth to take medical and horror photographs of disasters; he will only take pictures which 'leave people with some kind of dignity. Whenever I am in this sort of situation I try not to isolate the person in the photograph.'

Critical representations have also been made, warning of the effect on race relations if only inadequate, pitiable, unsuccessful black or brown people are featured in advertisements, thus reinforcing richer white readers' already well-developed sense of superiority. The inhabitants of developing countries are constantly liable to be patronised (even though aid workers who return home are frequently struck by the contrast between the cheerful courage of the people they have been working with and the depressed cynicism of Europe and North America). Would it not be good, for a change, to have posters displayed in Calcutta about unhealthily overweight white babies?

Robin Richardson of the One World Trust suggests in *Progress and Poverty* (in the excellent 'World Studies' series of educational books published by Nelson in 1977) the following guidelines as desirable for advertising about overseas development:

1. *We can learn from the developing countries.*
2. *We haven't got all the answers.*
3. *There are reasons for poverty: it's not just bad luck.*
4. *Tackle the causes, not just the symptoms.*
5. *Economic and political changes are needed, not just charity and aid.*

Lissner emphasises, in his thought-provoking study *The Politics of Altruism* (creditably published in 1977 by the Lutheran World Federation in Geneva, despite his criticism of some of their work), that the information about the developing world which voluntary agencies supply is uniquely valuable, because of the scarcity of such facts available to the general public. The great majority of people depend for their ideas and images of developing countries either on a handful of journalists or on propagandists, because few people have any first-hand knowledge of overseas life outside the tourist tracks. Victor Zorza's brilliant weekly column in the *Guardian* is virtually the only journalism being written anywhere of life in the villages where the majority of the world's population live.

Especially because most advertising today is extremely skilful, a particularly heavy responsibility rests on those who plan it. It would be dangerous, for example, if ordinary people were made to write off the developing world as being hopeless, because of a reiterated emphasis – however altruistic – on its tragedies. Every fundraising appeal and communication cannot escape also playing an educational role. They also say much – sometimes more than is intended – about the author's own stance. Too many such approaches still have an air of '*De haut en bas*'; or they imply that, if the rich have any fault, it is only a sin of omission (in failing to give more) rather than any structural sin of commission (by taking too much.) Few emphasise the solution which Tolstoy advocated, for the rich man to get off the poor's back.

The defence of aid agencies' staff to these charges are:

1. That tough, complex and controversial truths are best explained in talks or at meetings rather than in widely distributed literature where readers are easily alienated and switch off.
2. That the issues are too complex to simplify; education is a specialised field, and not their job (but see the next chapter).
3. That if the agencies changed their presentation, they would antagonise a significant part of their constituency: what is the use of having morally clean but financially empty hands?

Many fundraisers maintain the overriding purpose of a voluntary agency is to maximise its income in order to be able to give the most help to the developing world; and that a budget for education should be seen only as a means to this end. They disagree with those development educationalists who see intensive constituency education not only as a moral necessity, *but as the best way in which a voluntary agency can in fact be of help to the developing world*. Most voluntary agencies today agree to a minority education programme, provided that this does not jeopardise the agency's income. Many of them, as a compromise, adopt a varied spectrum of 'soft' and 'hard' publicity – reflecting the often conflicting views of their effective employees – so as not overall to alienate any important constituency.

On a different level, sophisticated assaults upon the whole idea of official overseas aid have been mounted and developed by critics of such widely differing politics as the leftwing journalist Richard Gott and the rightwing academic Lord Bauer. Both argue that the only people capable of helping the Third World are the inhabitants themselves, and these are liable to be hindered rather than helped by outside economic intervention. The reasoning by which they arrive at these objections, however, diverges.

Gott distrusts official aid as being likely to tie recipient countries into the present unfair international financial system, dominated by multinational companies; Professor Bauer criticises it for 'encouraging the belief that betterment depends not on self-help, but on helping oneself to the trough.'

But since the main cause of Bauer's suspicion of official aid is the support it gives to governments whose own policies may be responsible for impoverishment, he concludes that 'the effective way to relieve poverty and distress in the Third World is through voluntary, non-politicised charities.' Additionally, he concedes that 'development can be helped best by a reduction of western trade barriers. Some aid funds might be used to compensate some of those who would be harmed by this reduction,' although he has also on other occasions argued that 'Ideally official aid should be terminated . . . The Third World was invented by the advocates of foreign aid.'

Dudley Seers – a former director of the Institute of Development Studies – recently called for a reduction in the amount of outside interference and advice given to developing countries by the North, since it is so frequently based on colonialist and paternalistic attitudes; Teresa Hayter in *Aid as Imperialism* (Penguin, 1971) goes further and declares that official 'aid can be regarded as a concession by the imperialist powers to enable them to continue their exploitation of the semi-colonial countries'. The late Frank McElhone MP replied to Seers, 'Academics have interpreted the world; the point is to change it.'

At their worst, bad official aid programmes can amount to a tax levied on the less well-off people in rich countries which goes to help the rich elites in poor countries. But, even when true, this applies only to bad international organisations and government-to-government programmes, not to voluntary agencies' small-scale projects which are funded from voluntary donations and are directed to help the poorest.

Bodies like Oxfam have come to recognise that the real experts in deciding the most appropriate aid are in fact the needy themselves. In project after project of Oxfam's, villagers have been assisted to put their own knowledge and expertise to use. The necessity for development help, most often, does not arise so much from a lack of resources – which can be a symptom of the real problem – *so much as from a lack of any share of power*. While power remains unfairly distributed and often monopolised by an elite, any inflow of official aid is in danger of merely further enriching the same already privileged minority.

Another field where aid, which has been insufficiently thought through, can do the reverse of good is in the policy of food aid.

'Feeding the starving millions' is the most emotive and popular idea of overseas help. Nowhere, at first sight, is the inequality of the present situation more grotesque: south of the Sahara more than 150 million people are hungry, while in the EEC, to keep prices from falling, mountains of unwanted subsidised food are piled up or intentionally destroyed. The idea of the rich sharing their food with the poor is biblical in its appeal. Over £1,000 million worth of food aid is distributed annually. But Tony Jackson in *Against the Grain* analysed the reality of the results, and warns that food aid can foster dependency, besides adversely affecting attempts to grow local crops, and often not reaching those most in need.

Oxfam learned the shortcomings of food aid charity in the wake of the 1976 Guatemalan earthquake. In its place the Oxfam team helped to set up a proper development programme based on self-reliance and self-help. By assisting the local farmers to improve their storage facilities so that they could market their surpluses within their own community, while at the same time improving the quality of the seed grain they used, co-operative enterprises were started. These provided practical help to several thousand marginal farmers – whose livelihood might have been threatened by exported surpluses of North American grain.

'Hunger,' Brian Walker pointed out, 'is a symptom not a cause. The cause is poverty. There is enough food in the world to feed not only the world's present – exploding – population, but at least four times that population.' *This is a harder message to convey in charities' advertising than the simple image of a starving child.*

Food aid, although only a short-term palliative, will obviously always be a necessity in emergencies. And although it is right to criticise its limitations, there is a danger that such criticisms may be used by the selfish and the xenophobic as excuses for doing nothing. Rich countries consume over half the available world supply of food grains; feeding grains to animals is a wasteful way of producing protein for human beings. 'The rich white man, with his overconsumption of meat, which wastes the grain that could have saved them, last year ate the children of the Sahel, Ethiopia and Bangladesh. And we continue to eat them this year with undiminished appetite,' the veteran French development expert René Dumont has said.

Others have pointed out that Britain's 12 million pets, together with the United States's 40 million dogs and 23 million cats, consume more protein than the equivalent numbers of the human poor. But in telling the public the facts of world hunger and malnutrition, it is important not to convey either simplistic half-truths (simply shifting the EEC's surpluses to the Sahel would solve nothing) – or to give the impression that the situation is hopeless. Elizabeth Stamp, Oxfam's Information Officer and an economist, pointed out in *Growing Out of Poverty* (OUP, 1977) that the most densely populated country in the world, Bangladesh, now has a population one and a half times that of Europe in the Middle Ages, but is able to live on a land area only 1/35th of Europe. The quality of the soil in Bangladesh is as good as in Japan, but rice yields are only one-third of those attained in Japan. Similarly corn yields in India, Brazil and Thailand are only about one-third of those of the United States. Hence the importance of learning the lessons of the Green Revolution (which dramatically increased crops by means of new highyielding dwarf varieties of rice, maize and wheat, and turned Mexico for example from being a wheat importer into being a net exporter).

But another result of the Green Revolution has been further to widen the gap between the richest and the neediest farmers. The new hybrid seeds require relatively high inputs of fertilisers; vulnerable to pests and diseases, they also need pesticides and fungicides; and adequate irrigation remains an overall necessity. Unless accompanied by land reform or agricultural credit, the increased yields only serve to make the wealthiest landowners – who can best afford irrigation, fertiliser and storage – wealthier, so that as a result they have often bought out their smaller neighbours. 'Highly skewed rural incomes contribute both to widespread hunger, especially among the landless and near-landless, and also to stagnating food production,' said Prof. C. P. Timmer of the Harvard Business School. 'Without question, basic poverty – the lack of adequate purchasing power among consumers and food producers – is the most important cause of hunger. Eliminating poverty is the only solution to basic hunger.'

A growing awareness of the more fundamental causes that underlie hunger has led several aid agencies recently to change the emphasis in their advertisements away from emotional appeals in favour of raising the issues of North-South imbalances, and the agricultural and social problems of developing countries. Marcus Thompson of Oxfam says, 'Advertising recently has become much more straightforward in saying we must be prepared to make sacrifices, not just give crumbs from our table.' The frontiers where such political campaigns meet the charity laws are examined in the next chapter.

11

'. . . That Good Men Do Nothing': Politics and Education

Every gun that is made, every warship launched, every rocket fired, signifies in a final sense a theft from those who hunger and are not fed, from those who are cold and not clothed.

Dwight Eisenhower

Hunger is not debatable.

Graffito on wall at Chalk Farm, London

According to a saying attributed to Edmund Burke, all that is necessary for the triumph of evil is that good men do nothing. But the laws governing charities cabin, crib, and confine what men can do against the evils of the world.

'Infraction would be a breach of trust making the trustees personally liable for the expenditure in question' – thus, the British Charity Commissioners commenting in their Annual Report on the discussions they had with War on Want, Oxfam and Christian Aid about the boundaries between charitable and political work. Explaining their continuing refusal to grant charitable status to the Amnesty International Trust, the Commissioners cited with approval the judges' ruling in the case of D'Aguiar *v.* Guyana that just because a trust for the promotion of kindness towards animals is charitable, that is no reason why any trust for the promotion of the kindness of man to man should be charitable too.

If the layman, with 'all due respect' to the judges and the Commission, finds it hard to understand why it should be any less charitable to act benevolently towards human beings than towards our other fellow animals, one explanation is that British charity law is today still governed by a statute dating from 1601. Instead of the legal view of charity developing in step with the requirements of today, it is determined by dead hands from the grave; as Sir Arthur Hobhouse, an enlightened nineteenth-century Charity Commissioner, protested: 'Why should a man, whose opinion no one regarded in life, be able to dictate how posterity shall use part of the wealth they make centuries after he is dead?'

In an ideal world – or richer country – any benevolent activity might be awarded charitable status. But reality requires some boundary, since public funds – which help charities with over £120 millions a year on tax-exemptions – are unfortunately neither limitless nor self-raising. Because charitable resources as well as the nation's ability to give tax relief are finite, it might seem the sensible priority to concentrate these primarily on the most deprived, here or overseas. Ironically, however, the benefits of some contemporary charities such as exclusive schools and hospitals are restricted to precisely the opposite: those people who are already most highly privileged. One of Eton College's many trusts, for example, is 'for the sons of regular officers in the First Grenadier Regiment of Footguards' to be educated at the college. The fact that part of this is paid for by poorer taxpayers means that the net effect can be a *redistribution of resources from the less well-off to the rich* – a concept of charity which did not occur even to Jonathan Swift.

The numerous charities which benefit animals were not envisaged by the 1601 statute; their charitable status rests on a court case of 1915 in which they were pronounced charitable because they 'tend to stimulate humane and generous sentiments in man'. Yet in 1981 the Amnesty International Trust – whose ends might be thought similar, but whose means are more direct – was again refused charitable status in the Chancery Court. The World Wildlife Fund is a charity; but Friends of the Earth is not allowed to be. The United Nations Association also has been declared not to be charitable; but the Institute of Strategic Studies, Moral Re-Armament, and the Protestant Alliance have been accepted. The British Atlantic Committee (which campaigns against CND and to support NATO) is a registered charity, whereas CND is not. It is neither charitable, according to the Charity Commissioners, to promote 'international friendship or understanding', nor to promote better race relations; but rifle clubs (recognised to be training grounds for extremists on both sides) in Northern Ireland are accepted as charities.

Self-help is held not to be charitable. In effect that cuts off community action groups, working-class tenants' associations or claimants' unions from charitable benefits – but not professional associations or richer people's self-help to gain extra medical benefits or private schools for their children. Such anachronistic charity law serves to keep the poor powerless: it is a political law, enshrining a concept of poverty and altruism that reinforces the dependency of the poor.

The present cloudy charity laws' restrictions – real or assumed – on political campaigning results in most charities having to support the status quo, which is itself a political attitude. The law permits a degree of political activity, but in an anomalous and unfairly selective way. The Lord's Day Observance Society, for example, is allowed to have charitable status while lobbying in Parliament, whereas the Humanist Trust for many years has not been. Tax-exempt churches can and do campaign to influence both the government and voters about laws concerning family planning, divorce, abortion and other questions that equally affect those who are not their co-religionists. But in other fields, the law absurdly prevents a charity from seeking to remove the cause of the very distress it attempts to palliate. *Britain in this respect seems to prefer to apply cosmetics, rather than a cure, to its wounds.*

The present rule is that political objectives can never be charitable in law, although if political consequences flow from the primary humanitarian objective of a charitable act, and the subsequent action by the charity is therefore secondary, this may be permitted. The dissenting minority report of the Goodman Committee on Charity Law Reform (published by the National Council of Voluntary Organisations in 1976) said:

> It is not only the right but in fact the duty of charities in many areas to act as political pressure groups, and legislation must end the present uncertainty about this forthwith. The days of confining charities to pouring soup into faulty old bottles should be consigned to the past; such cosmetic philanthropy can in fact be capable of postponing the more fundamental reforms that may be needed. Campaigning for changes in laws is often not only the most cost-effective, but virtually the only policy for organisations . . . that cannot hope to finance the needs themselves . . .
>
> To further illustrate the point, it is worth recalling that when the British Government cut its overseas aid programme by £20 million in 1966 it did so by a sum greater than the total of all Oxfam's spending since its inception in 1942. It could be argued that if, instead of financing projects abroad, Oxfam

concentrated on education, propaganda and political pressure in Britain which resulted in the government increasing its present net aid budget by even 10 per cent, vastly more poverty, distress and suffering could be relieved overseas. Politics – as distinct from party politics – being a charity's responsibility, one important role for contemporary charities can be, for instance, to act as lobbies for the deprived, the unorganised, or the unpopular.

In 1968 the authors of the Haslemere Declaration on overseas development announced: 'We recognize the value and humanity of the work done by the overseas aid charities and the genuine motivation of many of those who contribute to them, but we refuse to accept the salving of consciences. Too often it is the equivalent of tossing sixpence in a beggar's cap: money given by those who have no intention of changing the system that produces beggars and no understanding that they are part of it.' The economist John Kenneth Galbraith, who also served as the US Ambassador to India, declared in his Gilbert Murray Memorial Lecture for Oxfam in 1971: 'And yet this assistance, vital as it is, provokes a question that no one can escape – or, I think, should try to escape. What a poor substitute this help is for action that prevents, arrests or reverses the error that makes it necessary . . . political action provides, in most cases, the only hope for remedy.'

But the UK Charity Commissioners at a private meeting of the overseas aid charities not long afterwards warned them that, whereas it was legitimate to try objectively to inform public opinion and to conduct research in order to do so, the borderline was crossed 'when so-called education of the public was particularly motivated towards a change in law or in government policy.' In 1982 the Commissioners listed some examples of the kinds of activities they have advised charities operating mainly overseas as being 'outside the permitted scope of legal charitable endeavour':

X The elimination of social, economic, political or other injustice;

X Seeking to influence or remedy those causes of poverty which lie in the social, economic and political structures of countries and communities;

X Protesting against alleged abuses by governments;

X Promoting or defending the human rights of a particular group where such rights are not recognised by the law or policy of the country concerned.

Martin Bax, the associate director of Christian Aid, commented: 'It really does seem very odd that it is OK to document torture of animals as a way of preventing further cruelty, but it is not OK for us to do the same for human beings.' Peter Burns, a former Director of War on Want, on the other hand alleges that 'The Commissioners are often used by charity directors as bogey-men to keep the reds quiet. They wouldn't "go political" even if they could legally do so. If the law were liberalised, they would find some other excuse.' Individual members of Oxfam and other charities of course remain free to campaign politically in any way they like. But warnings about sanctions against charities themselves cannot be dismissed as hollow threats. In New Zealand a comparable agency, CORSO, lost its tax-exempt status for showing a film about unemployment.

Most non-governmental organisations claim to operate in a politically neutral manner, whether at home or in their projects abroad. Oxfam makes a formal declaration that its work is done without regard for race, colour, politics or religion, and many other overseas agencies take a similar position. But the inescapable dilemma remains: in many countries, what the poor want, and what their governments want, conflict. The difficulties agencies face in political arenas such as civil wars was illustrated by their experience in Biafra, when having raised funds for a relief airlift, they encountered criticism for prolonging the war by strengthening Biafran resistance. Jorgen Lissner, in *The Politics of Altruism* says:

> The very existence of voluntary development agencies is evidence of altruism. But altruistic intentions must be translated into concrete actions. In a world of conflicting interests, that means making choices which are political, accepting compromises which are debatable, and influencing public opinion in one direction rather than another. In other words, helping people is a political art, just as politics is a way of helping people . . . Many (but not all) of the problems of the low-income countries originate in and are sustained by factors and policies in the high-income nations; and many (but not all) of the governmental and voluntary aid efforts 'out there' are of little use, unless those root causes located within the high-income countries are tackled simultaneously.

A study sponsored by the US Agency for International Development (*Problems of Voluntary Agencies in African Development*, Washington, 1973) argued the moral necessity of agencies' independence of action: 'If it is true that the ethical stance embodied in their programme is what most distinguishes voluntary agencies from governmental foreign aid and from the private sector's trade and investment with the less developed countries, then a loss or even a de-emphasis on ethical considerations may entail a cruel choice – going out of business or becoming "para-voluntary" organizations in the service of government . . . The unique value of voluntary agencies is neither the resources they generate from the private sector nor the programmes they fund and implement. Rather it is their ability to see things in a different light then the public sector and their courage in giving voice to this difference.'

Michael Harris, Oxfam's Overseas Director, accepts the challenge: 'I have always said that whatever we do, every project is a political move and has political implications. In my view – and I realise many don't agree with me – once we venture in development, going beyond support of the most simple one-off welfare undertaking, if we want to do the things we claim we should be doing, then we cannot avoid good projects just because they may be political. The query arises as to *how* we deal with such sensitive matters.'

The Oxfam Field Directors' Handbook gives the following advice about work abroad: 'As far as political considerations are concerned, Oxfam must largely accept them, although given persistence and tact, some progress may be possible in what appear to be most intractable situations. Offence to those in power must be avoided, but equally it may be that Oxfam can do much to encourage the weak and hesitant within the framework of the existing law.' Brian Walker has summed it up in this way:

Of course, all aid is political. The simplest grant . . . a new well in, say, a remote African village: clean water to drink, ample water to irrigate crops and water the cattle. A manifestly humanitarian gesture. But political, too – for a well belonging to the people *disturbs the balance of power in that village*. Whoever owned the watering place hitherto is now disadvantaged. Normally that means the landlord, the moneylender or the local political power boss. Sometimes all three in one. If the people have their own water they do not need to work for the landlord, or pay him a tithe, or vote for him in the election, or turn a blind eye when he looks lustfully on their daughters. The political power structure has been disturbed – with a measure of justice flowing towards the poor and away from the powerful. Even when multiplied many times over (and the combined annual income of half a dozen continental charities is greater than the GNP of some Third World countries), this remains a modest enough gesture, and is neither radical nor revolutionary. Nonetheless, it is a beginning – a threat to the power base of the rich and the powerful and hence profoundly political. . .

Oxfam has neither the wish nor the intention to support political parties, nor to be purveyors of ideology – whether of the left or the right – nor to support violent movements, whether designated freedom fighters or terrorists. But justice, human and legal rights and the arousing of a social conscience must continue to be part of our work. The communicating of this in a sensible professionally competent way, to our supporters at home, is constantly urged on us by our partners overseas. They see the development of public opinion in the United Kingdom as being as important as the payment of grants to their projects. But the Charity Commissioners consider that 'to seek to establish a climate of opinion or inculcate an attitude of mind or propound a particular thesis, are not charitable purposes', and hence would constitute a breach of trust. Charitable money, they rule, may not be used to promote reform. We have to thread our way, delicately, therefore, through a veritable minefield.

It is not always realised by our supporters how politically volatile the Third World now is. Many of our staff – the men and women who are looking after the money you raise – are at risk from death by bomb, bullet, or knife, in countries like Kampuchea, Uganda, Zaire, Guatemala, Chile, and even India. It is a sign of the times that more and more people seek a resolution to their problems through violence and armed conflict. Small as we are this is why Oxfam's commitment to nonviolence is an important strand in our work. It is why we support the World Disarmament Campaign. Ours is not a purist or absolute position, and we are well aware of what the political scientists call 'structural violence' out of which we cannot opt. Inequitable trading systems, unjust land holdings, biased or nonexistent court decisions, corrupt police forces, governments which protect the rich and despise their own poor, make up the reality of the world in which the money raised has to be spent by our staff. Short of entering a monastic order, there is no way in which Oxfam can remain clear of these pressures. But what we can do, and what we do do, is to try to make sure that the aid and assistance we give is channelled exclusively and directly into humanitarian work, and not into armed conflict . . . It goes without saying that we work within the law of our own country, and the law of the country in which we are operating. We scrutinise our grants within those two constraints. Of course, you will understand that in another sense every penny we spend can have a political effect. If we teach people the proper use of resources, if we encourage people to stand on their own feet, to develop their own communities and tackle the cause of poverty from within their own resources, whether as a family, a village, a community or a nation, then, as we have discovered in our own country, we are dealing with the stuff of politics. *Fundamentally, you cannot separate humanitarian action from concepts of social justice.*

What does this mean in practice? Adrian Moyes, who is the head of Oxfam's Public Affairs Unit and one of its more radical employees, explained in 1972:

Helping the poor is becoming fashionable. For a long time it wasn't; the most effective way of promoting everyone's development was thought to be to generate economic growth. Now economists and aid institutions are beginning to abandon their reliance on the theory of trickle-down and to concentrate on helping the poor directly: not just the generation of wealth, but its distribution. This can hardly be the field of voluntary agencies, let alone foreign ones . . . What we *can* do is to work on ways of reducing the bias against the poor – and the numbers of the poorest. Voluntary agencies are in a good position to run small scale experiments: the essence of experiment is failure – and voluntary agencies can better afford to fail than governments.

He frankly admits inevitable difficulties pave the path:

Oxfam, having raised its money from the public in the rich countries with the slogan 'Your money well spent' is under pressure to get the best value for money. Since it is almost always more expensive to help the poorest, a value-for-money policy is likely to perpetuate the bias against the poor. The difficulty about the usual policy of 'building on success' is that it may leave out the poorest – who have no success to build on. We can only counter this by increasing awareness of the real problems.

'Fundamentally,' Brian Walker sums it up, 'what our partners in the Third World need, and what all of us need, is an entirely new commitment to a Universal Declaration of Human Rights *as seen through the eyes of the poor.'*

Yet the Charity Commission remains adamant that, for example, charities may not fund legal services – so that the poor may not try to gain by constitutional methods even what rights the law of their country allows them. And David Carter recollects an earlier Chief Charity Commissioner himself telling him that it was improper for Oxfam to fund the building of an earth-road giving access to a new agricultural project in Kenya – a road essential so that the produce could be brought to market. A former Field Director in Latin America advises: 'To prevent alarming the Commissioners, the trigger words to avoid are "Trade Union" (which for them conjures up a spectre of Arthur Scargill) or "Legal Aid": but instead you are of course allowed to help an "Advice Centre for the Poor".'

There is increasing acceptance that human rights, disarmament and development are inter-connected. Oxfam once went to the Charity Commissioners voluntarily to consult them about a particular publication of theirs, and were pained to find themselves criticised in the latters' Annual Report for doing so. On another occasion the Commission pressed Oxfam's Trustees to cease its financial help for the *New Internationalist* (the excellent lively monthly magazine, started in 1973 by Oxfam, Christian Aid, the Cadbury and Rowntree Trusts, to campaign on development issues). Some of the staff wanted Oxfam to contest this, but it was decided not to, since Oxfam had no editorial control over the content for which its Trustees would be responsible. However, at other times the voluntary agencies have managed to criticise the British government's negative attitude to aid and development, for example, unscathed. Oxfam recently ran an energetic campaign under Evan Luard, the former MP for Oxford, on the Brandt Report (despite some of the staff being divided over whether the effect of the Report's recommendations would in fact help the poorest), and over 20,000 copies of its Brandt study-pack were distributed. It also published Dianna Melrose's book on the misuse of feeding powdered milk to babies *The Great Health Robbery*, and recently two detailed investigations of the marketing in developing countries of pesticides (*A Growing Problem*, by David Bull) and medicines (*Bitter Pills*, by Dianna Melrose). Both these last two books, which caused several hesitations among some members of Oxfam's Executive Committee, are critical of British commercial practices and call for the government to take action. Tony Jackson's book on food aid broke convention by criticising the activities of some other voluntary agencies. On another occasion, Oxfam itself experienced embarrassment from a political grant: the autonomous Oxfam Belgique campaigned in Belgium for relief to the Irish hunger-strikers, which caused consternation to a number of voluntary supporters of Oxfam in Northern Ireland.

In March 1979 Oxfam's Council issued a policy statement on 'Oxfam's response to need in the context of human conflict and political oppression', as an attempt to clarify what Oxfam's policy should be in such situations. The principal guidelines are:

a) 'Need' is the trigger ensuring a response from Oxfam;
b) Oxfam is a 'non-violent' agency, working within the 'rule of law' at home and overseas;
c) Monitoring and evaluating grants in conflict areas is essential;
d) Projects agreed for funding aim to support Third World partners in their struggle for justice;

e) We support people rather than organisations;
f) Our policy must be consistent on a global basis.

In 1981 War on Want changed its structure (with the Charity Commissioners' consent) in order to bypass the ambiguities of Britain's archaic charity laws. It set up a separate company, W.O.W. Campaigns Ltd, that – being noncharitable – can campaign politically. The brainchild of Terry Lacey (War on Want's Director), the company has separate finances but the same controlling personnel as its parent charity. The experiment is being watched carefully and, if successful, may be followed by other aid agencies.

The Controversy about Disarmament

Recently, increasing political challenges confront charities, including the renewed campaigns for disarmament. In 1981, the Joseph Rowntree Trustees reported they 'are prevented from supporting many activities directed toward creating a more peaceful world because this comes within the realm of political judgement'. In that year, the world's military expenditure was over £250,000 million – a fourfold increase in real terms since the end of the Second World War. Quite apart from the increased danger as a result, the diversion of resources from development has been tragic. The world overall is spending twenty times as much on weapons as it is on development aid; it is devoting an average of US $19,300 to each soldier compared with only $380 for each schoolchild; in 32 countries, governments spend more on military programmes than on education and health care combined.

Yet less than a third of one day's military expenditure would afford enough to banish malaria from the face of the earth. In the most recent two decades, military expenditure by developing countries has increased 4.5 times, while their growth in GNP has gone up only 3 times. *It has been estimated that during the last twenty years of this century, if the UN's member countries spent one-twentieth of what they spend on military resources on peaceful development instead, they could provide adequate food, water, education, health and housing for everyone in the world.*

Oxfam has given £10,000 to the World Disarmament Campaign

in each of the years 1980/81 and 1981/82, and this was upheld by the Charity Commissioners following a challenge from a Lieutenant-Colonel. The support has generated debate amongst a number of Oxfam's supporters, but is warmly welcomed by many of them. Ms B. Reid said: 'As a long-term covenanting subscriber, I feel very strongly that a better world for all can only be built on mutual trust, and that money spent on arms is, in a real sense, theft.' 'I am so heartened,' agreed Ms Cecily Eden of Birmingham, 'My fervent hope is that Oxfam and all similarly motivated charities will continue to press this point . . . you must disarm to develop.'

What Can Be Done

What, then, is a conscientious aid agency able to do? Jorgen Lissner suggests four main roles:

1. a *'Caritative' function:* activities which provide e.g. food, health care, or education directly to the victims of disaster, poverty or injustice in order to improve their material living standards;
2. a *'Sensitizing' function:* influencing people's attitudes and behaviour in socio-political matters, by public communication and educational work, and strengthening their ability to analyse their own situation critically;
3. a *'Tribunal' function:* actions to challenge those who have political authority or economic power in order to remove specific causes of human suffering, either by public protest or by quiet persuasion and pressure behind the scenes; and finally
4. a *'Hope-raising' function:* activities which contribute to people's spiritual strength and mental energy by encouraging a new sense of purpose in life. 'Critical analysis and empathy do not necessarily in themselves generate the human energy needed to trigger and sustain social change; hope and enthusiasm may be as important.'

Oxfam believes in attempting all four roles. Reggie Norton and Adrian Moyes suggest: 'Work on one front strengthens our ability to make progress on others: our aid programme gives us weight when lobbying the British Government, our lobbying at

Bangladesh: Oxfam's Bridge scheme is additionally valuable by helping the position of women through giving them employment. The goods made at this jute works will be imported to the United Kingdom and sold, 17 per cent by mail order through Oxfam's gift catalogue, 77 per cent in Oxfam shops, and 6 per cent wholesale. (See Chapter 9)

India: a bicycle rickshaw, parked in front of the hut that is the puller's home. Oxfam is helping pullers to buy their own rickshaws and to convert bicycle rickshaws to scooter-power. (See Chapter 8)

Bicester, England: volunteers at work in Oxfam's Stamp Unit.

The Good Neighbour scheme in operation in Britain: these toy bricks will be sold through Oxfam's catalogue and in its shops.

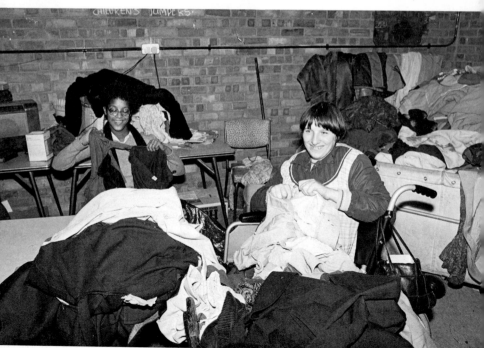

Huddersfield, England: Sorting clothes at the Wastesaver Centre provides employment for handicapped people. (See Chapter 9)

The familiar face of Oxfam to most British people: a modern-day Oxfam shop front, Wokingham.

Trafalgar Square, London, 1982: Campaigning on home ground outside the South African Embassy, in protest at the detention by the South African police of Alex Mbatha (seconded to Oxfam as a Field Representative) and his wife Khosi. Brian Walker and Sally Coles (Campaign Organizer) from Oxfam join others including Goodies, Tim Brooke-Taylor and Bill Oddie. (See Chapter 6)

UNCTAD makes it easier for us to work in the Third World, the projects we finance abroad give life to our education programme in Britain and point to our research and development work. More than almost any other organisation, Oxfam is in a position to attack poverty in many ways at once. There is another advantage in doing so: it's more honest – it better reflects the world as it is. To tell people the world can be saved by digging wells without doing anything about trade or monetary systems, is to kid them and thus to perpetuate the systems that must be changed if poverty is really to be reduced.'

The autonomous Oxfam Canada, like War on Want, in the 1970s gave priority emphasis to educational campaigning:

> We can no longer appear to be solely preoccupied in the intricate and demanding business of raising and dispersing funds while we know that fundamental social, economic and political injustices exist which all the aid in the world will never remove. We are at a point in our history when we run the risk of being seen as lacking in conviction and honesty if we do not show that we understand the underlying causes of poverty and underdevelopment, that we are unwilling to tolerate them and that we wish to help remove them insofar as we can . . . we must inform and involve the Canadian public so as to fundamentally alter its attitudes towards the Third World . . . If we are to adjust our priorities so as to emphasize this wider role of education, we must adjust mentally to a different approach regarding 'return on investments'. The style and basis of our aid programme may have to be amended which *may* result temporarily in a drop in income.

Most of the other agencies tried a different solution. In the words of Mildred Nevile, the able General Secretary of the Catholic Institute for International Relations: 'Instead of confronting the political issues directly themselves, the agencies encouraged – even financed – other groups to do the political work for them.' In 1966 Oxfam, with the other main British agencies, set up VCOAD (the Voluntary Committee on Overseas Aid and Development) followed in 1969 by WDM (the World Development Movement) to carry out political and educational campaigns on behalf of the parent agencies. After warnings by the Charity Commissioners, the parent charities were forced to disinherit the latter offspring (which was readopted as a noncharitable body funded by the Rowntree Social Service Trust); but, undeterred, individuals from the leading agencies united as the Independent Group on British Aid under Charles Elliott to campaign for Real Aid.

The Belgian Catholic agency Entraide et Fraternité offers one solution by giving its supporters a choice of donating their money to any of three different *troncs*. Money placed in *tronc* 1 (which results on average in just over half the total annual amount) is earmarked for development projects; money in *tronc* 2 (which receives about one-tenth) goes to finance development education in Belgium; while donations to *tronc* 3 (some one-seventh of the total) finance humanitarian projects sponsored by liberation movements. As the relative proportions of the donors' choices show, the importance of educational work is neither popular nor widely understood – compared with the more tangible appeal of the alternatives – although it is in fact the real key to getting any change in the North-South imbalance.

Why the Role of Education is Vital

The task facing charities and development educationalists in Britain seems hardest of all: a survey on 'The Perception of poverty in Europe' carried out by the EEC in 1976 found that Britain had the highest proportion of people of any European country who said they would not give even a little money or time to help the poor. Is this due to 'compassion exhaustion'? How much are such issues raised in General Elections? Peter Adamson of the *New Internationalist* adds: 'There is the almost permanent dilemma of the great gap which exists between the reasons why people give money to Oxfam and what Oxfam actually does with the money. This point is not meant to be critical of Oxfam – the gap exists in almost every agency that we've ever come across and I suppose that to some extent it is inevitable. But one could argue that the gap is a function of the different levels of knowledge about development issues and that Oxfam's educational task could almost be defined as the task of closing that gap.'

Education has been described as 'what I want to teach you; propaganda is what you want to tell me'. But the public's view of developing countries has been distorted by the media's treatment of disasters – which (like charities' agony-ads) sells copies, whereas development stories rarely do so. *Bursts of violence and terrorism hit the headlines, but less attention is given to the everyday violence of poverty which attacks half the world's population.* Gerald Priestland points to the effect of 'the passing of the old-style foreign correspondent who lived in the territory in which he specialised and soaked in its whole way of life. Today, with the jet plane, it is cheaper to employ the "flying fire-brigade" type of reporter, who can dash from one front page story to another, dealing only with surface appearances.' Tony Swift pioneered the excellent idea of Oxfam providing the press with background material and stories which increase knowledge about the developing world without publicising Oxfam. Much of this has to be non-attributable, in order to protect Oxfam's staff in the field overseas. An attribution to an anonymous 'aid agency' would provide no protection because Oxfam is often the only aid agency operating in a given area. Mary Worrall, who worked for Oxfam as an information officer, highlights another aspect of the problem:

> Those of us who are working towards a more just and harmonious multi-racial society, and those concerned with education for world development, are ultimately trying to move in the same direction. At the level of practical classroom innovation, however, it sometimes seems as though these two pressure groups are riding horses going in opposite directions: the first emphasising the achievements of other cultures and ethnic groups, the second stressing the poverty and disadvantage of the Third World poor . . . Led by the aid agencies, whose proper concern is with the poorest of the world's poor . . . in textbooks and materials, Asians and Africans are seen almost solely as victims and recipients, rarely as creative and capable people coping in their own way with the problems of their environment and evolving their own varied contribution to mankind's styles of living. These provide the dominant imagery affecting the expectations which white children have of black and Asian people . . . Even 17-year-old students have acquired very little knowledge about Third World countries. In response to the question 'what things do you tend to think of when the word "Africa" is mentioned?' virtually all answers could be summed up in one word: 'disasters'.

In addition, too much of the school syllabus remains parochial and ethnocentric, ignoring 90 per cent of the world. J. H. Burton, a volunteer working for Oxfam on education in Cheshire, believes: 'In secondary education there is such an emphasis on examination results that most teachers will only include in their teaching of senior pupils subject matter that will help examination success, so we should try to persuade examination boards to incorporate more material relating to development issues in their syllabuses.'

Sweden, Norway, Canada, Denmark, the Netherlands and West Germany spend much more on development education than Britain does. Sweden for example spends annually 24p per head on this, and the Netherlands 20p, compared with the United Kingdom's derisory 0.3p. This is especially shortsighted when Britain is probably more dependent than any other country on the rest of the world – importing half its food and 70 per cent of its industrial raw materials, and with one third of its workforce working on exports.

To try to remedy this situation, the Overseas Development Administration under Judith Hart started in 1977 a special Development Education Fund which grew from £150,000 to £750,000 p.a. – approximately matching the non-governmental agencies' combined effort. The Advisory Committee on Development Education pointed out some reasons why it was not desirable to rely wholly on fundraising agencies for such work: '(i) Each has its own constituency and goals: these could conflict with the need for a balanced and comprehensive approach; (ii) Their fund-raising background could affect the credibility of the material; (iii) The priorities within these organisations can be changed according to the pressures upon them, whereas development education requires a stable commitment; (iv) The "charity image" is perpetuated; (v) Charities may not engage in political matters, which restricts their choice of subject matter and treatment.'

One of the first actions however of the new Conservative government in 1979 was to terminate the United Kindom ODA's funding for development education. Hence the vital necessity for work in this area by agencies such as Oxfam. Many people who donate to them wish their money to go straight to the developing world; very few think it could be more usefully used at home in education. But this is arguably the most important part of all the programmes aid agencies can do – besides generating the best likelihood of future support for their work. A particularly important gap which must be tackled is the vacuum of interest by almost all trade unions and managements in such issues.

Elfed Jones, Oxfam's area organiser for South Wales, believes 'Oxfam often sits astride a gulf of misunderstanding: as a charity it tries to match the pity of the developed to the needs of the poor, while as a development agency it must try to reflect the causes of poverty in the social reflections of the developed world.' Peter

Burns, who used to work for Oxfam, makes the point: 'The question is, should the fund raising message tell the whole story or should it only try to generate funds? Should Oxfam lead public opinion and raise less – or follow public opinion and raise more? Oxfam's answer has usually been the latter: to raise the maximum and spend part of it on public education as a separate exercise.' Useful work is done by Derek Walker and others at the Centre for World Development Education (the successor to VCOAD, at 128 Buckingham Palace Road, SW1) together with the National Association of Development Education Centres: the commitment aroused by the scale and the crucial nature of the task has stimulated some of the best inter-agency co-operation.

A recent UN report offers a definition acceptable to most workers in this field: *'The objective of development education is to enable people to participate in the development of their community, their nation and the world as a whole. Such participation implies a critical awareness of local, national and international situations based on an understanding of the social, economic and political processes. Development education is concerned with issues of human rights, dignity, self-reliance and social justice in both developed and developing countries.'*

The work is conducted at many different levels. Some urges consideration of major policy changes: Claire Whittemore's report *Land for People*, published by Oxfam from its first-hand experience of working with the very poor, argues that the root cause of persistent hunger and poverty is 'the existence of unjust land tenure systems and the political, economic and social policies which enable these systems to prevail.' Professor Michael Lipton believes that the crux of the problem lies in urban bias compared with neglect of the countryside, and argues for diverting far more than the meagre 20 per cent of investment to the 80 per cent of people living in the rural areas of the Third World. A seminar held by Oxfam in 1975 at Tilonia in India, however, brought a different perception:

What we have may look like money, but in fact it is really power; power to arrange the world, or our bit of it to our advantage – or at least to maintain or to take advantage of the existing arrangements in our favour. So sharing will involve less power . . . backing development is a bit of a contradiction. For development is a process that you have to experience yourself – so any attempt to do it for other people is doomed to failure. Development agencies tend to supply 'outsiders' to think, and plan and implement for the people. But genuine development is when people learn to manage their own lives. It's not the well or the storage silo that matters, but the role of the people in planning it, making it, using it. So the development agency should be aiming to create the conditions in which people can do it themselves.

Such lessons are given immediacy in classrooms and other groups by simulation games, and Adrian Moyes has also drawn up simulation training for those who take Oxfam courses. Brian Wren, the administrator of Third World First (a development movement in universities and polytechnics, supported by Oxfam), has devised 'Giving and Receiving', a game simulating the preparation and funding of development projects, which conveys how it feels to be either a giver or a recipient. There is also a 'Trade Game', a 'Poverty Game', and 'Living Together – Survival'. In the 'Rich World/Poor World Meal Game', planned jointly with Christian Aid and the World Development Movement, two-thirds of the participants draw a Poor World meal card from a hat which reads:

> Hard Luck! You have been selected by the luck of the draw to receive a 'poor world' meal – you represent the poor world in which millions suffer from hunger and malnutrition. The 'rich world' diners are enjoying their meal at your expense, since your meal is worth less than you paid for it. This reflects the real world situation, in which rich nations obtain raw materials and tropical foods at less than fair prices from poor nations. You will notice that there are many more of you, and few of them. This also reflects the real world situation, in which the rich third of the human race owns three-quarters of the world's wealth. If you really feel compelled to do something to reduce your inequality, you may ask the rich for an amount of food proportional to what our country gives to help the poor world – less than half of one percent of our wealth, which is a quantity equal to one two-hundredth part (half a small carrot!) of what is on their plate!

Oxfam also offers teachers' packs, wallcharts, resource books, slides and films. Each month it publishes *Bother*, a magazine for young people. In 1982 it started the 'Oxfam 2000' grass-roots campaigning network, 'for people who are concerned about the British connections with Third World poverty'. It has not omitted to produce leaflets in Swahili and a number of other languages explaining to Africans what Oxfam is and does. Recently, the Education department also received this request from a school pupil in Berkshire: 'I would be very grateful if you could possibly send me some information on Oxfam, as I am doing a project on evil and suffering, and I would like to do something about Oxfam.'

An important new impetus that Oxfam and 63 other charities have supported is the International Broadcasting Trust, which is making films about development for Channel Four TV. Oxfam agreed to raise £25,000 of the £500,000 needed; its supporters instead gave £85,000 in their enthusiasm for this idea. In the struggle to arouse the public's concern, this could be the most crucial move of all. *There is certainly a need for it: government polls reveal that the proportion of British people who believe Britain should give overseas aid fell from 62 per cent in 1969 to 46 per cent in 1977.*

12

'All That We Can': Future Imperfect

Dear world: yes, you are sick and tired of all the suffering. But are
you so blind? Don't you realise that it is you and you only, each and
every individual that makes up our world, that is responsible and
no one is any more to blame than the next person? Face this fact
with braveness and boldness; our world is falling apart. Now is not
the time to despair and sigh but the time to get out and help your
neighbours.

Ruth Wolfgramm (aged 16, of Tonga)
(*From* 'Dear World', *ed. by Richard and Helen Exley*)

I just cannot understand how rich and powerful nations who inter-
fere so readily with poor ones when they are not wanted, can look
straight through them when the want is so desperate, and the time
so short.

James Cameron

In 1983, Oxfam appears to be swimming against a political mood
which venerates self-interest and is in danger of glorifying narrow
national and sectional selfishness. Many people react to the increasing crisis in world poverty – the news that, despite development efforts, the gap between North and South is not only
widening *but doing so at an accelerating rate* – either with despair,
or cynicism as an excuse for inert self-interest. But the fact that,
in the past, aid has often been provided in the wrong way, for the
wrong reasons, to the wrong people does not condemn development assistance any more than bad writing confirms that literature
is worthless. However, it does require that the lessons of both
the failures and the successes be learned, and their effects, like
their motives, clearly re-examined.

The cry of dogmatists that 'All aid harms' is as stupid as others'
belief that 'All aid benefits'. The subject has always suffered from
too many Pollyannas as well as too many Cassandras. Polemicists
of every hue have always found it easier to condemn than to
understand. On the other hand, oversold optimism can only
lead to disillusionment in both North and South. Instead, the

complexities and pitfalls, the conundrums and paradoxes – starting with the interaction of economic and social factors – need careful diagnosis leading to the continual adaptation and fine-tuning of policies. The first, most essential, place at which development must start is in the development agencies and workers themselves. A litmus test of the effectiveness of a NGO is the speed with which it can respond to new needs, and adapt itself. Oxfam, more than most, has changed – learning from its mistakes and becoming, as it matures from the necessity of experience, more flexible and realistic – in parallel with similar changes in the interpretation of what overseas 'development' really means.

Perhaps the first question which needs to be answered is why the North should concern itself with the South's problems at all. For some, the moral case for helping with overseas development is enough – though Shaw took pleasure in pointing out that the 'undeserving poor' need as much food as those who are thought 'deserving'. And Mahatma Gandhi wrote amongst the Rules for his Ashram at Sabarmati: 'Nature provides just enough and no more for our daily need. Hence it is a theft to possess anything more than one's minimum requirement.' But he added a caveat for overseas development workers: 'Man is not omnipotent. He therefore serves the world best by serving his neighbour. This is *Swadeshi* (local self-sufficiency), a principle which is broken when one professes to serve those who are more remote in preference to those who are near.' But David Owen, giving the Gilbert Murray Memorial Lecture when he was Foreign Secretary in 1978, advanced a counter-argument: 'A country that develops an attitude and an ethos which ignores poverty and inequality in the world soon ignores poverty and inequality on its own doorstep. It is a comfortable and seductive theory but a delusion that you can concentrate on your own problems at home first and only then look outwards to the world. If one once constricts the national horizon it will not be easy later to widen it out.'

Were he alive still, Gandhi might well be putting to British people the question, for example, what right we have to preach redistribution to other nations when in the United Kingdom the richest one-tenth of the population has four-fifths of all personal wealth, and the wealthiest 1 per cent still own 80 per cent of all held company stocks and shares. Yet his successor, Indira

Gandhi, reminded us in 1982 that no modern nation is entire to itself when she ruefully pointed out that 'to save a hundred jobs in an advanced country, a decision may be taken which sentences a thousand families to hunger in a far-off land'. (Furthermore 41 of the 98 largest economic powers in the world are now multinational companies, not countries: General Motors and Exxon indeed are richer than Switzerland, Yugoslavia or Saudi Arabia.)

In the forty years since Oxfam started, development agencies have changed from describing poverty delicately as 'disadvantage' or 'underprivilege' to the less morally passive term 'deprivation'. For many internationally-minded people in the rich North who believe the comfort they enjoy is based on the South's deprivation, the growth of agencies such as Oxfam helps the post-Fanon generation to express the feelings of those who agree with Jean-Paul Sartre: 'You know well enough that we are exploiters . . . with us, to be a man is to be an accomplice of colonialism, since all of us without exception have profited by colonial exploitation . . . A few years ago, a bourgeois colonialist commentator found only this to say in defence of the West; "We aren't angels. But we, at least, feel some remorse." What a confession! . . . The only chance of our being saved from the shipwreck is the very Christian sentiment of guilt.'

Léopold Senghor echoed this in his diagnosis: 'In brief, the proletarians of Europe have benefited from the colonial regime; therefore they have never really – I mean, effectively – opposed it.' Even after political independence, the benefits of economic colonialism continue to flow northwards, because of the imperial powers' legacy of primary commodity patterns, and because the structures of international trade and investment (except for the single case of oil) remain under the control of the North and serve its interests. Sékou Touré has warned that 'The major division in the world today is not between East and West, but between the underdeveloped and the developed countries of the world'. Frantz Fanon, who eloquently articulated the voice of the developing world in his book *The Wretched of the Earth*, concluded:

> The Third World does not mean to organise a great crusade of hunger against the whole of Europe. What it expects from those who for centuries have kept it in slavery is that they will help it to rehabilitate mankind, and will make man victorious everywhere, once and for all. But it is clear that we are not so naive

as to think that this will come about with the cooperation and goodwill of the European governments. This huge task which consists of reintroducing mankind into the world, the whole of mankind, will be carried out with the indispensible help of the European peoples, who themselves must realise that in the past they have often joined the ranks of our common masters where colonial questions were concerned. To achieve this, the European peoples must first decide to wake up and shake themselves, use their brains, and stop playing the stupid game of Sleeping Beauty.

Oxfam, War on Want, the Catholic agencies, Christian Aid, the World Council of Churches, the World Development Movement, contain some such awakened people – motivated less by guilt about the past, than by the recognition of the stark reality that, unless new measures are taken, the rich-poor spiral is bound to worsen. This is because those who already possess capital can invest to generate still more and dictate the terms of trade, while those who start with nothing have no chance or hope of doing so. But is there a danger that the private development agencies that provide conduits for such consciousness may, by cosmetic palliatives, unwittingly serve to postpone essential structural changes? When Oxfam was half its present age, Professor Peter Worsley charged in *The Third World* (Weidenfeld, 1964):

> For all their excellence, War on Want or Oxfam are, in fact, latter-day equivalents of Victorian organised charity, which in the end became a barrier to serious welfare reform, which only the State was fitted to undertake. The international attack on poverty, equally, will have to be carried out, ultimately, by the collective corporate action of governments, states and international organisations. The lasting contribution of the charity organisations will not be their material contribution, but the awakening of the 'conscience of the rich'. . . If only a little of the new-found enthusiasm and spontaneous popular support for famine relief causes could be harnessed for the far less personal and visible, but infinitely more important, task of turning our whole economy towards the development of the backward world, we would begin to enter human history and leave pre-history.

Nineteen years later, Worsley reassesses his view today:

> One big change is the shift in policy by such as War on Want from one of simply giving to the world's poor to one of enabling them to fend for themselves. My use of 'Victorian' wasn't meant to be disparaging: saving even one Smike from one Wackford Squeers is worthwhile. Better, though, to do what Dickens aimed at – abolish Dotheboys Halls altogether. These countries are not naturally poor; nor is their problem one of needing to be taught how to produce. It is that the wealth they produce ends up elsewhere. They receive

low prices for their products and pay high prices for what we sell them. What is called for is positive discrimination on a massive scale – reparation for the injustice of centuries. The present trend is in the opposite direction. Private aid, for all its virtues, does not change structures, which will continue to produce disasters – for which Victorian charity will still be needed.

However, it is – and always will be – more feasible to get international agreement and co-operation about specific problems such as disasters or diseases than on more fundamental political adjustments. The rich world's reluctance to change the rules they dictate stems from the fact that the power of money depends not so much on its absolute amount as on its amount relative to others': if international poverty were tackled in the way Fanon and Worsley advocate, this would result in less subservience, and the North would lose political control of the world.

Reluctance to change is therefore buttressed by emotions of patriotic and racial pride, as well as by the natural lure of economic comfort. As a result, more than three-quarters

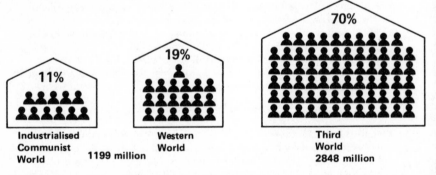

How many people live where?
(comparative populations)

The total world population in 1977 was 4,047 million. Africa had 426 million people (11% of the world's population). Latin America had 342 million people (8% of the world's population). Asia, excluding Japan and the Middle East, had 2,080 million people (51% of the world's population).

11%
Industrialised
Communist
World   1199 million

19%
Western
World

70%
Third
World
2848 million

The developing world has 70% of the world's people but only 10% of the world's weal‌

Source: World Bank Atlas 1977.

of the wealth created in 1981 went to the already wealthiest quarter of the world's inhabitants, and the income of the average person living in the rich world increased by £700 whilst the poorest quarter received merely an extra annual £15. The inflation rate in the developing countries, unlike in the richer ones, continues to worsen. *Despite the widespread belief that the developing countries have been given generous economic assistance by the richer North, the reality is that the worsening terms of trade due to the falling prices of their primary products have more than wiped out the value of all public aid.* For poor countries which have no oil and whose economy depends upon a single commodity's vulnerable crop, the outlook is particularly grim; to buy the same amount of manufactured imports, such countries need over three times the quantity of jute, maize, tea or zinc as they did seven years ago. Recently the amount of money developing countries have had to repay for past loans and interest has overtaken the total of all they receive in new aid and loans. Ironically, the North may be driven to begin for the first time to show serious concern about the South's economy, out of a wish to save their banks' enormous loans.

The Brandt Commission argued that, aside from morality, a change of course would be in the North's own long-term interest in order to build up future trading partners. Barbara Ward pointed out that after the Second World War the US donated to Europe in the Marshall Plan for five years about 2 per cent of a Gross National Product which was less than half its present size, thus restoring the consuming and productive power of their trading partners and potential rivals. 'It is perfectly possible to argue today', she said, 'that a comparable gesture – 2 per cent of GNP from the rich and OPEC nations transferred to the developing nations in order to revolutionize the productivity of the poor world – would cumulatively, have the same result . . . The critical fact today is that there are vast undeveloped resources and needs in the poor lands, large unused capacity among the rich, unsecured liquidity – from the OPEC surpluses and private bank lending – on a scale to threaten continued monetary instability, and so far barely a trace of the Marshall type of vision and statesmanship required to bring needs and opportunities together in a new global initiative . . . A 10 per cent cut in the world's lunatic arms spending would release more than the whole proposed sum and do so from the most inflationary of current uses' (*Progress for a Small Planet*, Pelican, 1979).

Unfortunately, the rich world has moved in precisely the opposite direction since Barbara Ward's plea not long before her death. The 17 members of the OECD's development assistance committee (DAC) gave only 0.35% of their combined GNP in 1981, compared with 0.38% the previous year, and 0.52% twenty years ago. (Holland – where aid is not felt to be a party political commitment that loses more votes than it gains, but a popular issue in which political parties vie with each other for imaginative vote-catching policies – gave the highest proportion, 1.08% of its GNP. Britain's fell to 0.43%, while the USA's was cut to 0.20%) The heirs of those political leaders and civil servants who said that the Great Irish Famine must be left to be solved by 'market forces' and 'natural (human) wastage' seem once again to be in control of governments.

Aid is far from the same as development (definable in this sense as desirable economic and social progress, and therefore liable to several subjective interpretations), though it can be a barometer of governments' internationalism. In the immediate future, it is essential to persist with efforts to reform international systems of liquidity and of trade. There is no point in giving aid with one hand while shutting out poorer countries' trade with the other. Trade, however, cannot be a complete substitute for development assistance: the former inevitably seeks areas of profit, which are not always the same as the places of greatest need.

Equally dubious is the assumption of the advocates of market forces that the benefits of economic growth will ultimately 'trickle down' to the poorest. The statistics of average per capita incomes can conceal more than they reveal, because a great proportion of poverty is caused by maldistribution. The World Bank estimates the number of people in 'absolute poverty' is 800 million (see 'How Much is Eaten in Different Countries?' below). In global terms there is no food problem – production has been expanding faster than population growth. The 1981 harvest was large enough to feed 1½ times the world's inhabitants. If the world's food were shared out equally, and food losses eliminated, the daily share for every man would be more than enough in both quantity

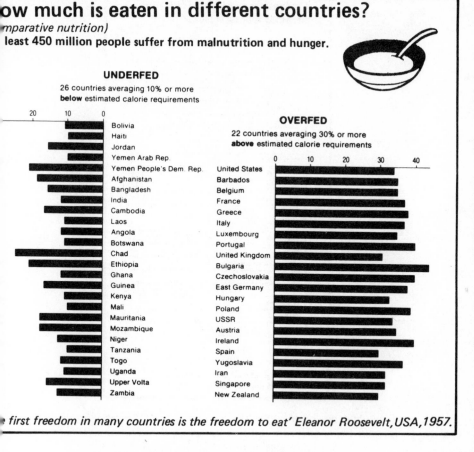

ow much is eaten in different countries?
(*mparative nutrition*)
least 450 million people suffer from malnutrition and hunger.

UNDERFED
26 countries averaging 10% or more **below** estimated calorie requirements

20	10	0			**OVERFED**
			Bolivia		22 countries averaging 30% or more **above** estimated calorie requirements
			Haiti		
			Jordan		0 10 20 30 40
			Yemen Arab Rep.		
			Yemen People's Dem. Rep.	United States	
			Afghanistan	Barbados	
			Bangladesh	Belgium	
			India	France	
			Cambodia	Greece	
			Laos	Italy	
			Angola	Luxembourg	
			Botswana	Portugal	
			Chad	United Kingdom	
			Ethiopia	Bulgaria	
			Ghana	Czechoslovakia	
			Guinea	East Germany	
			Kenya	Hungary	
			Mali	Poland	
			Mauritania	USSR	
			Mozambique	Austria	
			Niger	Ireland	
			Tanzania	Spain	
			Togo	Yugoslavia	
			Uganda	Iran	
			Upper Volta	Singapore	
			Zambia	New Zealand	

first freedom in many countries is the freedom to eat' Eleanor Roosevelt, USA, 1957.

Source: World Military and Social Expenditures, 1980.
© World Priorities, Leesburg, VA 22075, USA.

and quality. Yet Africa, the hungriest continent, is at present a net exporter of protein to Europe.

Why should this be? Gunnar Myrdal has argued that one major factor which causes the striking inequalities of power and wealth in much of the Third World is a built-in mechanism that almost automatically leads colonial powers to ally themselves with the privileged groups in any country (see 'Landlessness' chart below). These elites in turn seek Northern (whether of the Western or

Landlessness in selected Third World countries % of rural labour force

Country	10 20 30 40 50 60 70 80 90
Argentina	70
Bolivia	80-85
Brazil	59
Colombia	66
Ecuador	73
Mexico	50
Peru	60
Costa Rica	50
El Salvador	90
Guatemala	88
Dom. Republic	87
Jamaica	80
Bangladesh	89
India	79
Indonesia (Java only)	89
Malaysia	51
Pakistan	88
Philippines	81
Sri Lanka	73
Thailand	50

☐ Landless ▨ Near-Landless

Source: M. Esman and Associates, quoted in Lappé, **Aid as Obstacle**

Meanwhile, deserts are spreading at a rate of 80,000 square miles (about the size of Britain) each year. At this rate a third of the world's arable land will be gone by the end of the century.

Eastern variety) patterns of policies and imports, often totally alien and inappropriate to their country's real needs, besides being destructive of its culture. Brian Walker points to the lessons for development:

Poor people can become dependent upon development workers; they can also become dependent upon the resources which the aid agency controls – but to the debilitation of their own efforts and resources, however limited those might be. So much Western-type aid is utterly inappropriate to the conditions of poverty experienced at the very base of the human pyramid where the majority of the human family is condemned to live. High energy tractors and vehicles litter the countryside throughout Latin America, Africa and Asia. We have a view that windmills and solar pumps will be the equivalent of today's rusting tractors in the late 80s and 90s. *It is better therefore to see money as a lubricant in the development process rather than as a solution to the poverty trap. Aid input is the fertiliser rather than the seed of future harvests, and it must be used sparingly, and as a means to an end, rather than as an end in itself.* This is a very difficult discipline for the wealthy aid agencies to adopt and especially difficult for UN agencies or Governments to adopt once their own budgets are agreed and secured. Once you have an assured source of income the temptation to impose solutions is almost irresistible – irresistible, but fatal. People cannot grow under imposed solutions; they are never going to grow and develop their own humanity within their own cultural patterns, if they are manipulated by large sums of money, however well-intentioned the expenditure of that money was meant to be. Increasingly in Oxfam we have swung more and more of our programme into what we categorise now as 'programmes of social development', as distinct from the straight aid input aimed at generating more food, water, health, nutrition or whatever.

Economics as if People Matter

The ideas which have probably influenced Oxfam more than any other are those of E. F. Schumacher's *Small is Beautiful: a Study of Economics as if People Mattered*: the subtitle is the key to the book's message. Dr Schumacher mounted a crusade – with, like many prophets, a better response overseas than in his own adopted country. He argued that the pursuit of maximum profit and uncritical obeisance to accepted ideas of 'progress', leading to increased specialisation and giant impersonal organisations, besides the cost in ecological damage and pollution, have in fact resulted in economic inefficiency as well as inhumane conditions for work. Instead he advocated a radical reappraisal, based on smaller working units, partnership and co-ownership, making maximum use of local labour and resources: returning the focus from products to people, so that capital serves man instead of vice versa. He criticised many traditional development policies as merely transferring to the Third World the developed world's industrial system and technological mistakes with its myopic obliviousness to the human and ecological costs. He also warned that the heedless exploitation of finite natural resources was improvidently consuming irreplaceable natural capital as income.

Recent data confirm the truth of his warning. Of 30 fishing grounds in the northeastern Atlantic, 27 have been overfished. Nine-tenths of Ethiopia's forests have been felled during this century, causing increasing erosion; Thailand could be totally stripped of its forest by 1985 if present trends persist. As a result not only will several million poor people be without their basic fuel for cooking, but the absorptive capacity of trees, which is the antidote to carbon dioxide pollution, will be reduced to a dangerous level. If everybody in the world were to plant and care for at least one tree each year, there would be a chance of reversing this critical trend.

Aldous Huxley wrote that if it became the acknowledged purpose of inventors and engineers to provide ordinary people with the means of 'doing profitable and intrinsically significant work, of helping men and women to achieve independence from bosses, so that they may become their own employers or members of a self-governing co-operative group' the results would be 'a progressive decentralisation of population, of accessibility of land, of ownership of the means of production, of political and economic power . . . a more humanely satisfying life for more people, a greater measure of genuine self-governing democracy' (*Towards New Horizons*, Navajivan Publishing House, Ahmedabad, 1959).

Schumacher pointed out that by contrast to those who haven't enough to survive, the richest nations are eternally unsatisfied and incessantly demand more material riches. Having been Economic Adviser to the UK National Coal Board for 20 years, he warned: 'It is clear that the "rich" are in the process of stripping the world of its once-for-all endowment of relatively cheap and simple fuels. It is their continuing economic growth which produces ever more exorbitant demands, with the result that the world's cheap and simple fuels could easily become dear and scarce long before the poor countries had acquired the wealth, education, industrial sophistication, and power of capital accumulation needed for the application of alternative fuels on any significant scale.' Gandhi, who warned of the dangers urban concentration and mass-production were causing for village life and employment, and had advocated appropriate technology fifty years earlier, said 'Earth provides enough to satisfy every man's need, but not for every man's greed': economic policies based on personal greed, although often successful in the short-term, carry seeds of destruction germinated by envy, selfishness, competitive tension and frustration.

The lesson for development groups such as Oxfam (but one

which is equally true in the contracting employment of Northern countries themselves – by 1985 over 15 million people are likely to be out of work in Western Europe) is that it is best to spread the available jobs – however modest they may be – among as many people as possible. Schumacher argued:

> Their first need is to start work of some kind that brings some reward, however small; it is only when they experience that their time and labour is of value that they can become interested in making it more valuable. It is therefore more important that everybody should produce something rather than that a few people should produce a great deal . . . because this is a dynamic situation capable of generating growth . . . Workplaces have to be created in the areas where the people are living now, and not primarily in metropolitan areas into which they tend to migrate . . . The equipment would be fairly simple, and therefore understandable for maintenance and repair on the spot . . . far less dependent on raw materials of great purity or exact specifications and much more adaptable to market fluctuations than highly sophisticated equipment. Men are more easily trained; supervision, control and organisation are simpler. A plea might be made to supranational agencies which would be well placed to collect, systematise, and develop the scattered knowledge and experience already existing in this vitally important field.

Oxfam has successfully implemented Schumacher's ideas in a number of designs of appropriate low-cost prototypes by Jim Howard and others, such as the basic Sanitation Unit and the Oxtrike (see Adrian Moyes; *The Poor Man's Wisdom*, Oxfam Public Affairs Unit, 1979). Other simple basic needs could be filled: a cheap broad-tyred bicycle which could travel over sand, for example. But appropriate technology, as much as any other assistance, should be determined by local people's needs and not be 'dropped from on high'. What is required is something much more than signing a cheque and then departing. Training in use is as important as provision: nine-tenths of the pumps supplied to India by another aid agency were not being used by the end of two years because the users had not been given advice on maintenance.

Problems can arise from a suspicion in some Third World countries of any Northern-supported ideas. Might the Schumacher gospel's denial of support for more modern science in favour of primitive technology not be a plot to limit developing nations' economic and political growth and thus prolong their dependency? Are not Northerners – as with family planning – once again trying to tell Southern societies how to run their lives, whatever their motive may be? It is difficult for any development agency or worker wholly to deny a charge of interventionism, whichever type of development they support. Most of the Northern agencies originate from backgrounds of charity and relief or of social reform based on religious exhortation and preaching. But Oxfam – despite being still conspicuously white, like most British missionary bodies – has more than most successfully avoided the danger Virginia Woolf warned against in *Mrs Dalloway*:

> Conversion is her name and she feasts on the wills of the weakly, loving to impress, to impose, adoring her own features stamped on the face of the populace . . . she stands preaching; shrouds herself in white and walks penitentially disguised as brotherly love through factories and parliaments; offers help, but desires power; smites out of her way the dissentient, or dissatisfied; bestows her blessing on those who, looking upward, catch submissively from her eyes the light of their own . . . concealed, as she mostly is, under some plausible disguise, some venerable name: love, duty, self-sacrifice.

Equally, Oxfam workers' modest standard of living and often passionate identification with the poor they work with, has saved them from the other perils of development professionals:

> *Excuse me friends, I must catch my jet –*
> *I'm off to join the Development Set . . .*
> *The Development Set is bright and noble,*
> *Our thoughts are deep and our visions global;*
> *Although we move with the better classes,*
> *Our thoughts are always with the masses . . .*
> *We discuss malnutrition over steaks*
> *And plan hunger talks during coffee breaks.*
> *Whether Asian floods or African drought,*
> *We face each issue with an open mouth.*
> *We bring in consultants whose circumlocution*
> *Raises difficulties for every solution –*
> *Thus guaranteeing continued good eating,*
> *By showing the need for another meeting.*
> (Ross Coggins, quoted by permission of the author)

One of Oxfam's strongest beliefs is that *for any development to be successful, it must come from the bottom upwards and not be imposed from the top.* It is quite wrong to assume that the Southern countries want to become like the North, or indeed that this

"YOU SEE, THEY'RE TRYING TO FIND SOME UNDERDEVELOPED AREAS..."

Oxfam, like many private development agencies, is fair game for cartoonists in the national press, but here is a sympathetic example by Vicky.

would be desirable: Mother Teresa said the industrialised world has a 'different kind of poverty, a poverty of loneliness, of being unwanted, a poverty of the spirit'. (Peter Adamson in the *New Internationalist* has also satirised the idiocy of seminars where Northerners 'discuss the lives of people they do not know, whose cultures they do not understand, whose economic circumstances they cannot even imagine, and end up by passing resolutions telling them what they should do when they go to bed together at night'.) In place of Northern ideas of capital-intensive mechanisation, urban industries and sophisticated hospitals and academic institutions that benefit the few, most voluntary agencies now advocate self-help. This means labour-intensive and integrated rural development (the subject, like others, has generated its own jargon) together with relevant education and basic health care administered by local people trained as 'barefoot' teachers and doctors.

Such an approach has an appeal both for democratic socialists and for Samuel Smiles conservatives who believe in people standing on their own feet. Paul Harrison describes the aim in these words: 'A catalyst so that villagers can learn how to become individually and collectively, the major force for their own self-improvement . . . Self-help means that people are no longer the passive recipients of handouts or government provided services. Their participation cuts costs, provides a practical education, and spreads deeper attitudes of adaptability and creative change.'

The key (if unwieldy) words of the Third Development Decade, have become 'conscientisation and ensuring participation': taking steps to involve the people concerned – so that poor people are able to *be* more as well as *have* more. As *The Oxfam Field Directors' Handbook* says: 'The traditional aims of a voluntary society are to relieve the suffering caused by poverty and to reduce the total number of the poorest. Oxfam is doing this, but it is also trying to do something more; namely to encourage processes of change, and in such a way that the poorest can take charge of the improvement in their own living standards. In this way Oxfam seeks to reduce more permanently the bias against the poor in the development process.'

The spread of literacy is obviously useful to help this; much might also be done by radio and television. But Michael Behr is insistent: 'We must teach people, not to beg, but to demand their rights and their water. Anger is a necessary precondition for change. Peasants should be taught that their disadvantages are not due to any fault of theirs.' Xavier Albo warned Oxfam from Central America in 1974: '*Conscientisation is not enough – necessary, but not sufficient. Once oppressed groups have become aware of their problems, one has to look for means to solve them. Otherwise conscientisation leads to frustration . . . Conscientisation of groups in the First World (e.g. the United Kingdom) should aim at real commitment to solve problems of which those groups have become aware* . . . There is a danger that First World individuals will ease their consciences from the mere fact of having talked heatedly about the problems. This incidentally, is less applicable to Oxfam which certainly works towards solutions. It is important to ensure that aid acts as starter-motors so that, as rapidly as possible, the Third World can make headway in the direction it wants to go, and on its own. The help should not become a permanent umbilical cord, but like a power station.' Brian Walker describes specific examples of this work:

The kind of path such a development process might take could run as follows. Life cannot exist without water and so water is fundamental. Can wells be sunk and crops irrigated without damaging the natural water table or spreading water-borne diseases? Can ponds or tanks be constructed by the people to trap the rain water or syphon off the flood water? Can they be stocked with fish to provide protein to the people? Can fields be irrigated to improve crop production, and dairy cattle watered so as to improve their milk yield? Can mothers be taught the importance of clean drinking water to the lives and development of their children? Can water be stored for the dry months? Some mothers and daughters walk up to 6 or 7 miles a day in the Third World for every drop of water their family consumes. Water is crucial to development. Once it's there, can crops be planted and harvested twice or three times a year instead of once? Can improved seed varieties be used and new simple farming techniques introduced? Not tractors and petroleum based, highly capitalised equipment – but simple methods for arresting soil erosion, and weed growth; or is there a need for the use of manure and mulching to retain moisture and improve the structure of the soil? Can crops be stored safely and adequately? Rats, vermin and insects consume more food in the Third World than human beings consume. Simple rat-proof food stores, made of traditional materials, can make a significant contribution to development. And once there are food surpluses, can they be sold in the local market? Without cash in the pockets of the poor, no fundamental change can take place in the poverty trap. And so small revolving loan-funds, co-operative credit schemes, low interest loans, the marketing of surpluses are woven into the process. The relentless grip of the moneylender is broken, people become freer.

Personal Involvement

One growing response to the vast impersonality of the daunting statistics about world poverty with which we are faced, has recently been a significant take-off in the success of sponsorship agencies. A million 'foster parents' in the North now sponsor children in the Third World through agencies such as World Vision, Christian Children's Fund, Foster Parents Plan, Save the Children and Action Aid, donating an average of £10 a month. Action Aid, for example, started by Jackson-Cole (one of the founders of Oxfam), has evoked a ready response in the UK amongst many people who are moved to adopt a specific individual child in the Third World, rather than to give money to dig a well which would in fact save children's lives. Peter Stalker in the *New Internationalist* has argued the disadvantages of this method of helping: that helping individuals can cause divisions, create more inequality and a consciousness of humiliating dependence; and that providing and translating regular information about each individual 'adoptee' leaves less funds available for educative or other work.

Nevertheless, 'personalising' is obviously desirable – Aristotle described politics as 'the art of making people fully human' – particularly if the minds as well as the hearts of donors can be engaged. Sponsorship of a child or family appeals to the kindly emotions of thousands of people who have little time or inclination to think about the deeper problems of overseas development. It forms a small part of Oxfam's work, bringing in £60,000 a year.

Harold Sumption, an adviser to both Oxfam and Action Aid, believes '*the task is to remind people that we live in one world – to generate a continuing commitment, that is not bought off by a donation to a disaster fund*'. Reciprocal links through 'twinning' with developing areas are spreading in Britain: the London borough of Camden is twinned, not with some luxury resort where councillors enjoy freeload visits such as many councils choose, but with a part of Botswana. 900 households in Wood Green have twinned with Jailan village in Gambia; a wholefood shop in Covent Garden has twinned with the 146 inhabitants of the tribal village of Patra Toli in northeast India.

Nor should we ignore how much industrialised societies

themselves can learn from the so-called developing world. Action Aid now offers to arrange such village, community or school links as well as child sponsorship, while Oxfam in 1981 started Project Partnership, which is intended to overcome some of the disadvantages of individual sponsorship, while answering people's need to identify personally with the communities they are trying to help. Under this scheme, Project Partners who give £100 a year are invited to choose an individual Oxfam-supported project which is of particular interest to them; in return for his or her regular support, the donor receives four times a year information about the project's people (who have all been consulted beforehand and agreed to participate) and progress, in the form of letters, photographs, tapes, slides, reports and background data, so that he or she can build up understanding of the project and the people it affects.

In development work, as in every other field, an ounce of personal commitment is beyond value. Mr and Mrs Alan Weaver of Shrewsbury decided to auction every possession in their home – starting with their colour television set – to raise funds for Bangladesh: 'After seeing how bad conditions are in Bangladesh we had to do something to help', said Mrs Weaver. 'We have no savings and the only thing we could think of to raise money was to sell our possessions. It will probably take two years to get back to where we were, but at least we have jobs, food and a roof over our heads.'

The generous public response to natural disasters habitually puts governments to shame. Unemployed men from Skelmersdale travelled to help victims of the 1981 earthquake in southern Italy, despite forfeiting their social security by doing so, and a marked lack of co-operation from the British and Italian Governments. Northern Ireland, despite its own problems and poverty, gives more per head to Oxfam than any other part of the United Kingdom: old ladies doggedly sweep up glass in Oxfam shops after a bombing and carry on selling secondhand clothes. '1 per cent Groups' have been set up at the United Nations and elsewhere, whose members regularly give at least one per cent of their income to world development. (Details can be obtained from O. Gulbrandsen, Office E 10041 at the UN in Geneva, or from 161 Bishopscote Road, Luton, England.) In Norway, 20,000 people have gone further and formed a movement committing themselves to a simpler lifestyle as well as to take part in educational and political work about the problems of the Third World; a similar Lifestyles Movement has now been started in Britain by Horace Dammers, the Dean of Bristol, with a thousand members.

'Progressive' groups have far from a monopoly of personal outrage. Gut feelings are something different from effective action; it is temptingly easier as well as more pleasant to try to change others than to change oneself. But it is from such wells that voluntary agencies often draw their strength. Voluntary action is usually a matter of personal commitment and choice, rather than the performance of a duty carrying a substantial salary, perks, privileges and power with it. George Verghese of India warns, however, 'A voluntary agency can regard itself as successful if it becomes redundant in the area and for the purpose for which it was started. But do-gooding can be habit-forming and some voluntary efforts unconsciously create dependency instead of encouraging self-reliance. Development should be not merely for people, but of and by people, so that the logical successor to external voluntary intervention is local community action.'

The Next Phase for Oxfam

How will Oxfam develop in the future?

'This peculiarly British body' derives its nature from a compound of several tensions. In some ways it is a highly idiosyncratic organisation: in other ways, a very simple one. On the one hand it enjoys an atmosphere like an extended family or sect, quite unlike the synthetic attempts to replicate such feeling occasionally attempted in business corporations. It is an impressively democratic charity, without any of the trappings of royal or aristocratic figureheads so many British charities ape. Geoffrey Wilson suggests that what keeps 'this extraordinary diversity within a more or less coherent organisation, is that it answers a remarkable range of human needs at many different levels, both at home and abroad.' Peter Wiles, working in it, said he was pleasantly surprised by the permanent 'bubble of debate' there; the problem is to channel this into practical action. Some personality differences are inevitable in any charity, because feelings outrun the scale of ascertainable results and motives are more mixed than expectations. Talented people of a wide spectrum of politics and idiosyncrasies join, hoping to change the world. 'I wouldn't have Brian Walker's job for anything', said one of his colleagues. 'Oxfam by its very nature attracts highly motivated individualists, few of whom find it easy to accept teamwork.'

Several of the staff would like Oxfam to be the fully-fledged co-operative it often urges as a model on others. Many of them are worried lest the growth in its size may cause it to lose its human atmosphere: 'The sheer problems of management of the organisation start to dominate one's days, rather than concern for the poor. And there's the danger we may take decisions, particularly in the areas of publicity, which are more in the interest of Oxfam than those of the people we are meant to serve.' Some are worried lest the increasing commercial character of the shops loses something valuable from the past; others consciously want to leave amateurism behind them. Several people were worried by Oxfam's high profile in the Cambodia operation, and the press-hype which they fear tempts fate and could lead to an equally spectacular Icarus-type fall: 'We shouldn't compete with other agencies', though not all agree.

There is wider consensus on the desirability of trying to reduce the gaps between the perceptions of Oxfam's funders and its work. The overseas tours organised by Oxfam for volunteer workers at their own expense are widely praised, and very often produce a renewed enthusiasm for proselytising as witnesses on their return. Wilson is particularly anxious for more of the local groups to involve themselves in the wider issues as well as fund-raising. One school of approach argues 'We also have responsibilities to our donors, 80 per cent of whom have old-fashioned ideas about development'; while for the radicals, donors should have no rights, only commitment: 'Either you're on the side of the poor, or you're not.' A third view is that the scale of Oxfam's actual projects is so small that it could best use its funds by exporting its ideas, such as the 'giving ideal', to other countries. Just as Oxfam has given several hundred ordinary people a new meaning and purpose in life, so it might do the same for rich, bored societies elsewhere.

Frank Judd (a former British Minister for Overseas Development – who has suggested that this Ministry should best operate as a BBC-type quango) believes that NGOs like Oxfam could be much more influential with the government than they are at present, without infringing the charity law. But Jeremy Swift, a consultant for the UN in Africa, outlines one paradox faced by Oxfam and other NGOs:

> Their field projects are often successful because they can get around the problems faced by the big multilateral and bilateral aid agencies – bureaucratic inertia, vested interests, poorly motivated 'experts' etc. NGO projects are often small scale, run by dedicated people with good local knowledge and contacts (often Church people who have been there for years and speak the language), and do not threaten too many interests, and that is why they often succeed where the bigger projects fail. But it is precisely these characteristics that limit the effect of NGO projects and make it difficult for them to spread. There aren't enough highly qualified people to go round: small-scale projects tend to remain just that *unless* you change the bureaucracy and overthrow the vested interests. So unless the NGO type of approach can be translated into a larger-scale move after the successful project, not much has been achieved.

Recently, in response to almost continual crises such as those in some parts of central and eastern Africa, Oxfam has become more 'operational'. On occasions it runs its own projects – since needs can be undeniable while an infrastructure of indigenous applicant organisations sometimes does not yet exist – as for example in the pioneering work by OXWORP in Orissa. In response to emergencies, Oxfam is also having to employ more professional engineers and medical staff on short-term contracts. This will probably lead to an increase in Oxfam's Field Directors, resident throughout the Third World, accumulating knowledge and experience of local conditions and needs. These people are in the best position to judge which people have the necessary '*dynamique*' to help their community, and they enable Oxfam to take much more flexible and rapid decisions than can other bodies administered from Northern capital cities. This network could be combined in the future with greater use of local people as advisers and assistants, as has happened in India. So that Oxfam's operational initiatives do not breed dependency, these could be given an optimum limit of three years before either being handed over to local control or ended. It was noticeable when Cambodia brought many people – including at the very top – in Oxfam's Oxford headquarters the opportunity for direct action, they felt re-enthused and younger through escaping from their usual administrative insulation. The gap between field and headquarters staff may widen as the price however if more local staff are recruited, since these are less likely to want transfers to Oxford to work outside their home areas.

Because of the rush of short-term demands, it is always difficult in any busy organisation to find enough time to stand back and evaluate comparative lessons. One present gap which could be filled is in the better exchange of development ideas learned in different parts of the world (for example, to help women – in which crucial field Oxfam has no co-ordinating specialist yet). Jim Howard who first went to India with the Quakers says he found to his surprise he'd more to learn than to give, such as about the dignity with which people there treat each other. He sees a particularly useful role for Oxfam in acting as a hinge between relief and development – helping longer-term reforms to emerge through the catalyst of an emergency.

When in the next short period of time Oxfam's present leadership – Wilson, Walker, Stringer and Harris – all retire, the organisation will again come to one of its periodic crossroads. Some staff question whether it will be sensible for so many disparate activities to continue to co-exist in one body. A number of them would prefer its disaster relief role to be dropped in order to concentrate on development work, but recognise that to do so would risk decimating Oxfam's income, size and publicity. One former staff member, Glen Williams, foresees it will increasingly be necessary for Oxfam to help more action groups to reduce extremes of inequality, which will bring it into growing problems with governments, and that one day Oxfam will have to face the decision to stop being a charity.

Many radical groups abroad however might be reluctant to be compromised by receiving foreign support. In addition, Brian Walker foresees it is unlikely that NGOs will be allowed to operate freely abroad in the future: 'Armed conflict is already severely interrupting work throughout Central America and has caused major problems in Uganda, Somalia, Ethiopia, and the Lebanon. And several Third World governments are beginning to realise that the poor's heightened awareness of their own oppression is political dynamite.'

Nevertheless, to ignore politics is both impossible and in itself a political decision. 'Don't rock the boat' can lead to self-censorship. But a majority of Oxfam's activists believe, 'The

British public can empathise with justice, but not with revolution. And there is Oxfam's original pacifist Quaker ethos to remember. If Oxfam became another War on Want it would probably lose its constituency.'

All groups of opinion however are united in wanting to widen Oxfam's basis of support – by making greater use in Oxford itself for example of not only the students but the Cowley car-workers: extending its active membership more outside the traditional charities' middle-class catchment areas. Perhaps it would help if voluntary agencies were called 'non-profit' instead of 'charitable'. The recession at home should not necessarily be a deterrent. Marcus Thompson of Oxfam believes that hardship can increase a person's consciousness of others' deprivation. (And poverty means something different in the Third World from when it is used in Europe by a man still spending significant sums of money on cigarettes or alcohol.) Murray McLean, one of the able businessmen who help Oxfam on a voluntary basis, believes that the recession might have a beneficially cathartic effect by necessitating the adoption of new strategies: 'Oxfam's value is, and always must be, qualitative, because quantitively it can't make much of a dent in the size of the problem.'

Co-operation between NGOs could, it is hoped, also be developed still further in the future. With or without government assistance, they might usefully pool their specialist advisers and professionals, research, information, educational work, management and accountancy services, appropriate technology development and even share their representatives in the Third World. Governments and international organisations could help by allowing NGOs better access to the data banks of information on development problems which they possess. The same principle applies worldwide: international co-ordination is even more desirable in this field than it is for Amnesty International.

At present, besides the Disasters Emergency Committee (composed of the British Red Cross Society, the Catholic Fund for Overseas Development, Christian Aid, Oxfam and the Save the Children Fund), a certain amount of co-operation, including some joint funding is achieved through Euro Action-ACORD, a consortium of 19 NGOs; but a number of major agencies are not members of this. Dom Thomas Cullinan warned: 'We must be very, very careful not to be more interested in our organisations than in the people we are existing to serve. Sometimes even amongst voluntary agencies, one feels a certain competitive approach of one agency to another. Sometimes it slips out by mistake in the way we talk, betraying what might be going on at the back of our minds, that we're more interested in Oxfam than the people who are destitute and in need. This is very dangerous, because the organisation becomes what we exist for and not the people, and in the end it's only people that matter.' A senior man at Christian Aid gave generous praise to Oxfam in general: 'They are a brave new world – and politically a good sight braver than most other agencies. They are very respected in the field – which is where it matters most. They co-operate closely with us on overseas subjects, perhaps less so on domestic ones. At times they behave more like a progressive company than an aid organisation: some agencies envy them for this; others look the other way.'

A woman working for another NGO said, 'Most of the reservations you hear about Oxfam are envious or in fact are compliments – that it is pushy, etc.' Nor does every aid agency start from the same premise: International Christian Relief, for example, is connected to the anti-communist mission Underground Evangelism.

Looking to the Future

Terry Lacey, the General Secretary of War on Want, can see a time – perhaps ten years hence – when his organisation will not be funding anything abroad: 'All funding of this nature is neo-colonial and as such must stop. Ultimately, the countries will have all the expertise and contacts to raise such funds for themselves. Meanwhile we must get used to the idea that a Third World charity should be spending money in Britain.'

Meanwhile, what are among the likely areas of emphasis for Oxfam in the future? Help for *agrarian land reform*; the provision of *cheap credit facilities* to help below the levels assisted by banks; encouragement for *marketing co-operatives*: these remain major unfulfilled needs for millions of people. One solution might be to recycle such help through a rural development trust fund, but the scale required would need at least a consortium of agencies.

More projects are likely to be helped as part of *integrated* plans. There might be further general pioneering initiatives along the lines of the *Vegetable Gene Bank*, and the *Home Pharmaceutical Factory* Oxfam has supported in Bangladesh to help poor countries escape multinational prices. *Indigenous peoples* – such as the Indians of both South and North America – and *refugee concentrations* face particular difficulties. 'Ethnodevelopment' requires that culturally distinct societies be given the autonomous chance to direct their own development.

In developing *internationally*, one major gap is that there is as yet no real equivalent of Oxfam in France – which would obviously be valuable for helping projects in francophone Africa and elsewhere. But there is an Oxfam America, Oxfam Belgique, Oxfam Canada, Oxfam Quebec, and an Australian equivalent – Community Aid Abroad. An Oxfam support group was established in Hong Kong in 1975 (which in 1980 raised HK$950,000 [£415,000]) and there are others in Eire, Gibraltar, the Bahamas, Denmark, Italy, and Malta. The other five overseas Oxfam organisations however are now completely autonomous from Oxfam, and attempts to administer them as a unity have been abandoned. Oxfam Quebec specialises in appropriate technology; Oxfam Belgique believes it is crucial to change the multinational companies; Oxfam Canada has been influenced by Marxist intellectuals and concentrates on trying to radicalise public opinion in Canada. In the United States, Oxfam America is increasingly successful: begun in Washington in 1970 in response to the famine in Bangladesh, it now has its small headquarters in Boston. In 1980 it raised $5.6 million (£2.5m.), much of it for Cambodia, on which it gave influential evidence to US Congressional committees. Like the original Oxfam, it is unbureaucratic and operates on modest overheads, spending only 12 per cent on administration. It refuses to accept any funding from any part of the US Government, and criticises US aid for having caused increased dependency rather than self-sufficiency. It has organised tours by journalists of Nicaragua, Guatemala and Cuba. The chairman, Newell Flather, is opposed to seeking money or support by any method that demeans the people who will receive it: 'If the message Americans get is of people living in deprived, decrepit conditions, they miss the fact that these are fundamentally similar human beings to themselves. If you provide negative images of these people, that breeds condescension and lack of respect.'

A shift of emphasis is overdue to give greater help to *the situation of women* in Third World countries – many of whose living conditions have worsened rather than been improved by development projects. The realisation has come late to all the male-dominated aid agencies that many women and children form the ultimate exploited classes of the world population: just as aid channelled to a repressive government or elite can serve to tighten its hold on less privileged people, so development projects can unwittingly widen the gap of economic and other opportunities between men and women. Most frequently invisible in economic statistics, the female half of the world's population already do two-thirds of its work for only 10 per cent of its income; development can have the effect of further increasing their work-load while reducing what limited status they possessed. *As in family planning, too often it is the men who take decisions and the women who take the consequences.* Tony Vaux believes 'Funding agencies also need to look at themselves. To what extent do women play a role in their decision-making processes? Should the voluntary agencies employ more women at field level? Changes are certainly likely to be needed closer to home.'

Dramatically increased support for *family planning* projects, which Oxfam first began as one of the pioneers in 1965, is more controversial. The acceleration in the growth of the world's population has recenty moderated, but even so it is projected to reach 6 billion by A.D. 2000. To some this is a nightmare prospect: they point out that each time our hearts beat, there are two more births than deaths in the world, and predict that on present forecasts there is liable to be standing room only on the earth in 22 more generations. Nevertheless, to many Third World inhabitants, for white people to finance population control campaigns amongst non-white nations can seem the ultimate in cultural imperialism. Zimbabweans still remember the white farmer's wife who gave all her black female staff contraceptive injections without telling them what it was. Providing the opportunity for family planning by consent, however, increases people's (and especially women's) control

over their lives, and could reduce the present enormous incidence
of abortions. But research has shown that lower birth rates will
only result if people want smaller families – because their health
situation has improved so that they think their children will
survive; because their income has increased so that child labour
is no longer necessary; and when they feel that their children
are not the only means of support for themselves in illness or old
age.

In any event, new programmes are going to be needed to
relieve abuses of *child labour*. The International Labour
Organisation estimates that in all 75 million children between
the ages of 8 and 15 work in the labour forces of the developing
world, surrendering their childhood to survive, while often
underfed, underpaid and unprotected. In India, where children
overall account for 23 per cent of family income, 40,000 children
are working in dangerous factories for a daily wage of less
than 20p. James Grant of UNICEF suggests that projects, such
as those being tried in Brazil where working children are provided with safeguards, schooling and meals, could offer some
solution.

At home in Britain, Oxfam could press for a *Fund for Industrial
Change*, which would assist United Kingdom manufacturing
companies to change over from the production of goods that
are better produced in the Third World. Tony Swift has also
suggested that consumers should monitor the methods of production of overseas goods, to help discourage unsafe places of
work. But undoubtedly the priority task remaining to be tackled
is *to increase public concern about the overseas world* generally. The
Brandt Commission spoke of the need to move from enlightened
charity to new world structures: 'a rearrangment of international
relations, the building of a new order and a new kind of comprehensive approach to the problems of development', since
governments have shown themselves unwilling to implement
any such proposals, the support of such changes can only be
generated by non governmental campaigning. The Commission's
report was criticised by Third World First and by some in Oxfam
for confusing growth with development, and for paying in-
sufficient attention to inequalities *within* nations. But it argued
that the current recession, far from being a pretext for timidity,
is precisely the time that requires bold and imaginative

new initiatives. Many components of the present world crisis – worsening unemployment, growing pollution, the arms spiral – are hurting nations of every political and economic character alike.

The concept of an international community has not yet matured enough for it to take effective remedial action: the idea of global responsibility is still only at an adolescent stage. World society today is still like a magnification of nineteenth-century England, that had been made aware by Dickens and others of the poverty and social problems in its midst, but is still reluctant to levy the tax to deal with them. *Perhaps it will not be until there is some world form of universal franchise that the earth's resources will be more fairly shared.*

But let us not be in any doubt: we have it within our power now to abolish absolute poverty on the earth today. Technically it is easier to do so than to send two astronauts to the moon; the cost could be financed by a tax on arms sales or on luxuries, or from the wealth of seabed minerals.

We are still learning that our world's responsibilities are indivisible – or divided at the peril of all of us. Will the growing North-South confrontation be the most likely cause of the third – and possibly final – world war, or will Northern people accept any voluntary restraint upon the growth of their living-standards?

Moses Maimonides counselled 800 years ago that it is best *to anticipate charity by preventing poverty.* The object of development assistance should be to help create a world where the giving of it is no longer necessary. William Clark – who describes today's world as being like a ship, on which the steerage passengers report the stern is sinking, to receive the reply from those in the first-class lounge that they'll consider helping, but first they must deal with the rise in the price of fillet steak – praises Oxfam for 'digging down into individual people and convincing them of their obligations and responsibilities.'

Donne said *'This only is charity, to do all, all that we can.'* Many people today think they have done something positive just by watching a disturbing documentary on television. But if we know the reality and still do nothing, are we not accomplices in what has been called the 'hidden holocaust'?

Our response tells us all we need to know about ourselves.

During the time you have taken to read this book, several – perhaps 500 – people will probably have died *unnecessarily*. *The rich world could do so much, at the cost of so little sacrifice*. Many of the tragedies mentioned in this book are preventable – and comparatively easily.

If you would like to find out what you could do about this, one way you could start would be to contact Oxfam at 274 Banbury Road, Oxford.

Appendix:
How You Can Help

Locally:

Consider the following opportunities: look up OXFAM in your telephone directory and ring the local organizer – he or she will be pleased to hear from you and advise you.
Or write/telephone to the Volunteer Co-ordinator,
OXFAM House,
274 Banbury Road
Oxford OX2 7DZ
(tel: (0865) 56777)

Joining a Group: The local groups are the hub of local Oxfam activity. Organizing events, writing to the papers, putting on exhibitions are just a few of the things they do. Some are responsible for running the Oxfam shops too.

Working in Shops: Thousands of people work in Oxfam shops every day. Most put in a few hours' voluntary work, helping to serve, price and organize. It's a friendly place to be and at the same time helps generate funds for Oxfam's work overseas.

Pledged Gifts: For those who like getting out and about for an hour from home or at work, the Pledged Gift scheme can be the answer. Hundreds of people go out to collect the small 'pledges' from their friends, neighbours and colleagues. Put together, it all adds up to a really worthwhile amount each year.

Doing your own thing is what many supporters prefer – whether it is to organize a sponsored walk, to have a coffee morning or think up some unusual event. There's plenty of scope for the independent minded to use their energy and enthusiasm to help Oxfam.

Give and Take: You don't have to work in an Oxfam shop to help them. They are only effective because of the continuing flow of good clothes, toys, books, china and other gifts from well-wishers. Why don't you look in your loft and look out something you could give to your shop? Everything that will sell helps – and you might take away a bargain at the same time too!

Centrally:

Join thousands of other supporters by becoming a member of our register, receiving three informative mailings a year and our mail-order catalogue. There are other versions of this:

Making the Government help more: Many people make simple donations to Oxfam – and very welcome they are too. But there is way in which you can get the tax man to add an extra 43p to every pound you give. Its called the Oxfam Tax Recovery Scheme. If you agree to give just a few pounds each month for a period of four years, we can recover the tax you will have paid. It is an effective way of helping – 30,000 people already do.

Project Partnership: Find out about the daily routine of the Village Health Worker in Tanzania who bicycles long distances over rough tracks to reach the next isolated clinic. Or the Indian mother employed as a labourer on a building site in Delhi – forced to leave her young children to fend for themselves while she works.

Become closely linked to one project getting to know the people involved. Receive up-to-date information from your project three times a year. Visit Oxfam House in Oxford to see the organization at work.

Take the opportunity of booking a place on Oxfam's success-ful Supporters' Tour overseas.

Will Power: Often overlooked is the importance of making a will. For if you don't mention it in your will, nobody will make a final donation to your favourite charity. If you haven't done so, it's important that you make a will in any case – it's also a good opportunity to make your last gift your best. Write for Oxfam's helpful leaflet "Will making simply explained".

For these ways of helping – write or telephone to:

> Patrick Wise,
> Appeals Department,
> Oxfam,
> 274 Banbury Road,
> Oxford OX2 7DZ.

If none of these suit you:

The Volunteer Co-ordinator (address below) has many specialist jobs – suitable for retired accountants, property experts,
shop merchandising advisers, legacy team visitors, electricians
and so on – waiting to be filled.

*Oxfam needs you: you will not regret the decision to join us – Please
act today:*

OXFAM
274 Banbury Road, Oxford OX2 7DZ
Telephone: (0865) 56777
Telex: 83610

Index